Epic Continent

Also by Nicholas Jubber

The Prester Quest
Drinking Arak off an Ayatollah's Beard
The Timbuktu School for Nomads

Epic Continent

Adventures in the Great Stories of Europe

NICHOLAS JUBBER

nb

NICHOLAS BREALEY
PUBLISHING

London · Boston

First published in Great Britain in 2019 by John Murray (Publishers)
First published in the United States of America in 2019
by Nicholas Brealey Publishing
Imprints of John Murray Press
An Hachette UK Company

2

© Nicholas Jubber 2019

Internal artwork by Rodney Paull

A CIP catalogue record for this title is available from the British Library

UK Hardback ISBN 978-1-47366-572-9
UK Trade paperback ISBN 978-1-47366-573-6
UK Ebook ISBN 978-1-47366-574-3
US Hardback ISBN 978-1-52937-434-6
US Ebook ISBN 978-1-47369-525-2

Typeset in Bembo by Palimpsest Book Production Ltd, Falkirk, Stirlingshire

Printed and bound by Clays Ltd, Elcograf S.p.A.

John Murray Press policy is to use papers that are natural, renewable and
recyclable products and made from wood grown in sustainable forests.
The logging and manufacturing processes are expected to conform
to the environmental regulations of the country of origin.

John Murray (Publishers)   Nicholas Brealey Publishing
Carmelite House   Hachette Book Group
50 Victoria Embankment   Market Place Centre, 53 State Street
London EC4Y 0DZ   Boston, MA 02109, USA
Tel: 020 3122 6000   Tel: (617) 523 3801

www.johnmurray.co.uk
www.nbuspublishing.com
www.nickjubber.com

For Milo and Rafe

Contents

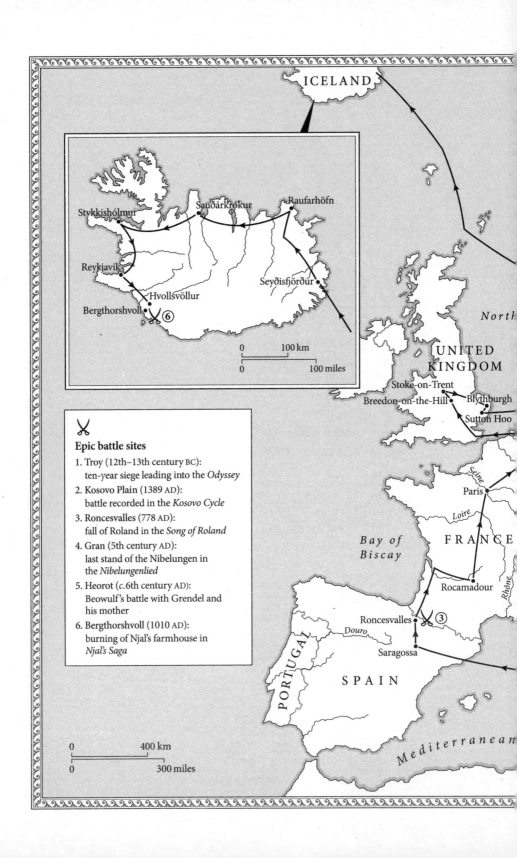

ICELAND

Stykkishólmur   Sauðárkrókur   Raufarhöfn

Reykjavik
          Hvollsvöllur
Bergthorshvoll   ⑥

Seyðisfjörður

| 0 | 100 km |
| 0 | 100 miles |

✂

Epic battle sites

1. Troy (12th–13th century BC):
   ten-year siege leading into the *Odyssey*
2. Kosovo Plain (1389 AD):
   battle recorded in the *Kosovo Cycle*
3. Roncesvalles (778 AD):
   fall of Roland in the *Song of Roland*
4. Gran (5th century AD):
   last stand of the Nibelungen in
   the *Nibelungenlied*
5. Heorot (*c.*6th century AD):
   Beowulf's battle with Grendel and
   his mother
6. Bergthorshvoll (1010 AD):
   burning of Njal's farmhouse in
   Njal's Saga

North

UNITED
KINGDOM

Stoke-on-Trent
Breedon-on-the-Hill   Blythburgh
                  Sutton Hoo

Seine

Paris

Loire

*Bay of
Biscay*

FRANCE

Rocamadour

Rhône

Roncesvalles   ✂ ③

PORTUGAL   *Douro*

Saragossa

SPAIN

Mediterranean

| 0 | 400 km |
| 0 | 300 miles |

Timeline

Some of the dates that follow are speculative.

1188 BC	Troy is sacked by the Greeks and Odysseus sails back towards Ithaca
1178 BC	Odysseus returns to Ithaca
8th century BC	The *Odyssey* is composed
AD 437	The Burgundian Kingdom is sacked and King Gunther is killed (see *The Nibelungenlied*)
AD 451	Burgundian troops fight against Attila the Hun
AD 516	Hygelac, chief of the Geats (and Beowulf's overlord), falls in a raid against the Frisians
AD 778	Roland dies in an ambush at Roncesvalles
AD 990	Gunnar of Hliðarendi is killed by his enemies in Iceland
1000	The manuscript of *Beowulf* is written down
1010	Njal the lawyer's farmhouse is burned in Iceland
Mid-11th century	The *Song of Roland* is composed
Late 12th–early 13th century	The *Nibelungenlied* is composed
1280	*Njal's Saga* is composed
1389	The Battle of Kosovo and death of Prince Lazar of the Serbs
15th century	The first songs of the *Kosovo Cycle* are composed
1488	Publication of first Western edition of the *Odyssey*
1755	The *Nibelungenlied* is rediscovered
1772	First printed edition of *Njal's Saga*
1787	*Beowulf* is rediscovered
1814–15	Publication of *Serbian Folk Songs*, edited by Vuk Karadžić, containing songs of the *Kosovo Cycle*
1835	The *Song of Roland* is rediscovered

Prologue

WE TEND TO think of epic stories as remote: faraway tales set long ago. But over the course of a few years, immersed in the epics of Europe, I grew to understand that these stories are all around us. As immediate as news reports, as explosive as blockbuster movies, as twistily compelling as the tales of a campfire bard.

The idea for this book started on a road trip across Europe. My wife was on maternity leave, and I was editing a book, so there was no reason we couldn't, as she put it, 'have fun for a few months'. At the end of the summer, our eldest would be starting school, so this was our chance. We lurched from one mini-disaster to the next, rolling through seven countries in the space of four months, staying with friends, relatives and budget homestays through Airbnb. There was a visit to a mechanic after we punctured our tyres on a Sardinian dirt track, and we spent most of the ferry crossing to Sicily in the sick bay, after I forgot to strap our baby into his highchair. But we weren't doing *too* badly: the kids were in one piece (each), we were still talking to each other and our ten-year-old Peugeot 206 was just about roadworthy.

It was an innocent, balmy time, flushed with the joy of exploring Europe through the eyes of small children. In Nuremberg, we revelled in the model trains at one of the continent's finest toy museums and plodded, more soberly, around the site of the Nazi rally. In Syracuse, we attended a puppet show after wandering around an ancient Greek amphitheatre. Occasionally, signs of a hardening continent seeped through our little family bubble – from racist graffiti in Hanover to African migrants asking for help in Sardinia. But dirty nappies and grazed knees tended to distract our attention. If the headlines got us down, we could always focus on the adventures of the Octonauts, or marvel at the brilliant wood-work of the German *kindergartens*.

How I loved Europe that summer: the brassy light beating down on the Mediterranean beaches, where the sea coddled our feet in blankets of turquoise; the dusty golden green of pine forests; the rituals you can still witness, from Sicilian *signoras* touching our baby's feet and our older son's blond hair, then doing the sign of the cross, to graduates celebrating their degrees by kissing the bronze lips of the Göttingen goose-girl. Great coffee, delicious ice cream; and as their quality deteriorated, the sausages got bigger and so did the beer mugs.

But the talk back home was of severance. Identity politics was being marshalled for political gain; historical terms like 'Anglo-Saxon' and hoary concepts like 'sovereignty' were being triggered to canvass votes; Facebook profiles were being mined and divisive videos unleashed on YouTube by political strategists who derived their tactics from Sun Tzu's *Art of War* and the nineteenth-century brink-manship of Otto von Bismarck.

By the time we reached the Bavarian Alps, it had already happened: Britain had voted to end its forty-two-year political union with the mainland. Squeezed into a horse-drawn carriage clopping towards the castle of Neuschwanstein, I found myself brushing elbows with a friendly Düsseldorfer. 'You guys made a big mistake,' he helpfully announced, scrolling down his iPhone to show me the freefalling pound. The castle was a Romantic folly built for the nineteenth-century aesthete, 'Mad' King Ludwig, but we were in no state for castle touring. My wife managed to lose her purse in the carriage, and I wandered around in a daze, the words *mad* and *folly* bouncing around my head. Fortunately, at least one member of our party was on the ball.

'Daddy,' our three-year-old exclaimed, 'it's a dragon!'

My eye followed his finger across a vaulted arch towards a scaly, curly tailed beast, its breast pinned by a golden-armoured hero with a gleaming sword. We looked at each other and smiled, standing there under the mural.

And that was the moment when it clicked.

The hero was Sigurd, or Siegfried, from the medieval tale of the *Nibelungen*. The story occurs in several versions. A couple of weeks earlier, I had downloaded the twelfth-century epic version – the *Nibelungenlied* – on to my Kindle. King Ludwig's paintings followed another version, set down in thirteenth-century Iceland. Gazing up at the painting, I thought of Siegfried's tale: he kills the dragon, claims a magnificent treasure, marries a beautiful princess . . . and during a woodland hunt, he falls to a spear in the back from a treacherous murderer.

Over the subsequent days and weeks, like a ball of wool played by a mischievous cat, this grim story spooled around my head, threading itself around other tales. I thought of its influence on the Anglo-Saxon epic *Beowulf* and the Icelandic sagas, and later the writings of J. R. R. Tolkien (whose dragon-telling explains why the image of a scaly winged beast is so recognisable to three-year-olds today). And I thought about Siegfried's connections with the great Homeric heroes – he's a master of disguise, like the wily Odysseus, but he's also a nearly immortal strongman, like Achilles, with his own Achilles heel – a leaf-shaped patch on his back.

'Epic is about wandering in search of something,' said the poet Derek Walcott. 'You know: the knight leaves, goes forth and encounters different dragons, et cetera, on his quest.' More than two millennia earlier, Aristotle defined it more formally: 'an imitation of serious subjects contained in a composition of some compass', employing 'the steadiest and most dignified of metres'. What sucked me into the European epic wasn't so much its form as the symmetry of its motifs and plot strands, sewing the continent together in a patchwork quilt of storytelling.

Theorists have bolted labels on to these connections, from Jacob Grimm's search for the *Zusammenhang* or 'together link' to the twelve stages of Joseph Campbell's mono-myth (and they've been going at it for so long that George Eliot parodied them all the way back in the 1870s, with Casaubon's 'Key to all Mythologies' in *Middlemarch*). Many of their insights are illuminating, but I found them too mechanical for the intricate connections burrowing between the tales' mythical and folkloric underpinnings. For me, the stories joined together in so many surprising ways, linking so organically, that the ties between them were like roots criss-crossing under the trunks of a vast, intractable forest.

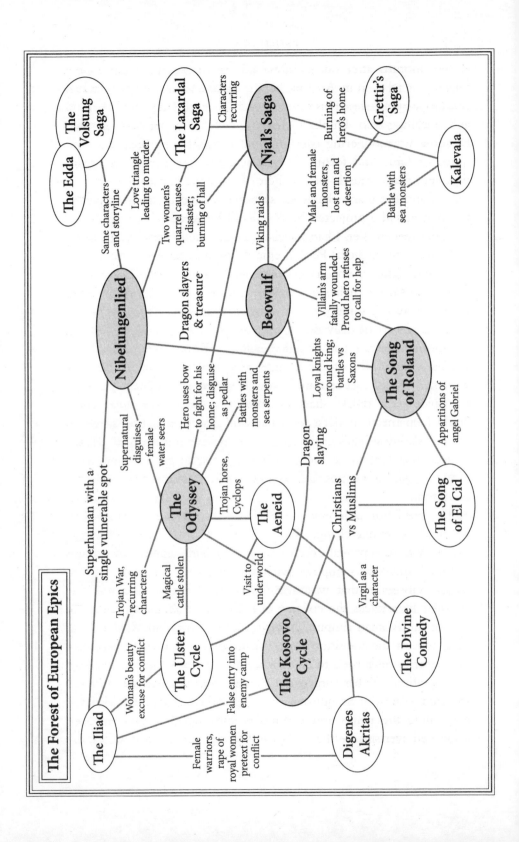

The Forest of European Epics

The Iliad
The Odyssey
Nibelungenlied
The Edda
The Volsung Saga
The Laxardal Saga
Njal's Saga
Grettir's Saga
Kalevala
Beowulf
The Song of Roland
The Song of El Cid
The Aeneid
The Ulster Cycle
The Kosovo Cycle
Digenes Akritas
The Divine Comedy

Superhuman with a single vulnerable spot

Same characters and storyline

Love triangle leading to murder

Two women's quarrel causes disaster; burning of hall

Characters recurring

Burning of hero's home

Male and female monsters, lost arm and desertion

Battle with sea monsters

Dragon slayers & treasure

Viking raids

Villain's arm fatally wounded. Proud hero refuses to call for help

Loyal knights around king; battles vs Saxons

Supernatural disguises, female water seers

Hero uses bow to fight for his home; disguise as pedlar

Battles with monsters and sea serpents

Dragon slaying

Trojan War, recurring characters

Trojan horse, Cyclops

Magical cattle stolen

Visit to underworld

Christians vs Muslims

Apparitions of angel Gabriel

Virgil as a character

Woman's beauty excuse for conflict

False entry into enemy camp

Female warriors, rape of royal women pretext for conflict

A few months after our family road trip, I was planning a new journey: a relay from Anatolia to the Arctic Circle, in the shadow of Europe's epic tales. This time, I would be leaving my family behind and travelling solo. Unlike Odysseus, I wasn't being strong-armed by some warmongering overlord; and I wasn't on a Siegfried-style hunt for fame and fortune. I'm a scrawny, bespectacled scribbler type, not some muscle-bound hero. It was the stories I wanted to follow, and the many characters scattered within them. I hoped the journey, and the projected book, would be worth it.

Some years earlier, I had travelled around the *Shahnameh* or 'Book of Kings', the medieval Persian epic. I had met farmers who recited its episodes during the harvest and war veterans who followed its narrative in the trenches of the Iran–Iraq War. Ancient storytelling, for them, wasn't some precious artefact stored in ivory towers, but a pulsating part of daily life.

Until recently, I had assumed Europe was different, its history sterilised behind the orderly casings of its museums. But the last few years had eroded that certainty. Now, I wondered if a journey among the epics – the oldest, shaggiest, most dog-eared tales out there – could help me to understand what being European is all about. If the epics were still alive, still influencing people outside the palisades of academia that make them so intimidating to new readers, then surely it would be possible to follow their trail right across the continent?

The great European epics were all composed during, or based on, moments of seismic change. The *Odyssey* tells of the aftermath of the Trojan War, the primal conflict from which the Greek nation was spawned; and it was composed when the heroic age was being replaced by the city-states that would dominate the European future. The *Nibelungenlied* tracks the collapse of a Germanic kingdom at the fag end of the Roman Empire. *Beowulf*, the only surviving Old English epic, reflects the transition from paganism to Christianity. Many of these stories refer back to an epoch that has been labelled the 'Age of Migration'. Tribes surged out of the steppes of central Asia and the archipelagos of Scandinavia, crossing the rivers of central Europe and filling the plains and peninsulas with which they have been associated ever since – the Franks and Danes, the German tribes, the

Anglo-Saxons. Amongst many other things, these stories are Europe's foundation myths.

As a literary reference, Europa first appears in Homer's *Iliad*: Zeus' captive, winged to Crete so the god could ravish her, displaced like so many of the tribes that would dominate its story. Nothing unusual there – dispersal is the starter signal on which early history ran its races. The name was used by Greeks to distinguish their territories west of the Aegean, later adopted by the Romans for their western empire, used by encyclopaedists and cartographers into the Dark Ages and deployed by Charlemagne's propagandists as a catch-all for his imperium. But it wasn't until the rise of humanism in the fifteenth century that it became common practice for people to call themselves 'European', as a way of distinguishing themselves from 'Christendom'.

None of us knows what 'Europe' will mean in the future. But what we can do is look at the stories from which its constituent parts were fashioned: the tales told over fireplaces, chanted across the halls of kings; the stories that inspired armies to march, thrilled the imaginations of their rulers and offered motivational imagery for revolutionaries.

Many of us, still, are easily bewitched by tales of heroes slaying the dragon, battling together against the odds. *Jaws*, *Apocalypse Now*, *Game of Thrones* . . . or, to take the epics with which these modern classics share uncanny parallels: *Beowulf*, the *Odyssey*, the *Nibelungenlied*.* As the kindly swineherd Eumaeus puts it in the *Odyssey*, 'you can stare at a bard in wonder – trained by the gods to sing and hold men spellbound – how you can long to sit there, listening, all your life when the man begins to sing'.

How to make a selection, with so many epics to choose from? I was drawn especially to those with an oral background, stories I might be able to hear in some form of public recital. The word *epic*

---

* A man-eating monster haunts a blessed community until a hero takes it on and sets out to the deep to complete his task (*Jaws* and *Beowulf*). A man ventures out with his ill-fated crew on a perilous journey, confronting many horrors along the way (*Apocalypse Now* – or 'The Idiocy', as Francis Ford Coppola quipped during the fraught filming – and the *Odyssey*). A king and his followers are tricked into a celebratory feast and butchered in a massacre of revenge (the 'Red Wedding' episode of *Game of Thrones* and the *Nibelungenlied*).

derives from the Greek verb *epein* – 'to say'. In order to be truly 'epic', a story must be sayable. Words spoken aloud have power – to the ancient Greeks it was *kelethmos*, or 'enchantment'. Because these stories were spoken aloud, long before the age of printing, they were able to sink deep roots, entangling themselves around the core of European culture.

The European epic tradition starts with Homer, and so would I: specifically, the *Odyssey*, that beloved tale of a cunning hero's long journey home from a war. From there, the ground would become less familiar. Travelling north into the Balkans, I would explore the *Kosovo Cycle*, the story of Christian knights fighting against the Ottoman Empire. Crossing the Adriatic, I would move around western Europe with the *Song of Roland* – about the deeds of Charlemagne's paladins in the bosky passes of the Pyrenees. Central Europe would be represented by the *Nibelungenlied*, which tells of dragon-slaying Siegfried and the terrible revenge that follows his murder. Heading north, I would explore Britain and Scandinavia through *Beowulf* – that eerie tale of monsters and mead halls, and a hero who must stand brave against a dragon's fire. And finally, I would approach the furthest flung of European nations through *Njal's Saga* (and its verse companion, *Gunnarsrímur*), the story of two Icelandic friends and the feuds that rip their lives apart.

Europe's epic heritage is too rich to squeeze into a single book, and this one cannot cover every region, nor every great epic tale. There were many I was sad to miss, but if I could trail these six stories across the continent, I hoped I would be able to answer a cluster of nagging questions: What did these stories do to create Europe? Are they still worth reading? And can they help us to understand Europe today? Setting off for Greece, I wasn't sure what to expect. There probably wouldn't be any dragons, and, fingers crossed, I was unlikely to get transformed into a pig by a wily sorceress. But nor was I expecting to take part in drinking rituals with poetry-singing war veterans, sleep in a Bronze Age tomb chamber, meet flag-waving secessionists at a Dark Age battle site or wander around an embryonic temple with a pagan high priest. The epics gave me a path. I had lived my whole life as a European. Now I wanted to ride the continent of my birth and find out what that meant.

PART ONE

The War that Launched a Thousand Ships

The Odyssey

The Trojan War is over and Odysseus wants to get home. After seven years as a captive of the nymph Calypso, he is sent off on a raft towards the island of the Phaeacians. There, he narrates his adventures since plundering Troy – the battle with the Cyclops, the alluring song of the Sirens, the Cattle of the Sun (which his men mutinously roasted, resulting in their deaths in a storm whipped up by the gods). The Phaeacians pity Odysseus and send him home to Ithaca, laden with gifts.

Disguised as a beggar, he makes himself known to his son Telemachus, who has just returned from a journey of his own. Together, they plan how to overcome the suitors who have descended on their home, squandering Odysseus' estate and vying for his wife, Penelope. When she announces an archery contest – with her hand in marriage as the prize – they know it's time to strike. Several suitors try to wield Odysseus' bow, but none can manage the feat until he takes up the challenge himself, shooting an arrow through twelve axe heads.

But the contest turns out to be target practice. Assisted by Telemachus, Odysseus slays the suitors and hangs the maidservants who consorted with them. Finally, he presents himself to long-suffering Penelope, who tests his identity with intimate questions. Husband, wife and son are reunited, and all that remains is for the goddess Athena to descend, pacifying an angry mob of islanders and the suitors' relatives.

I

O would to God this drifter had died before he reached us,
And then from all this chaos we'd been spared!
The Suitors, *The Odyssey*, Book Eighteen

RACE OFF OR start slow? I had eighteen countries to cross — a span of more than 3,000 miles — but before I hurtled around the continent, I needed to place myself. European epic begins with the Greeks, and the *Odyssey* is the most famous of all travel tales, so this was the logical beginning for a journey into epic. Composed roughly at the end of the eighth century BC and attributed to the bard known as Homer, this story is so familiar — with its Sirens and Cyclops and the great battle in Odysseus' hall — it's easy to forget that it predates the invention of mealtimes or the minting of coins. And yet, reading it today, the *Odyssey* feels *now*. The playfulness of its looping, non-linear narrative, the range of its characters, the viscera of its violence; so much that's prized in storytelling today can be found, just as fresh, in Homer's epic. Think road movie or disaster movie, slashed with setbacks and sudden deaths, climaxing in a shoot-out as blood-spattered as a spaghetti Western.

The *Iliad* may have preceded it, with its brittle depiction of the Trojan War and the rage of Achilles, but it's the *Odyssey* that established the template still followed by Hollywood screenwriters: the cycle of misadventures spinning towards a bloody confrontation with the enemy; the happy ending reuniting the lovers. If greatness is measured by imitation, the *Odyssey* is surely the greatest story ever told. Which makes it a tricky story to journey round. The clue's in the name: all those *Odysseys* filling the shelves in any library or bookshop. *New Odyssey, An Odyssey, Ithaca, Circe, Odysseus: The*

Return, The Odyssey: Missing Presumed Dead . . . And those are just a few of the titles published this decade.

Why does this story, above all others, keep sucking us in? And what does it tell us about Europe – the continent whose cultural tendencies it did so much to shape? In order to explore these questions, I decided to follow the *Odyssey* on three tracks. One would take me amongst Greeks, people with a native connection to the story. Sometimes it's through the particular that we uncover the universal, so I wanted to meet the people in the eye of the storm. But the *Odyssey* is also the iconic tale of travel and adventure: in order to get to grips with it, I needed to have some adventures of my own.

But first I wanted to visit a single island (according to some, the very island where Homer composed this epic) which is at the heart of a modern crisis. Because the *Odyssey* isn't dead literature – that's the exciting thing about the most enduring stories. They keep going, regenerating as the world changes around them. Imagine the plot as a series of news headlines: men rushing away from a war zone, stranded on the islands of the Mediterranean, desperately seeking a place to call home. Comparing present-day trauma to long-ago tales from the past doesn't insult either, so long as you recognise the value of both.

Chios, just a few miles from the Turkish mainland. An island once famous for its mastic and black wine, until the Ottoman Turks massacred its population during the Greek War of Independence. Now it's a hub of the 'refugee crisis', currently holding nearly four thousand 'unprocessed' asylum seekers.

A fortress muscles over the sea. Grass and ragwort coil out of cracks in the bastion, like tattoos on a bouncer's biceps. Wedges of sky peer through the loopholes and gaps in the rubble; sunlight glances off the lids of storage containers that house many of the refugees. Past a cluster of tents, men are playing cards around a trestle table. Behind them is a queue for supper. Some of the men are fingering relit cigarette stubs, thumbing the pockets of donated jackets for their ration cards. We are in the Souda refugee camp and tonight's menu is rice and runner beans.

'Teacher,' says Yassin, 'you must eat with us.'

I peel off my high-vis jacket and leave it scrumpled beside my shoes, inside the door of the tent. I don't want to eat their food. Nothing against runner beans – it's just that I know the food has been earmarked for the refugees. But Yassin is insistent, and I've never been much good at saying no.

'*Laziz*!' I dip my hand in the rice and nibble a few flecks. 'Tasty!'

'Thank you, teacher. But I want to invite you to my real home. We would eat a big sheep!'

Two years earlier, Yassin was a medical student at Homs University – until the Syrian war closed the university. Back in his family's village, he worked as a private medic, but his meagre income was leached by local chiefs – representatives of the ruling Alawite sect. One tried to blackmail him, another warned he would soon have to enlist.

'But I didn't want to go in the army. If you go in the army, you don't even get a weapon – you are just for throwing away. I climbed over the mountains to Turkey, I went very low so the soldiers couldn't get me.'

He found work in Bursa, but he had his eyes on Europe. His meagre salary, along with money sent by relatives, eventually added up and he approached the smugglers. The first time he tried, the boat never materialised. It took several months to collect enough funds for a retry. This time, coastguards stopped the boat and he was pulled out of a hatch. Another crossing was thwarted when the vessel was stolen by a rival smuggler. So it continued, until the sixth attempt.

'It was a calm day,' says Yassin. 'I thought this is the day for chance.' But halfway across, he started to have doubts. 'There were too many of us in the boat. The water was around our ankles. We tried to get the water out with our hands, but it was impossible.'

Fortunately, they had made it far enough. Horn blast filled the air, like the audible answer to a prayer. A local fisherman had alerted the Greek coastguard. They were brought to Chios, logged on to the UN Refugee Agency (UNHCR) system, given forms to fill in, billeted to tents and container units, to wait for the long process of asylum. Back in Syria, Yassin had lived in a three-storey house with a satellite TV and decent Wi-Fi; now he had to adapt to life in a tent, watching out for the rats that infested the camp, along with the snakes that came for the rats; waking up to the sloshing of waves, the rattle of wind in the UNHCR canvas, and the screams of fellow refugees struggling to shake themselves free of the past.

I knew I would bump into refugees along my way through Europe; I would be following a similar route to many of them. But I didn't want to encounter them in complete ignorance. I hoped that by spending a few weeks among the camps, I could learn something about the issue igniting so much passion across the continent. So, with a vague hope of making myself useful at the same time, I volunteered with a school for refugees run from a converted hair salon.

The old stone building was divided into a couple of classrooms, with a curtained-off lobby and a small kitchen. Rules of conduct and papier mâché models hung alongside refugees' paintings and portraits of teachers (for some reason, which I'll put down to felt-tip availability, I was depicted with a face the colour of seaweed, ears like handlebars and a long crimson neck). Most evenings there were meetings, which could be as long-winded and nearly as tense as the war councils in the *Iliad*. Everybody pitched in, arguing over disciplinary procedures, throwing out project ideas, exchanging anecdotes about the frequent fighting between Syrian and Afghan students, who were acting out the rivalry between their elders for dominance of the camps.

Given what they'd been through, it's amazing how balanced most of the students were. But amongst them, there were a few who struggled: boys who used their ninety-euro monthly allowance to drown their memories with drink, guys who fell for the camp drug dealers, kids whose arms were scarred by fights or self-harm. Looking into their eyes – these were old eyes. I knew something about mental health from personal experience, but not enough. Suffering from variations of post-traumatic stress disorder, these guys needed experts. Cooped up in the camps, their asylum hearings unscheduled, many were struggling to deal with their frustrations and anxieties about what lay ahead.

But when you sat with them to play a game of chess, saw their drawings and poems, played 'duck, duck, goose' with the younger ones and their laughter sizzled in your ears, the world felt very cruel for penning them in, trapped like the ancient Ithacans when the sorceress Circe transforms them into pigs.

To be a refugee is to be unwanted, an exile, suspected by the authorities and the locals, and worst of all by those around you; like Odysseus, returning to Ithaca in disguise, 'a brazen, shameless beggar' in the words of the suitor Antinous. Another pedlar accosts him and, egged on by the suitors, they end up wrestling for the prize of a sizzling hot goat sausage. Odysseus throws his rival, 'so that blood gushed purple from his lips and with a shriek he fell on the dust'. A rare case in which the Homeric details sound comparatively tame.

The *Odyssey* is rife with fugitives, outsiders wandering in from elsewhere. Reading of the kindliness towards the dispossessed shown by Odysseus' son, Telemachus, who harbours a fugitive on his ship without expectation of reward, or the swineherd Eumaeus, who hosts a penniless tramp (his master in disguise) and tells him the poignant tale of his own enslavement, one suspects the poet understood something about the pain of dispersal.

'Have we not vagabonds enough, paupers whose pestering turns our stomachs while we feast?' asks the suitor Antinous, rehearsing an argument that's been at the heart of anti-immigration rhetoric for the last three millennia. I heard something similar in a waterfront bar one evening, sharing a bottle of wine with a retired fisherman called Michaelis. 'They leave rubbish everywhere,' he said, 'they take drugs and get drunk. They are like animals!' He clasped his wine glass between rope-calloused fingers, scrunching his nose tight. 'If you want to help these people, why don't you take them back to *your* country?'

He had a point. If ever there was purpose to political union in Europe, surely this was it: to find an organised way for a well-off continent of 500 million to absorb a population increase of just 0.3 per cent. But European leaders had been swinging more wildly than the Olympian gods, allowing domestic survival to suppress the more urgent task of pan-European policy making. Hungary had built a razor-wire fence, Angela Merkel had U-turned on her refugee policy and British Eurosceptics had distributed posters of immigrant 'swarms' to drive the vote for Brexit. As a result, Greece had been boxed unwillingly into the role (to quote its prime minister, Alexis Tsipras) of 'a warehouse for human souls'.

Once, during an intermediate English class, I narrated the plot of the *Odyssey* to a young Afghan student. 'That sounds like my journey,' she said, with a wry smile. It wasn't part of her cultural inheritance, but she could see the echoes. More voluble was a 'project' class, in which we read an adaptation from the *Odyssey* alongside Bob Dylan's *Rolling Stone*: two tales of wandering souls. To my surprise, it was Homer and not the Dylan classic who got the students talking.

'This is about something,' said a student called Nouri. 'This person has a difficult experience, but he tries to survive. I can understand this.'

'But I think our experiences are harder,' said another student, Faizullah. 'We are not captains with many slaves to do all our wishes.'

It wasn't so much the lit. crit. that engaged the students as the chance to express themselves, and that came to the fore during a workshop on poetry composition. Far from the self-consciousness that might have stifled students in a comparable class in the UK, these young refugees were itching to get their compositions out: the scratch of pens, paper scrumpled in dissatisfaction, heads tossed back, whispered recitations, slowly curling smiles . . .

There were poems about nature, about springtime and 'the season of kissing'; surreal poems about endless journeys (one student wrote about 'the scream' that nobody could hear); satires about the hygiene levels in the camps and the never-ending bureaucracy of the asylum process; memorials to the people left behind. One wrote about mothers standing in empty rooms, another remembered sitting on the roof of his house, listening to the voices of his family. I wrote verses as well – it was important to make the sessions as collabora- tive as possible. There were images from those classes – a heart decanting blood into the sea, a voice simulated by the wind blowing through the flaps of a tent – that I would remember throughout the coming months of travel.

We weren't reciting long verse tales to each other (although I'm sure some of the students could have carried on that far). But we were enjoying the solidarity of spoken word, treating poetry not as something static, silent in the pages of a book, but flying off our tongues, like the tales sung at the Homeric feasts. *Epein*: to say, to speak aloud, the origin of 'epic'. Verses shared, like a joke or a snack or a smile shining across the table. A symbol of companionship.

One free afternoon, I followed the rocky coastline, past seafront apartments advertising vacancies and terracotta houses with fences of prickly pear. In a pebbled cove, a couple of fishermen were caulking an upturned dinghy. Steps twisted above the beach, past a sanctuary to the Phrygian fertility goddess, Cybele. I climbed higher, until I reached a grass-flecked outcrop pimpled by a two-foot stump of limestone.

'Homer's Stool', they call it, whatever that means. Some barefoot, bearded bard in a pleated chiton, reciting the lamentations of Andromache for her slain husband Hector, or thrilling the children with the grisly man-munching Cyclops? Entertaining the youthful, and the comically minded with the mock-heroic *Battle of the Frogs and Mice*? Or laying out the *Thebaid*, one of those long-lost epics that's vaguely attributed to him? Whether anyone called Homer existed, whether the epics were composed by a single bard or clans of them, is immaterial. What matters is the surviving epics, and 'Homer' is our shorthand for the sensibility behind them.*

The location of Homer's Stool, so near the temple to the Anatolian goddess Cybele, underlines a point that has some bearing on Homeric composition. No matter if the poet lived on Chios (according to Herodotus), Smyrna (following Aristotle) or elsewhere, he was likely orientated towards the Near East. This is borne out by the epics. It wasn't just Troy in Homer's sight but 'the story climate of the Near

---

* Chios's claim as Homer's home-place is threefold: from the ancient tradition of *Homeridae*, rhapsodes or bards who recited his epics on the island; the connection drawn by scholars between the language of the epics and the 'Ionian' dialect spoken in ancient Chios; and a fragment of ancient verse known as the *Homeric Hymn to Delian Apollo* ('He is a blind man, and dwells in rocky Chios: his lays are ever more supreme').

East which taught Greece so much', to quote the pre-eminent scholar of epic, Albert Lord. This blossomed especially in the *Odyssey*, which contains compelling resonances with various Asian myths and tales, not least the much earlier Sumerian epic, *Gilgamesh*.★ Chios was a fitting homeland for an Iron Age storyteller, for the same reason that it draws refugees fleeing warfare today – it's at the edge of Europe, eavesdropping on the dramas of Asia.

Before I headed west, I needed to go east. To the place where it all started. So, on a weekend off from teaching, I made my way to Troy. A ferry puttered across the sea and a couple of buses rolled along the Turkish mainland towards the famous alluvial plain. I hiked between tomato plantations and grazing sheep, stalking my Cyclops-sized shadow along the tamarisk-haunted banks of the Scamander. Reaching the sea at last, I swam around the barrow where Achilles was legendarily buried and sat on a tuft of rock to dry myself off. When Alexander the Great came here in 334 BC, he danced naked around the barrow and sprinkled it with wine; but I figured that probably wasn't allowed these days. Just a few yards away, local women in burkinis and *abayas* were wading in the shallows, splashing and laughing. The *meltemi* wind blustered at their coverings, which flapped and rustled as if they were about to auto-sail themselves across the Aegean.

Troy is primarily the setting of the *Iliad*, but it haunts the *Odyssey*. It is the ominous place that Penelope hates to name; the ruin sung about by Sirens and bards, driving Odysseus to tears when he hears it recited in the hall of the Phaeacians. And just as its shadow looms over the *Odyssey*, so it looms over Europe. In his *History of the Kings*

★ Like Achilles, Gilgamesh is heartbroken by the loss of his friend; like Odysseus, he travels to the underworld and is directed there by a sorceress; and like Odysseus' crew, his friend's demise is caused by the theft of holy cattle. A more distant connection can be forged with the Indian *Ramayana*, which also narrates a hero's journey to reunite with his wife and climaxes with the wielding of a mighty bow. Closer to Chios is the *Book of Dede Korkut*, drawing on the ancient legends of the Oghuz Turks, in which a one-eyed giant is blinded with a red-hot spit and the hero escapes by hiding in a ram skin. But since there are more than two hundred known versions of the 'blinded ogre tale', accusations of plagiarism can swing back and forth from East to West until the end of time.

of Britain, the twelfth-century chronicler Geoffrey of Monmouth derived the ancient Britons from the Trojan Brutus (a mythical genealogy that's repeated in the medieval tale of *Gawain and the Green Knight*, linking King Arthur to the Trojan bloodline). The seventh-century Frankish King Dagobert claimed ancestry from King Priam, the Norman chief Rollo traced his line to the Trojan Antenor and the Roman poet Virgil wrote one of the most influential epics, the *Aeneid*, about a rare Trojan survivor. Tellingly, it is the losers they identify with, not the winners; the Asians, the refugees, scattered from their homeland. Loss and destruction are not simply the themes leaking out of the epics, they are the foundation on which European culture was built.

Scarred and deeply cratered, Troy languishes on the Hissarlik hill like a body that's been serially disembowelled, under the mortuary glare of the sun. I spent the afternoon wandering around, from the great propylaeum (temple entrance) to the sloping rampart wall, firmed by alternated joints, which archaeologists have identified with Homer's tale (supported by the discovery, in the 1930s, of hastily built 'siege' structures behind the wall). Teasingly, this four-metre-thick limestone shield suggests a city resistant to enemy might – the reason, as recalled in the *Odyssey*, that Odysseus comes up with the 'crafty device' of the Trojan horse to smuggle the Greek ambushers inside the city. Now, a model Trojan horse stood near the entrance turnstiles. Children brimmed inside, shrieking out of the narrow windows, while their parents watched from below, iPads and iPhones raised: Homeric imagery broadcast by Instagram.

Behind the rampart walls, poppies scarleted the fractured earth, fruit of a century and a half's soil churning. Wading between them, I thought of Priam's son, Gorgythion, falling in the *Iliad*, 'as on the stalk a poppy falls, weighed down by showering spring', as well as of the poppies that became such a defining image of the First World War.

> *And Priam and his fifty sons*
> *Wake all amazed, and hear the guns,*
> *And shake for Troy again.*

So wrote Rupert Brooke in 1915, shortly before succumbing to sepsis and a few weeks before the fighting at nearby Gallipoli. For Troy isn't just *a* war but *every* war. Which is why Homeric epic is still supplying military terminology, from Operation Achilles (Afghanistan, 2007) to Operation Odyssey Dawn (Libya, 2011). Verses like Brooke's, and many others in the Great War, speak not only of Homeric resonance but also of the self-aggrandising of combat, cloaking itself in history, overlooking the 'relentless, heartbreaking grief' expressed by the war veterans of the *Odyssey*. Other wars may have predated it, but in terms of Western consciousness, Troy is the blood-stained maternity ward – which is why I would find its imagery flashing from the graffitied walls of the Greek capital.

2

But still the night is young and seems to have no end,
No snoozing time for us who dwell within this palace.
So tell us more adventures — they are wonderful!
Alcinous, *The Odyssey*, Book Eleven

FORGET ABOUT MAN-EATING giants, the temptations of the Sirens, or even the becalming that maroons Odysseus' crew on the island of the Cattle of the Sun. For the modern-day Aegean island hopper, the chief hazard is industrial action. There would be other delays to come, but for now, at the end of my month in Chios, it was the Panhellenic Seamens' Federation that was holding me from Athens, protesting against changes to their pension fund.

After a couple of days' loitering on the waterfront with recent arrivals from Turkey, I switched tickets for the next passage out. I needed to get moving: there was an Odyssean event taking place in Athens in a few days, a musician to meet and adventures to have on the way to Ithaca.

At last, we were off. On deck, burly men with barely any hair chain-smoked under the radar stanchions, ash dancing with gobbets of spray under the lamps. A woman in a leopard-print suit stood beside me, one hand on her cigarette, the other stroking the lapdog peeking out of her handbag. The sea roiled through the night, and early in the morning the horizon laced itself in necklaces of amber light.

Burrowing out of the Metro in the district of Exarcheia, I strolled between reinforced concrete splashed with graffiti and the glass panes of antique booksellers, gleaming with gold tooling. A spray-paint horse stencilled a metal panel beneath a grid-glass window, and I buzzed the intercom. Graffiti blossomed across the walls around me: tendrils of blood-red, delphinium-blue and matt black, vines in a forest watered by political rage.

Exarcheia is Athens's beating heart, with a knack for setting off nationwide protests, from an army raid on the Polytechnic University in 1973 to the police shooting of a fifteen-year-old, Alexis Grigoropoulos, a few blocks from the university, which sparked the 2008 riots. This is an area that tattoos its politics across its chest, frothing with soup kitchens, recycling projects, guerrilla parks, squats and social centres. It also happens to contain one of Athens's finest museums, the Archaeological Museum, which was due to host a reading from the *Odyssey* in a couple of days' time. Waiting for this event, I killed time exploring the neighbourhood, although I wasn't expecting to find Homeric iconography so alive here, amongst all these symbols of twenty-first-century protest.

'Welcome to Exarcheia!' said Lewsha, my American host, leading me up the rickety stairs inside her block.

Through the Airbnb website, I'd booked myself into a marine-blue storeroom with a mattress on a pile of pallets. Lewsha was married to James, an Anglo-Greek art curator with a fondness for polysyllabic expostulations that I couldn't help admiring.

'Those jet-set curators,' he fumed, 'they're coming here with this didactic mentality, using us as an abstraction! Documenta – you heard of them? They've set up their state-funded exhibition, and they're presenting it as some kind of antidote to austerity!'

He was thrashing out proposals, exhibition lists and schedules, a desk-bound warrior. All over Exarcheia, people were at battle, whether with leather coshes and plastic shields, fingers hovering over their laptops, or tagging their protests with well-aimed cans of spray paint. This is an age of protest and you're never far from one, but few places manage it with the panache of Exarcheia.

Spiderman was a few blocks from the flat, tilting across a concrete wall, under a punnet of falling eggs. A wrinkled tramp spanned a derelict apartment block, dedicated to 'the poor of the world'. 'Barack O'Mama' was nursing a baby version of himself, while a silhouette figure was drowning in a giant egg timer and a clawed, mechanical dragon was swallowing a euro. To walk the streets of

Exarcheia is to swim in the luridly coloured pages of a comic strip, with dialogue written by left-wing polemicists. Classical images mingled with pop art and runes of political affiliation: a Cyclopean one-eyed head with its brain chopped out; the owl of Athena; the goddess Artemis, her bow raised across a bared breast.

Wandering the covered walkways, alongside shutters scrawled with slogans, I stopped to look at the posters: tirades against the local police, the 'betrayal' of Syriza, the EU and the Troika. Locals carried brooms to paste up their latest posters – flyers for Athens Pride, economic manifestos, a collage of photographed demonstrations (Palestinian slingshooters, stick-wielding Mexican tribespeople, Kurdish separatists firing behind sandbags, Greek rioters wearing bandannas – a globality of rebellion).

In this semiotic jungle, the image that kept stopping me in my tracks was the ubiquitous stencilled horse. High-maned, with a ladder dangling from its belly, this wasn't just *any* horse. It was an artificial horse, mounted on rollers; a wooden horse. To be precise, it was Odysseus' 'cunning trap', another iteration after the one I'd seen in Troy. But what did it mean, here in Athens?

After talking to protesters in Exarcheia Square (men in motorbike helmets and balaclavas, wielding leather coshes around burning oil drums) and bumping into a few Homerphiles in bookshops piled with left-wing classics by Chomsky, Bakunin and Slavoj Žižek, I was none the wiser. But sometimes you don't have to look all that far, and this was one of the serendipities that travel occasionally throws up. For the source of the Trojan horse graffiti was in the very flat where I was staying.

There it was, spread across James's desk in black-and-white A5. The stumpy tail, the ladder dangling under the belly. The only difference was this horse was stuffed with words: 'hegemony', 'aesthetics of resistance', 'the othering gaze'; dozens of phrases, the kind that get bandied about in arts councils and well-meaning social enterprises. It was a project James's collective had initiated, and Lewsha was their frontline guerrilla – she was the one who'd been printing the stencils all over Exarcheia. 'We're trying to reclaim the language of the discourse,' said James, puffing on a Camel. 'Documenta is an expression of the global art market machine, and we're challenging this power dynamic. We're dragging the discussion into the streets and squats.'

By turning the interlopers' weapons against them, James believed his collective was mirroring the effect of the Trojan horse. But it was a complicated, contradictory image. Greeks had become Trojans, defending their own cultural spaces against the invaders. And weapons no longer cut it. By making words the stuffing of their Trojan horse, James and his colleagues were deploying an idea that simmers in the *Odyssey*: the power of words to bite just as hard as steel. After all, in the most iconic of Odysseus' adventures – the encounter with the man-eating Cyclops – it's word guile, not steel, that saves the hero's skin.

'Nobody [*Oudeis*] – that's my name,' Odysseus tells the Cyclops after the monster has gobbled down several of his crew. It's a brilliant pun echoing his own name. When he's blinded the giant with a red-hot staff, this clever wordplay saves him. 'Nobody's killing me,' Polyphemus roars, and so nobody helps him: a single word becomes the hero's shield.

'We are all Greeks. Our laws, our literature, our religion, our arts, have their root in Greece. But for Greece . . . we might still have been savages and idolaters'.

So wrote Percy Bysshe Shelley in 1822. Nearly two centuries later, his words were echoed by a banner hanging over Omonia Square, on the edge of Exarcheia: 'Welcome to the Barbarians'. And yet still the philhellenes, the 'lovers of Greece', keep coming.

Shelley was a firm devotee of Homer, perceiving the Greek epics as 'the column upon which all succeeding civilisation has reposed'. He was writing during the peak of Homerphilia, an enthusiasm that both nourished and fed off one of the most influential events of the nineteenth century: the Greek War of Independence.

Between 1821 and 1829, Greece was flooded with over a thousand well-meaning activists from all over the continent: exiled officers who'd been on the wrong side of the Napoleonic wars, former fur traders back from the Americas, a French fencing teacher pretending to be a cavalry officer, a Spanish girl dressed as a man, hundreds of Germans who saw themselves as citizens of a new 'Hellas' (culturally strong but politically disunited) and England's most famous poet.

That was Lord Byron, who did more than anybody to propagate literary philhellenism. He was drenched in the romantic love of ancient Greece, which he'd poured into *Childe Harold's Pilgrimage*, the poem that made his name, after hiking around Troy and visiting Odysseus' Ithaca. Setting out to join the war, he designed his own uniform, inspired by descriptions in the *Iliad*. But he died before his illusions could be shattered, struck down by malaria in Missolonghi. Others weren't so lucky.

'I said to myself, "you are going to fight under the standards of Achilles alongside the heroes of the siege of Troy"', recorded a Prussian officer called Bollmann. 'But the ancient Greeks no longer exist . . .'

Slowly, they discovered the grubby truth behind their romantic fantasies. Already disillusioned by the failure of their Greek compadres to converse in the language of Homer and dispirited by a death rate of one in three, the philhellenes watched Greek war bands fouling mosques and churches with their horses, prostituting Turkish boys, cutting pregnant women open and stuffing dogs between their legs. All this contributed to the visitors' growing schizophrenia: revering Greece while reviling the Greeks.

The philhellenes stuck with the cause, and at Navarino Bay, muddled orders led to the unintended bombardment of a combined Ottoman–Egyptian fleet, which left the Turks incapable of recapturing the Greek island bases. The war would stutter on, but Greek independence had effectively been won (it would be confirmed in 1832, at the Treaty of Constantinople). It became a model for independence movements all over the continent. 'The Greece that Byron fought for – the Greece that still exists,' writes the historian Roderick Beaton, 'with all the continuing problems inherited from its violent birth – lies at the very foundation of the Europe that we know today.'

This complicated relationship has coloured interactions between Greece and western Europe ever since, including Greece's mismanaged absorption into the Eurozone. If European culture has its 'root' in Greece, as Shelley claimed, how could Greece be excluded? When the very symbol of the union – the euro itself – is derived from the Greek letter *epsilon* (a reference, according to the EU website, to 'the cradle of European civilisation')?

Debate still swings on the Greek crisis: internal differences or a crisis in the neoliberal welfare capitalism model? A systemic failure of the currency union or the fault of one nation in the Eurozone? The country that did more than any other to create Europe continues to have the most contradictory relationship with it. Like Brits crossing the Channel, Greeks talk of 'going to Europe'. They may have given Europe its name, its foundational literature, philosophy and political concepts, its earliest maps and scientific discoveries, but they remain outsiders in the European project. Which makes the pan-European intimacy with Homer all the more problematic. Do we have the right to claim these stories when we remain so ambivalent about the nation that forged them?

It was time to listen to Homer. At the edge of Exarcheia, behind a row of policemen with riot shields, I crossed a formal lawn and stepped between the ribbed Ionian pillars of the Archaeological Museum.

Inside, an exhibition had been arranged on the theme of Odysseus' wanderings. Looming over Bronze Age amphorae and a lekythos jar on which Circe dispensed her potion was a statue dredged in 1900 from a two-thousand-year-old shipwreck. The marble was corroded and pitted, nibbled by marine bacteria to the crumbly texture of stale Weetabix. Stooped, his mottled face sunk beneath a pointy *pilos* hat, this was Odysseus as the penniless tramp, the self-declared 'toiling and suffering man'. For the ancient sculptor, it wasn't the cunning weapon deviser or island king who intrigued, but the wanderer stripped to the lowest position in society.

From James Joyce's *Ulysses* to the Coen Brothers' *O Brother, Where Art Thou?*, from Fenelon's *Les Aventures de Télémaque* (an eighteenth-century bestseller about the travels of the hero's son) to Margaret Atwood's *Penelopiad*, the great and good of Western literature have lined up to do their cover versions, squeezing Odyssean plots and characters through the ideologies of romanticism, modernism, feminism, absurdism, post-colonialism. Odysseus the everyman: a hero of everywhere and every-when. It's hard to think of another story that's been aped so often.

How easy to forget this is a Greek story – composed by a Greek, deeply engaged in what it means to be Greek. When Homer sang about the union of various Aegean kingdoms for a common goal (the recovery of Helen and revenge against the Trojans who'd 'captured' her) and the struggle of that union's most ingenious member to 'get back to the land of his fathers', he established the foundations of Hellenic nationality. In short, he invented Greece. Regular Homeric recitals at the pan-Athenaeum (along with special games and sacrifices to Athena and Poseidon) became part of the imperial project that clawed Athenian authority over the disparate islands and peninsulae we now think of as Greece. Without Homer's epics, Greece as a nation might still have existed, but it would have needed to find another thread to bind itself.

That crumbly statue – the penniless wanderer – is pretty much Odysseus' condition when he turns up at the Phaeacian court. Helped by the kindly and charming Princess Nausicaa, he tells his tale like any wanderer arriving out of the blue, so effectively that the Phaeacians warm to him. 'You frame and bedeck this tale,' declares King Alcinous, 'as knowingly as any bard.' Odysseus may be a warmonger, a crew leader, a weapon deviser, but he's also a storyteller.

But if the soldier can be a storyteller, how do we distinguish between the magic of his poetry and the bloody deeds executed with his bow? It's a conundrum that threads through the great epics, joining their blood-stained heroes to the more problematic blood shedding in which so many are implicated. What lured the philhellenes to swing their swords for Greek independence? Homeric heroes were still inspiring the men who made themselves cannon fodder in the nineteenth century. Which is why Socrates, all the way back in the fifth century BC, warned that Homer would make calamitous reading for young men in the ideal city.

Odysseus isn't the only storyteller that night in Alcinous' palace. The Phaeacian bard, Demodocus, has such a gift 'that he charms his hearers with every song to which his heart is moved', accompanied by his own playing on the lyre. Now, sitting in a gallery in the museum, I was waiting to hear a modern-day lyrist, Nikos Xanthoulis, one of Greece's leading classical musicians. Unfussily dressed in jeans and a blue shirt, he stood out from the marble reliefs around us, aligned to the setting by his lyre. Resting it on his left leg, he leaned in to pluck the first watery notes, and I thought of an image from the climax of the *Odyssey*: the hero, stringing his giant bow before he launches his vengeance against the suitors, like 'a skilled musician who makes fast both ends of twined cat-gut and strains it to a new peg in his lyre'.

It was no passive audience that day. Gripping her transcript, a woman with a beehive of grey hair rose from her seat and read Homer's description of the lavish Phaeacian court: the dogs crafted from gold and silver, the maids' distaffs fluttering like poplar leaves. She made way for a lady in horn-rimmed glasses, who recited the passage about the land of the Lotus-eaters. The lyre floated its notes, swooshing with ripples like falling water. A woman in a purple blouse and scarf took the reins of the narrative and the lyre glided faster, splashing out dramatic flourishes at the tips of the verse:

> τὸν δ' ἀπαμειβόμενος προσέφη πολύμητις Ὀδυσσεύς
> *Now spoke up many-sided Odysseus:*
> Ἀλκίνοε κρεῖον, πάντων ἀριδείκετε λαῶν,
> *'Lord Alcinous, who shines amongst your island people,*
> ἦ τοι μὲν τόδε καλὸν ἀκουέμεν ἐστὶν ἀοιδοῦ
> *What a good thing it is to listen to a bard*
> τοιοῦδ' οἷος ὅδ' ἐστί, θεοῖς ἐναλίγκιος αὐδήν.
> *Like this one here, whose voice is like a god's.*

It was like a neighbourhood book club – devoted to the *Odyssey*! Half a dozen voices rattled along the polysyllabic flow of the hexameters, hard consonants bouncing off the tripping rhythm, a sound that was physically robust and ghostly at the same time: ancient and immediate.

As Xanthoulis put down the lyre, I could see the audience looking around with buoyant expressions. I picked up my notebook and approached a couple of the reciters, eager to know what it meant for them.

'We see this as our story,' said Vera, the lady in purple. 'Coming through many problems with the Cyclops and all these things, it's like us. We are living the story when we read it! All our troubles in Greece today, all the things we are suffering.'

The grey-haired Alexandra was more cerebral: 'It is a journey into the soul. Reciting it is like a spell.'

'The *Odyssey* is a never-ending story for us,' added a woman called Ioanna, who had brought her children with her. 'It is not from that time only, but every time. But also it has a happy ending. He gets home and when you read this, it gives you a good feeling. It gives you hope.'

Later, I sat with Nikos Xanthoulis in the atrium cafe, sipping sweet gritty coffee. We mixed up a stew of subjects, from Nikos Kazantzakis's *Zorba the Greek* and his sequel to the *Odyssey* (Nikos believed *Zorba* was a better match for the Odyssean spirit) to his grandmother's ability to recite a lengthy Cretan epic – a reminder of the long-enduring span of epic traditions.

'Odysseus is one of us,' said Nikos. 'That is why we can understand him. He has a sympathy for everybody, he's trying to survive.'

This is why he appeals to Greeks today, and why he's appealed across so many different milieus. It is what makes the *Odyssey*, in Nikos's view, particularly well suited to public recital.

'We could have done it differently. We could have read the *Odyssey* with classically trained actors. But doesn't the epic belong to everybody? I was talking to the lady who read about the Cyclops, and she commented on Odysseus' "human" qualities. Look at how he behaves. He has beaten this monster, he's blinded him, escaped, he's back on his ship, all he has to do is sail away . . . and then he calls out his name!'

It's a critical moment. Too proud to keep his identity a secret, Odysseus exposes himself to the wrath of the Cyclops' father, the sea god Poseidon. A strategic mistake, perhaps, but for Nikos this is the moment when the hero reveals everything about himself.

'He can't help it,' said the musician, his face stretching in boyish delight. 'And isn't that so human?'

3

My dearest son, what brings you down into this world
Of death and empty dark when you are still alive?
Odysseus' mother, *The Odyssey*, Book Eleven

OUT OF ATHENS on the road to hell. Which, when you're in Greece, is a mappable location. Dawn 'rose-fingered' – just the way Homer likes it – glancing between giro stalls and billboards. The Corinth Canal glistens under the highway, which snakes into the Peloponnese, guided by palisades of sticky black pine and tall firs. Beach resorts swing frayed signs out of cypress groves, parasols peeling inside the warped frames of yesterday's paradise. At Areopoli, I switch to a local minibus, admiring its goat-like grip on the stony track of the Mani; as dexterous as an elderly, black-cowled woman, who drills the driver with the hard tack of her consonants, then hurls herself into a thistle field to make her way home.

In Athens, I experienced the *Odyssey*'s continuing resonance for modern Greeks, and in Chios I learned about the immediacy of its storytelling, echoed in the traumatic experiences of refugees. Now, I want to feel the story and its spirit for myself. En route to Ithaca, my plan is to dip into two of my favourite episodes. One is associated with the darkest of all Odysseus' adventures, the other with a glamorous city visited by his son Telemachus. Between them, I hope they will teach me something about the relationship between the epic and the landscapes from which it was conjured.

The hero's visit to the underworld is a key episode in his journey. Directed by the sorceress Circe, he seeks out the dead seer Tiresias, hoping to learn how he can find his way home, and in the process he encounters a panoply of the dead. Not only significant in plot terms, this is a dramatically powerful episode, poignantly reuniting Odysseus with his dead mother, along with the shades of his comrades-in-arms, Achilles and Agamemnon, and his hapless crewman, Elpenor, who fell from Circe's rooftop after drinking too much wine.

From Gerolimenas, a stony, shelving plain tapers towards the narrow waist of Cape Tanairon, which fans out before shrinking into a bony ridge swallowed by the sea: a ramble of about ten miles. As isolated as Land's End, its sinkholes and underwater warrens rationalise the long-standing local associations with the underworld. I've read about a cave here, known locally as 'the cave of Hades', and a cult to the sea god Poseidon, who throws so much trouble at Odysseus.

As I stride out from Gerolimenas, the heat is pricking my neck – a mischievous acupuncturist with red-hot needles. I relish the blades of shadow dropped by the stone towers, the walls of rising cliffs bristling with prickly pear and yellow candlesticks of broom. After a few miles, I'm in marching mode. The only audible sound is the slap of footfall, skin lubricated by sweat, tenderised against the leather whips of my shoes. The road slides down a mountain ledge towards the isthmus that chains Cape Tanairon to the rest of the Mani. An African wind blasts along the scarp, grumbling through tangles of spurge, howling over the chattering cicadas.

Ahead shimmers the sea in bands of turquoise and quartz. Nuzzling at the sandy inlets, either side of a thorny buff, the water tingles with invitation, and I race towards it. A sea-polished ledge does the job of a swimming-pool locker; a moment's plunge and the water absorbs me. The blistered soles of my feet protest against the salt, but the water is deliciously soothing. I could hang here all evening.

The gods are remembered at Cape Tanairon. Inside a dry-stone wall near the beach, spirals wheel around circled petals, framed by chalky white tesserae, like a diagram of the cape. Identified with a sanctuary to Poseidon, its foundation stones have been absorbed into a Byzantine chapel, whose ruins squat on the bluff. Under horseshoe arches and the slate red pediment of a narrow doorway, I step inside a prayer chamber that looks like it's holding a rummage sale. Amongst the offerings are a jewellery box, a bottle of Nemea wine and a toy Shrek. Should I leave something? I've packed thriftily and I don't fancy letting anything go this early in my journey. But as I climb out of the chapel, I can't help wondering if I've broken a taboo. 'Ever jealous the gods are,' as Menelaus warns Telemachus, 'that we men mind their dues.'

For a sailing nation, no god is more relevant than the sea god. So it's hardly any wonder that Poseidon wields such a dramatic influence over the *Odyssey*. On the Mani, Poseidon was even more terrifying than elsewhere, for not only was this narrow peninsula wracked by the sea, it was haunted by earthquakes – the dealings of the 'Earth-Shaker', to use one of Poseidon's most common sobriquets.

After spending the night under the lighthouse, lulled to sleep by the rhythmic booming of the waves, I wander back across the beach, past the Byzantine chapel, and dip into the adjacent cove, where an oval cavern yawns beside a couple of battered fishing dinghies. Behind a vaulting fig tree and cairn-like projections, waves of soot-stained rock ascend to tangled grasses and belly towards the muddy earth. This is the mouth of Hades, associated with Hercules' mission to drag out the hell-hound Cerberus, which is mentioned in the *Odyssey*. But this cave is also connected to Poseidon, for a nearby oracle of the dead doubled as an asylum for fugitives: under-water overlapping with underworld. The *Odyssey* dramatises this association, dragging Odysseus towards the underworld in order to untangle the sea god's wrath.

Scholars have located Homer's Hades all over the place, from the Souli gorge in north-western Greece to a volcanic crater near Naples to Extramadura in Spain. In the *Odyssey*, Hades is on 'the Earth's verge', 'where no flashing Sun-God shines down a living light'. I'm not concerned with locating the unlocatable. What I want is an underworld experience. Hercules' grotto was disappointingly shallow, a mere three metres deep. Talking to the lady who runs the tavern, I learn of another cave associated with Hades, and she shows me a photograph. 'But this is not an easy place to reach,' she warns, tapping her knee. As it turns out, she's quite the Sibyl.

★

Ahead is a steep rise speckled with loose rock that looks like chunks of petrified feta cheese. I tiptoe along wobbly dry-stone walls as if I am a child testing a new climbing frame, occasionally jumping off when I lose my balance or the wall shakes beneath my weight.

The brow of the upland teases its distances, peaks drifting back across paths that reveal new, surprising folds. Finding a summit at last, I peer down the stony slope, towards a cleavage in the hills. To the west, spiky basalt jaws are hanging over the mouth of a sea cave. There it is! I brace my backpack under a slant of limestone and trench my feet in the soil, braking my descent with fistfuls of thistle. It would be suicidal to drop too close, so I use the cleft as a guideline, carefully weighing my feet on pinnacles of rock. A treacherous cliff-side, jagged rock below, a cave mouth gulping at the sea – this is something! After a few moments' hesitation, I wedge my clothes among the crags and lever myself down.

The swell bobs me at the mouth, cool in the embrace of shadow. Slowly, I breaststroke deeper into the cave. Under weapon-like stalactites, the slap and suck of the water echoes against the walls; the light turns powdery. This is what I've been looking for – the childlike thrill as imagination mingles with the landscape. But as I breast deeper, a queasy unease nudges like backwash. I'm not quite bold enough, and after a few more strokes I turn around.

Confronting the infernal is a staple of heroic storytelling – a cliché as well trodden as the casino scene in a spy movie. Christian epic hesitates on the threshold of hell, so medieval epic tends to reconstruct it symbolically: Beowulf's descent to the mere-cave of Grendel's mother, for example. But the ancients had no such qualms. 'How will you find some madder adventure to cap this coming down alive to Hades . . .?' asks the shade of Achilles. As travellers' tales go, a visit to the underworld beats them all.

But the eeriness of the Homeric Hades is peculiar to itself. This isn't so much a place to be travelled to, more an atmosphere that Odysseus ritualises into being. What rises around him is a vampiric no-man's-land, where shades communicate by drinking the blood of sacrificed sheep, where Odysseus cries bitter tears when he's unable to feel his mother's touch. Nowhere is the pain of his journey more palpable; his exclusion not only from home but from the years that have been lost, years in which loved ones have aged and died, and the traveller has missed their passing. Here, at the furthest extremity of his journey, Odysseus comes closest to his loved ones. And far from lingering among the dead, he is fired with a renewed determination to get back to them.

Dressed again, I scale the pinnacles and look around for my backpack. When I set it down, the tuft looked isolated enough. But climbing from below, the perspective is different. So much for a solitary outcrop. It's camouflaged amongst dozens – no, hundreds! – of rocky protuberances.

Where is my backpack? I make for the most obvious spot, but the rock is a different shape, less of an aperture. I slide sideways. There's no track, no goat droppings or herder's footprints. Just thistles all around, and brutal fists of rock. Everything looks different.

I can feel myself growing less steady, struggling to judge the distances between the rocks. Once, I topple on to my backside, and slide about ten feet downslope. Picking myself up, I concentrate on a more strategic approach: dividing the hillside with invisible cross hairs, raking along a north–south axis, then climbing to the next level.

For a couple of hours I scour that hillside, cursing my stupidity. Fortunately, I've kept my valuables, including my passport and diary, in a smaller string bag over my shoulder. But the prospect of losing my sleeping bag and bivvy bag, chargers and clothes, some pills I need . . . that's not so easy to digest. The pulse is throbbing in my temples, the sun hammering down and my desire to find my possessions rapidly diminishing. I have a bottle of water, at least, which feels for the moment more precious than anything I'll have to abandon.

Solitary ramblings can mess with your head. *It's the underworld, I've failed to pay the toll!* Giving up on my baggage at last, I trawl around limestone tufts, hacking between thorny burnet and yellow shafts of broom haunted by hornets as noisy as helicopter gunships, looking for a short cut back to Gerolimenas. Walk due north: can't be more than an hour's hike, right?

If my experiences in Athens illuminated the *Odyssey*'s resonance in modern Greece, this adventure is showing how stories are cooked in particular places. Read the *Odyssey* and you're sucked into Greece, then and now. Laundry is laid out to dry on pebbly beaches, the hero rests under olive bushes, fences are constructed from wild pear. Odysseus, swimming to the 'riptooth reefs' of Scheria, surviving the backwash of breakers and roaring combers, ventures inland, mindful of wild beasts and the thrashing of the elements.

Gashed by thorns and grazed by stones hidden cunningly under sun-browned burdock, my fingers and elbows are bleeding, stinging in the sunlight. I reach the base of the hill, hoping I'm past the worst. But the next incline is just as perilous, and far higher than I estimated. My ability to judge distances has collapsed: a third brow soars, mischievously hidden until I scale the second crest. My head is tingling, and a couple of times my vision glazes over, punctured by the brutal sun. I'm grateful whenever I find a trail of stones. But they are rarely stable, and my balance is too weak to hold the line. Twice I fall into the gorse, leaping up quickly in case of snakes. Homer would describe my state of mind as *aporia* – 'uncertainty' or 'perplexity', literally 'without a path'. Which is exactly the problem I'm up against.

Clumps of burnet brush against my knees and a dry-stone wall grazes my palms. At last: a bridge across this thorny wasteland. Olive ledges wobble under my feet and a gate of iron strips sags against the ground. Sun flares crackle in my vision, out of which snaps a furious-looking dog – calling out in no uncertain terms. Grabbing a length of withy, I scramble towards another gate, which guides me on to a dusty track. Below an uninhabited farmhouse, a cockerel is peering through a covert of pine. I look into its eyes, warmed by a strange feeling of gratitude.

Homer, like other epic poets, blurs the line between nature and the supernatural. A shearwater transforms into a sea goddess to guide Odysseus to Scheria; a hawk ripping the feathers off a dove is taken as a providential sign. Nature is the language through which the gods express their will, offering threats but also resources. I hobble down a dirt track towards the main road and stick out my thumb, begging for a lift away from that nightmarish hill country.

This evening, I make it to Areopoli – hitch-hiking with a kindly German couple, who offer me Oreo biscuits and mineral water. I pay for an en suite room with an overhead TV (thirty-five euros – the most expensive of the whole trip) and channel-surf on a lovely soft mattress. What a mess I've made of things – so early in the journey! I went looking for adventure – looking for the underworld! – and, in a way, I found it. Be careful what you wish for, as the old saying goes, or the gods may just grant it.

Odysseus' underworld experience is known as the *nekyia*, which is the name Carl Jung used for the 'descent into the land of the dead' associated with unconscious psychological distress. Lying on my bed in Areopoli, I fret over my lost possessions, the pills I've lately depended on, my lost Sim card pin code (which has put my phone out of action), and wonder how much of that shifting landscape I've carved from my own subconscious. The frizzy-haired concierge at the hotel commiserates with my experience and offers a weary shrug: as far as she's concerned, this is textbook Mani.

'You know,' she says, 'there's a reason we have so many places associated with Hades. This whole region is very unstable. There are a lot of caves and waterholes under the surface. In old times, they built stone towers to survive the earthquakes and they must have done it well, because a lot of these towers have survived. But now we have regulations, so we reinforce all our new buildings against the earthquakes.'

She's rationalising Hades for me, but I'm not feeling rational; and later, channel-surfing on the overhead TV, I spook myself all over again. The events onscreen are strangely familiar: a hero sacrificing a sheep, venturing between cavernous walls, surrounded by wraiths . . . I'm watching the *Odyssey*! Greek epic retold as an American TV movie, dubbed back into Greek. Here is Odysseus (a beefcake Italian-American called Armand Assante, looking like he's walked out of a shampoo advert), striding towards an encounter with the blind seer Tiresias, played by that master of spookiness, Christopher Lee.

Like some B-movie horror cliché, the TV is speaking to me. And if I ever return to the Mani, I'll be sure to observe the lesson: before anything else, I'll make a beeline for the livestock market and pick up a couple of sheep.

4

Telemachus, the time for shyness now is past,
We sailed the seas for this, to hear news of your father.
Athena, *The Odyssey*, Book Two

WHEN I THINK of Telemachus, I think of the reunion – the young man returning from Pylos and Sparta, where he's been seeking news of his father. Visiting the loyal swineherd, Eumaeus, he sits down in his servant's steading and greets the tramp-like stranger Eumaeus is hosting. Touched by the goddess Athena, the mysterious tramp is transformed: taller and suppler, his jawline firmer, a dark beard clustering around his chin. Telemachus takes him for a god; it requires considerable reassurance to convince him this is 'your father, the Odysseus for whose sake you have grieved'. At last, we are told, 'Telemachus with a cry folded his father in his arms and burst out weeping.' There's no other passage in epic literature that moves me like that one. Every time I read it, it gets me.

Sixteen years earlier, barely out of university, I was working as an English teacher in a school in Jerusalem and the West Bank when I was called back home. I slung down my bag in the hospital corridor. Lights blinked on consoles and screens, electric data dancing around the still figure in the bed. When I held my father's hand, I knew he was already gone, and all that remained was to turn off the machine. I had left home thinking he was on the road to recovery, and I would often wonder if I had made the wrong choice.

Of all the characters in the *Odyssey*, it's Telemachus who really speaks to me. Gawkishly unsure of himself, shambling in the adult world he can't quite understand, trying to negotiate a life without his father . . . until one day the impossible happens and the father he'd given up for lost comes back to him. The stuff of dreams. Epic isn't just about the public, the making and breaking of nations. Sometimes it can probe the deepest feelings inside us, reaching in with the raw shock of familiarity.

In Kalamata, I stocked up on provisions: a new Sim card and phone charger, a towel, some clothes, a cheap replacement backpack. But some things couldn't be so easily replaced. I was . . . I've hesitated to write this, but it's part of the story, it needs to be told . . . I was missing my pills, and I wasn't sure if I could manage. For a few years now, I had needed a serotonin regulator. Oh, the irony . . . don't go looking for the underworld, or the gods might just take you there. Still, I wasn't too far down to miss the joke.

No chance of getting a new batch sent out. Where could I pick them up? *No: I'll be on the move, nowhere to send them.* Maybe I'd been reading too many old tales, but I felt like this was some kind of test. If I couldn't even control the chemical imbalances in my own head, what business did I have trying to understand all these ancient heroes and the epic obstacles they faced?

After Hades, I hankered for civilisation – and Pylos was the answer. Another bus, under the limestone folds of Mount Taygetus, tracing the Gulf of Messenia. The soil was softening, the hills less bony, blossomy with oleander. Riding towards Pylos treated me to one of Greece's most magical views – the descent to Navarino Bay, resting placidly like a perfectly cut sapphire. Strange to think that here, 190 years earlier, a chaotic sea battle took place that sealed the Greek War of Independence. Now, the bay sits not so much like the setting for the battle as a trophy commemorating it. Gaze at it long enough and all the world seems to harmonise.

Pylos was a waterfront idyll, ringed in cafes and memorial cannons. I could have stayed for days. Which meant there was only one thing to do: get the next bus out. A road darted up the Engliano Hill like an arrow shot between the cypresses and currant plantations, and the bus dropped me by the 'steep crag' where the palace of King Nestor was built. Here, according to the story, Telemachus arrives searching for news of his father, and receives the most comprehensive hospitality available to his age.

The palace was closed until the next day. But hidden nearby, amongst oleander and olive groves, was a tholos – a Bronze Age memorial, partially buried under a mound of earth. A bedrock corridor flared out of a beehive-shaped vault where corbelled rows of mud bricks tapered towards a massive capstone, like the stopper on a jar of sweets. I felt a frisson of excitement standing inside it. No point digging around for a room: my night's shelter was ready and open.

Xora was the nearest village, three miles in the tracery of shadow cast by the olive trees, a twisting, dog-yapping road flanked by vineyards budding with enormous *fileri* grapes resembling purple gobstoppers. That afternoon, in a wood-panelled bar in the heart of the village, I tumbled into another world. Men sat around baize tables playing cards; others were telling prayer beads, practising the underrated art of making a grainy cup of coffee last the whole afternoon. Occasionally, they broke off from slow-motion sipping to fondle the long strings of vegetables carried inside by onion farmers.

There were twenty-four men in the bar, and a single woman – she was behind the bar. She lit up with a kindly smile when I asked about the carton of 'Nestor wine' propped beside the fridge. She took out a plastic bottle and poured a tumbler of honey-sweet white wine. I doubt Telemachus could have been any more refreshed when King Nestor mixed him 'a cup of wine which had mellowed eleven years in its jar before the good-wife broke the sealed wrappings and poured it forth'. I drank it down, relishing the sweetness of the *fileri* grapes.

'Our wine,' she explained, refusing any money. She passed across a tray of peanuts, launching into a rhapsody about the local wine-making co-operative. The talk was beyond me; what stuck was her sad, full-lipped, heavy-eyelidded smile. She fended off, indulged, mothered and scolded the men who crowded the bar with a combination of exuberance and melancholy that felt quintessentially Greek.

Hospitality is a key feature of Homer's world. The very suggestion that Telemachus might spend the night in his ship appals King Nestor: 'as if I were a naked, needy man who had at home neither cloaks nor coverlets for the soft sleeping of himself and his guests!'

Nestor rolls out the full gamut of hospitality, feasting Telemachus on heifer meat and golden tankards of honeyed wine; sending him off to his bath to be anointed with olive oil by his daughter, Polycaste.

This is where my Telemachus connection becomes shaky. Unconnected to a princely network, subsisting on a tight budget, I would have to be content with a tumbler of Nestor wine, a bowl of peanuts and a kindly smile. After my hapless ramble on Cape Tanairon, it had been good to connect with people again. I shuffled back to my sepulchral lodging and lay down under the corbelled vault of the tomb chamber with my new backpack for a pillow, slumbering to the racket of angry dogs.

Pylos is one of the great Mycenaean palaces. It was reopened, in June 2016, after a three-year, multimillion-euro refurbishment, with a steel roof arcing over a catwalk. Wooden slats groan underfoot, metal wire and piping soar above. Peering down from the catwalk, you look on a tidily designed grid of storage chambers and corridors, the hearth slab of the throne-room, the H-shaped entrance hall and a bathroom with a spiral pattern wheeling round the terracotta tub. It feels like you're hanging off the outer rigging of a space station, peering through a telescope at ancient Greece.

So evocative is Nestor's Homeric hospitality, the eye is drawn towards anything that fits the scene: the terracotta bath, the fragments of two-handed drinking vessels in the storage chamber, the wine magazine, the clay benches where pithoi jars of olive oil were kept. And this picture is supported by the archaeological research. A cache of clay tablets, unearthed in 1939, revealed details about palace entertainments. Amongst these was a feast at which eleven cattle were sacrificed in honour of Poseidon, which has been corroborated by animal bones found on the site. This is echoed in the *Odyssey*, when Telemachus first encounters Nestor, sitting on a sheepskin rug with a tankard of wine, offering jet-black bulls to Poseidon, 'in whose honour the leg-bones were now burning with fire while the assembly ate of the entrails and organs'.

If you had to be blasted back to the Bronze Age, this wouldn't be a bad spot to land. But for all the wealth associated with Pylos, recent discoveries suggest we may have been underestimating it. As

I walk around, a team from Cincinnati is pulling back tarpaulin covers and handing out tools. In 2015 they dug up a shaft grave near the palace, revealing bronze basins, gold cups and carved stone seals predating the Mycenaean era of King Nestor. The highlight – so freshly discovered it wouldn't be publicly announced until several months after my visit – is an agate seal-stone just 3.6 centimetres long, depicting a muscular, long-haired warrior plunging his sword into a helmeted opponent's neck. So intricate is the technique, so astonishing, it bears comparison with the poetic craft of Homer.

'It's gonna take us years to assess it all,' says one of the archaeologists, pushing a wheelbarrow between rows of oleanders behind the palace. 'And there's still more, there's still places we haven't even dug.'

His supervisor is calling out – a new trench is about to be dug and she wants help putting together a 2-D profile. As I watch him go, I think: isn't this what makes history so exciting? Recent discoveries have shifted our understanding of key Odyssean sites such as Pylos, Ithaca and Troy. The past is still changing – and who knows what its future holds.

5

I cannot credit this as shiny Ithaca,
I must be roaming round another foreign land
And you are telling me these tales, mocking me,
To make me lose my way.
    Odysseus, *The Odyssey*, Book Thirteen

'As YOU SET out for Ithaca,' wrote the poet Constantine Cavafy, 'hope your road is a long one, full of adventure, full of discovery.' More tussles with the gods of Greek transport – a cancelled bus from Pylos, a change at Kalamata, a night ferry to Cephalonia following a misdirection to Patras – and I was plunging towards Sami harbour, only a ferry ride away from Odysseus' home. Signs for 'Extreme Water Sports' hovered over groves of wild pear trees, where goats were clawing at the trunks, as if they were training themselves to go bipedal and try out the waterskis.

The ferry was delayed, but only by a couple of hours. Passengers sank into leatherette couches or congregated on the stern to be branded by ultraviolet. A row of tree-furred pyramids expanded across the sea line, their contours so acute they turned the sky to an azure sawtooth. I thought of Telemachus' description: 'our islands which rise rock-like from the sea, not one is fit for mounted work, or grass-rich: least of all my Ithaca'.

At the climax of the *Odyssey*, it is on Apollo's feast day that Odysseus avenges himself on the suitors. The god is often invoked in prayer, so it's no wonder the Ithacan temple to Apollo has been associated with a cult to Odysseus. Archaeologists have found bronze and copper coins showing a thickly bearded head squeezed under a *pilos* hat, the trademark image of the wily traveller. Minted in the fourth century BC, these coins suggest a continuity of local tradition, tantalising clues to the rich mythology from which Homer reaped his story.

Long after the convoy of ferry passengers had sped towards Vathy, the island's main town, a buzzard wheeling over the ancient temple site might have caught sight of a limping straggler, turtle-backed with sweat. Picking my way between limestone boulders and mastic bushes, wafted by the scents of sage and wild thyme, I imagined Odyssean devotees reciting the hero's adventures. The masonry hinted at former majesty, but nothing matched the robust practicality of a carved marble basin, stained with loam and goat saliva, at the base of the hill. A farmer was using it as a trough, under a length of piping fed through a traffic cone.

Currant groves and vines jungled along the road towards Vathy, and a broken-down minivan squatted over a farmstead, reconstituted as a hayloft. I stopped occasionally to rest my limp and admire the vista. For a first-time visitor, the landscape of Ithaca is eye-wateringly exotic, its hogbacks and summits furred with cypress and pine, its angles as unlikely as a sketch by Escher. But that's for the outsider – the native shouldn't be flummoxed, surely? Yet Odysseus' return is a fug of disorientation. Waking up after his Phaeacian taxi ride, the hero finds himself blinking at Ithaca's 'unaccustomed face, the pathways stretching far into the distance'. Surely this can't be Ithaca! He curses the Phaeacians for deceiving him, and it takes the insistence of the goddess Athena to persuade him of the truth. Here is one of Homer's psychological masterstrokes: the unfamiliarity of homeland, which has been noted in veterans of Vietnam, Iraq and many other conflicts. Home, the nostalgic stuff of travellers' dreams, revealed as something more complicated.

That winter, sixteen years earlier, I came back to an unfamiliar home. I wasn't returning from a war (although the West Bank had been rocked by the intifada, and I'd seen plenty of skirmishes); it was the change at home that threw me. Not just the loss of my father, but the subtle alterations between the rest of us.

Well-wishers orbited the house, bringing lilies and lasagne, cards warm with signatures and kindness. Many of them I had never seen in my life; many I would never see again. There were critical adjustments in our family chemistry, new roles to adapt to. There were stories, so many stories, of things I had missed. I found myself falling as family life reorganised itself around the mythology of a few months when I hadn't been around, and wondered if there was any way to pull things back to how they used to be. The past was receding like a departing ship that's landed you in the eerily unfamiliar world of the present.

All around me I heard the voices of strangers, their words of comfort and kindness; and the strange new tones of those I thought I knew. At the school in Jerusalem, or amongst the tanks and tirades of the West Bank, I had never felt so abroad. And now, reading the *Odyssey* all those years later, I recognised that feeling of dislocated homecoming. It's often the greatest risk of travel: the fear of what may change back home.

The long walk from the port brought me, later in the afternoon, to Ithaca's principle town, Vathy: a picture-postcard seaside port sprawling around its gentle bay, under hills lush with olive and pine. Between waterfront cafes and artists' workshops, souvenir stores were making a brisk trade in the old tale, handing out miniature wooden horses, busts of blind Homer and T-shirts with the legend 'Nobody is My Name'. There was a Nausicaa jewellery store, a Calypso studio, paintings of sea storms and erotic-looking Sirens in an exhibition beside the town hall. The kitsch was a joy. It pulled Homer down a couple of pegs, celebrating the *Odyssey*'s three-thousand-year-old popular appeal. Forget the literary canon, this is the tale that can charm *everyone*; inspiring the French underwater explorer Jacques Cousteau (who sailed a ship called *La Calypso*), retold by bands such as Cream, Steely Dan and Florence and the Machine. As a child of the eighties, my first Odyssean experience was a sci-fi cartoon set in the thirty-first century, and I wandered around Vathy humming its theme tune: '*Ulyse-ee-ee-ee-eees, no one else can do the things you do . . .*'

Wandering the harbour, I could feel the Odyssean enchantment all around me, bouncing between yachters and antiquarians, package holiday pensioners and ouzo-sozzled party-goers stumbling against the hero's bronze statue. But one group had taken it to the next level: a group so immersed in the *Odyssey* they made me feel like a superficial dilettante barely giving Homer's story a passing glance.

It was there in the name of their yacht, so easy to pick out amongst all those dreamy monikers: *Sama Cherie, Sun Fizz*. Of all places, it made sense in Ithaca. The *Odysseus* was crewed by Hungarians: sinewy guys with anchors and hearts inked on their forearms. I talked to a couple of them, and they introduced me to their captain. Moon-faced in a stripy shirt, Tibor Vass had the bluff, stubborn look of Captain Ahab. Arms folded over his chest, he threw a few answers back, in between inspecting cleats and checking the foresails. His voice was calm and toneless: a pragmatic captain's voice, ready for all eventualities.

'We started in Troy,' he explained. 'So we've been following the *Odyssey*. All the way. And now here we are!'

'But where . . . what route did you take?' I scooped my pockets for my notebook.

'It's all there in Homer,' said Captain Vass, leaning over the guard-rail. 'I've studied the *Odyssey*, I've looked into it. We went along the African coastline, up past Italy. We stopped at Sicily, Malta, back to Greece. It's taken us several months, of course. If you do this journey properly, you can't rush it.'

I felt a rebuke against my own hasty itinerary. In a few days, I'd be ditching the *Odyssey*, spinning off in pursuit of another epic. I admired the intensity, the integrity, of Captain Vass's focus.

'Of course, it's been hard,' he said. 'We had some very rough weather. Storms at sea. There's a lot of rocks you have to watch out for. And we were sailing at night, mostly, because we were filming in the daytime. But this is a modern ship, of course. For Odysseus, it would have been much worse!'

Hungarians pursuing a Greek epic: here is the trans-European appeal of the *Odyssey* in a nutshell. The story that we like to think belongs to all of us.

I wanted to visit some of the places associated with the *Odyssey*'s final chapters – the palace where the final showdown takes place, a cave where Odysseus stashes his loot, and first of all the spring where his loyal swineherd Eumaeus waters his pigs, under the 'Raven's Crag'. Here Odysseus learns what's been going on in Ithaca during his twenty-year absence, and here he meets his grown son for the first time.

After a drink and some food in Vathy, I found a bike hire store behind a statue of Poseidon and scribbled out the paperwork for a GT Karakoram. Crepuscular light flickered through olive groves, brushing the corrugated roofs of the farmsteads sliding down the steep skirts of Mount Neriton. Despite the isolation of the distant southern stretch, the farmsteads were guarded by yapping dogs, their gates heavily padlocked, topped by razor wire. The 'wild-looking dogs' and prickly pear recalled Homer's description of Eumaeus' farmstead. But after the gentle atmosphere of Vathy, there was something sinister about the security.

Olive, laurel and cypress thickened over the soaring road. Following the signposts for the Raven's Crag, I locked the bike around a wooden post and followed 'a rugged path through timber along high ground'. Bushes bulked around me, dense to the skyline and down to the bay. Stones formed steps, then a slope, before fading into naked dirt. My feet sounded clunky on the narrowing stone, chided by the whispering cicadas.

The path looped around a pair of hillsides, a double-ridged bow, intermittently swallowed by gorse. Spiderwebs hung like fencing between the branches, impressively tensile. I remembered a line from the epic, uttered here at Eumaeus' farmstead, when Telemachus imagines his parents' bed 'abandoned . . . for spiders to defoul with their webs'. Far beneath were less gluttonous creatures: beetles scuttled, amber-coloured centipedes crawled between the rocks and there was a cameo from a mud-coloured snake, eyes flashing like beads in one of Vathy's tat stores.

The wrinkled Raven's Crag droops from the Marathia plateau like the haggard face of an anxious god. Drops plinked under a hood of rock, suggesting the 'dark pools' that quenched Eumaeus' pigs. A hole in the rock looked like the mouth of a large animal's burrow. Goat bells played nursery tunes in the valley, hidden below a cascade of fig trees. I wanted to imagine the swineherd, one of the most likeable characters in the story, not only loyal but hospitable, a character so relatable that Homer addresses him as 'you'. But there wasn't much to connect to round here. I should have twigged from the name: 'Raven's Crag' isn't exactly an invitation to camp out. My plan to spend the night like Eumaeus, 'under the overhang of the crag', was undergoing some rapid revision. When I spotted a femur bone on the ledge above the burrow, I decided to look elsewhere for a night spot. The bone had been licked clean.

Heading blindly with a stick – too dark now to detect the spiders – I was racing against the dying light. When I glanced over my shoulder, the turn of the hill was already black. I was looking frantically for clues of progress: the track reassembling in stone, the gradient rising. The steady chorus of the cicadas was a welcome back to the land of life, away from the brooding menace under the crag. Gasping by the roadside, I draped my towel over a picnic table and in a state of wonder peered into the darkening bay.

The spring was a refuge. A suitable HQ for a hero-in-hiding, where he could reveal himself to Telemachus and plot the suitors' demise. But it's up on these promontories that a returning adventurer could feel his homecoming: the whole island at his feet, gnawing at his appetite to reclaim it. At moments like these, it's hard to see the epic as mere fabulation. The contours of the story seem to wind, eternally, out of the shrubs and rocks around you.

'If this isle were mine,' said Byron when he visited Ithaca in 1823, 'I would "break my staff" and "bury my book." – what fools we all are.' In the morning, I could see where he was coming from. I sped towards Odysseus' palace, to the sound of pebbles crackling under my tyres, the crowing of cockerels and dogs snarling against wire stockades. In the glades and hillsides where I stopped to rest, horse-flies and damselflies were humming together like motor cars at the start of a race. Butterflies were nectaring amongst brambles and bees were spinning cat's cradles under sun-bloomed clouds of pollen. A delicious smell of sap oozed from the trees they were reaping for their honey, under blossom exploding like popcorn. Many of these elements had disturbed me on Cape Tanairon, but perspective is everything. I wasn't pathless any more, dwelling on the underworld. Here, in the bright light of morning, it was beautiful.

Crossing the narrow isthmus that links the island's northern and southern swells, I paused beside a roadside mural: a curved trireme of painted stone and mirrorwork, engulfed in flowering waves, under the words 'ΕΥΧΗΝ ΟΔΥΣΣΕΙ' – 'Blessings of Odysseus'. These words were discovered, all the way back in 1868, on a fragmented clay mask pulled out of the Cave of Loizos, in a bay near the village of Stavros.

I saw the mask itself, uphill from the spider-haunted cave, when I visited the Archaeological Museum in Stavros. It's an influential phrase, which I had seen reproduced on paintings and postcards in Vathy, and engraved under a bust of Odysseus in Stavros's main square. The original mask was discovered along with a statuette of Athena and a set of clay tripods, uncannily similar to the tripods that Odysseus carries as gifts from the Phaeacians, which have been dated to Homer's time (roughly the eighth century BC). Some observers have taken this as proof that Odysseus was a historical figure. But it doesn't prove historicity, only the power of his story. This is Odyssean fan art, testifying the hero's ancient popularity. As for the hero himself, he remains out of reach, tangible only in the verses of the epic. Words, not clay or flesh, are the true frame of his life. But there was one more place I wanted to find, which offers the most beguiling of all links to an Odysseus embedded in the whispers of historical reality. It was time to pay a visit to his palace.

'If it looks like a cat, sounds like a cat and smells like a cat – it's a cat!'

The museum curator was sure about it, and an increasing body of evidence backs her up. Overlooking three seas, surrounded by three mountains, dated roughly to 1300 BC, this multi-level Bronze Age ruin has led the excavation leader, Professor Thanassis Papadopoulos, to declare, 'We believe we are before the palace of Odysseus and Penelope.'

'See how it rises stage beyond stage,' declares Odysseus, 'with its courts all properly walled and coped, and its double doors so securely hung.' Several millennia later, this grandeur is a little harder to pick out. After walking my bike down a pebbled trail and stashing it under a holm-oak, I climbed up several tiers of broad stone steps, like a grovelling petitioner on his way to the royal court. So far, all I could see was cypresses, oaks and the odd stony tuft. Thorns scratched my arms as I squeezed into a pine thicket and crept inside the shell of an old chapel with marble slabs half hidden under the foliage. But this was no Bronze Age wreckage.

Had I come all this way only to be rebuffed? What a downer it would be to leave Ithaca without even glimpsing the hero's palace. I could feel a tug of negative thoughts, and I was having to work a little harder to push them away. Sitting down on a rock, I pulled off my T-shirt so the wind could blow-dry my sweat and tried to cheer myself up with an apple. Then I peeled myself off the rock and carried on the search.

It was back down the path – a stony track peeling towards the sea, bearing me on to a terraced plateau. After struggling to find the right access point, the scale of it came as a shock. Square-cut boulders piled over the bedrock, forming arched niches, raising a lookout over the sea. A well sank into the bedrock and a carved staircase plunged, past column bases and pillars, down a craggy cliff-face, spreading clues of habitation across the lower plateau. It didn't look like a castle so much as a pirate's mansion; a place to stash his loot, with plenty of escape routes. Which made it an apt home for Homer's trickster-hero.

Wooden planks straddled the crevasses. Beyond them were the remnants of a large *megaron*, or hall. Creaking and splintered, the planks looked like they hadn't been used for a long while. Homeric archaeology was paying the price of the economic crisis. The funds had run out, and the team from the University of Ioannina had downed their picks in 2012, after eighteen years of labour.

What they had left behind was turning into a meal for nature to slowly ingest. Wandering around, it was hard to distinguish between the boulders and stony clumps, the thistles and wild grasses tethering the masonry, what was manufactured, and what organic. I thought of Pylos – the shiny gangways, the state-of-the-art archaeological equipment. No such glamour round here. Nature was gobbling up the archaeologists' hard-won discoveries. It reminded me of Penelope's shroud – the one she weaves for her father-in-law Laertes. To keep the suitors at bay, she promises to choose one of them as soon as she has finished it, but each night she unpicks the work she's done. It's one of many acts of subtle cunning, which show why she's a perfect match for her 'wily' husband.

Sometimes we forget this: without Penelope's delaying tactic of the shroud, without her loading the dice in her favour and arranging a 'bridal contest' that requires the slothful suitors to wield her warrior husband's bow (a pretty tall order, given they've been pigging out on her estate for several years), the story would never reach its climax. So here it is, the template for thousands of stories that have followed. We've all seen it: the hero takes the enemy by surprise in the grand hall, reveals himself and picks them off, one after another. Bond movie, Western, sci-fi spectacle: the *Odyssey* gives them all their final act prototype.

An arrow pierces the chief suitor Antinous' throat; blood sprays from his nostrils like veiny egg yolk. His chin smacks the floor and so does his wine goblet. Another arrow takes Eurymachus in the nipple and rips through his liver. Leocritus is speared in the groin so deep the bronze shaft emerges from his back. Swords and spears are slashed left and right, grisly screams erupt from skulls cracked open and the whole floor is splattered with blood.

Odysseus stands, covered with blood, gore on his hands and thighs, granting no quarter to the last suitors' pleas for mercy. The treacherous servant Melanthius is bound with rope, his limbs cut off piece by piece, and savage dogs jostle around to gobble at his severed penis. And when the slaying is over, we follow Telemachus (gentle, self-doubting Telemachus – oh, how things have changed!) across the yard to watch the 'wanton' handmaidens hanging from the vault until their feet stop twitching.

Is this the 'happy ending' some of the reciters in Athens had mentioned? Perhaps they were talking about the poignant reunion between Odysseus and Penelope, united by shared memories of their olive tree marriage bed (another piece of cunning from Penelope: she tells her servants to pull out the bed, a bluff she knows would irk the real Odysseus, since he constructed it himself around an olive tree – his indignation is the proof of his identity). In one of his most perfect similes, Homer compares Penelope's relief to the survivors from a shipwreck, 'their bodies all crusted with salt spume, but happy, happy, for the evil overpassed!' It's a stroke of genius, grafting the experience of the husband on to the long-suffering wife, imaginatively binding them as mutual survivors of Poseidon's wrath. For a moment, it is possible to forget the terrible slaughter and relish the reunion of a husband and wife after being apart for so long.

But the story isn't quite over, and for all the heroic rage of Odysseus' revenge, it fails to draw a line under the narrative. A mob sets out for the palace, restrained only by the last-minute intervention of Athena. 'The vast mischief this man has worked against the Achaeans!' roars Eupeithes, father of the slain Antinous. 'Think of the many stout warriors he took abroad with him, only to cast away his ships and all their crews; while he returns, only to butcher the very best leaders of the Cephalonians that remained.' Here is Homer's wisdom, to the very end: relishing Odysseus' victory, but aware that others might see it differently.

My Odyssean adventure was nearly out of sand. The next day would carry me back towards Athens, to ride across Attica and the plains of Greek Macedonia, deep into the Balkan Mountains. As darkness fell, I lay down on the floor of the megaron, resting my back against the pillar stub. The hall was on a raised level, out of reach of burrowing creatures. But it was unroofed, open to the elements, and that night they decided to visit.

A shot of thunder. Whip-cracks of lightning on the far side of the island. The salvoes grew more frequent, transforming the stone walls to flashes of zinc or silver; like photo negatives of the palace's prime. Still, the rain took its time. The deluge didn't come until a few minutes before midnight.

I picked up my meagre possessions and hid myself under a wooden shelter near the foot of the stone steps, ushered out by the gods. It was a sodden, uncomfortable, occasionally alarming night. But something was glowing inside me . . .

This is Odysseus' palace!

I had glimpsed the *Odyssey* in Bronze Age ruins and the landscape that nourished Homer's tale; but also, more surprisingly, in modern protest art, a Homeric reading group, a vintage of wine, a long-cherished blessing, a Hungarian crew retracing Odysseus' journey. The *Odyssey* doesn't just speak to us today – it covers every eventuality:

from the economic principle of minimum cost choice (explained by Circe when she advises Odysseus to sail closer to the monster Scylla than the whirlpool Charybdis or the Clashing Rocks) to the grief-numbing drugs taken in the aftermath of war; from the virtues of hospitality to the nymph Calypso's outburst against sexism ('You unrivalled lords of jealousy!'). Sure, some of its values can be disturbingly alien, like the extravagant sacrifices to the gods or the hanging of the handmaidens. But their strangeness gives balance to the story. Showing just how far-ago it is, they push the more resonant moments all the closer.

This questing tale of an adventurer who can fashion a weapon out of an olive wood branch to beat a 'barbarian' on a foreign isle, who can entertain his hosts with charming tales from overseas and slay without mercy the intruders in his home, is a blueprint for European literature, but also for its history. It anticipates the restless searching, the storytelling relish and the violence that underpin the continental story, from Crusades to colonialism, from the Age of Discovery to the Atomic Age.

Another roar of thunder broke the sky, and excitement swooshed around my belly. The weather was stirring up so much drama, it felt like the gods were talking to me – or to anyone else who happened to be abroad. I clambered on to the table, wearing my towel like a headscarf, and yelled at the brawling sky: 'Ha! I made it! I made it to Odysseus' palace!'

Let it roar, let it rain. Tomorrow, I would turn my back on Greece. I would soon be out of the Olympians' orbit, at the mercy of other gods.

PART TWO

Elegies for an Everlasting Wound

The Kosovo Cycle

Prince Lazar of the Serbs has been ordered to hand over the keys of his cities by the Turkish Sultan Murad. But the Turks have not accounted for Serbian defiance. Lazar assembles an army against the Muslim leader and sets out for the battlefield. He knows that defeat is inevitable: he has spoken to a heavenly hawk, pledging himself to the 'Kingdom of Heaven'; and he has denounced his most courageous fighter, Miloš Obilić (pronounced Milosh Obilich), as a traitor.

The next day, Lazar marches from his stronghold at Kruševac to Kosovo Polje, the 'field of Blackbirds'. Before the sun has risen, Miloš races ahead, approaching the Sultan's tent and presenting himself as a turncoat. He bows to the Sultan, but instead of allegiance he brings death, pulling out his dagger. It is too late to turn the battle: Miloš is hacked down and Prince Lazar is captured too. He dies beside his most faithful knight, realising that he was mistaken and Miloš has been loyal to the end.

News of the disaster spreads back to Kruševac and the mourners gather. A young woman tends to the dying, giving them wine to drink before they breathe their last. Prince Lazar's widow hears of the catastrophe from a pair of talking crows and bemoans her family's tragedy. A noblewoman stoically accepts the deaths of her nine sons until she is shattered by the fall of the tenth. The shadow of grief falls across the Serbian lands, along with the conquering Turks.

6

My lord, I beg of you, beloved lord,
Towards the troubled field do not ride,
For fear an evil falls on Kosovo.
Jela, *The Kosovo Cycle*, 'Song of
the Battle of Kosovo'

M Y GREEK JOURNEY had been focused on the edges — islands
and headlands, for the most part. Boarding a train across the
Attic Plain and a bus into the hill country north of Thessalonika, I
was moving to a different altitude: I would be spending the next
few weeks among mountains and rivers, under a cloudier sky lacking
the translucence of the coast. I had encountered the *Odyssey* in many
surprising ways, but apart from the reading at the Archaeological
Museum in Athens, Homeric words were rarely on people's lips.
Now, I was venturing into Europe's most combustible region. If
anywhere is likely to broadcast long-ago verses as communal experiences, it's here, in the pine-furred valleys of the Balkans.

Of the epics I was following, the *Odyssey* was by far the most
ancient. This next stage of my journey would carry me into the
most recent — a tale barely six centuries old. Less cohesive than
the *Odyssey*, the *Kosovo Cycle* is more an anthology, a series of
episodes loosely connected to the central drama, which concerns
a fourteenth-century battle between a Christian army and the
Ottoman Turks. Sung by bards or *guslars*, who performed on a
(usually) single-stringed instrument known as a *gusle*, the semi-
historical, semi-legendary stories of the *Kosovo Cycle* evolved
during the long centuries of Turkish occupation. They weren't
formalised until the early nineteenth century, when philologists

collected the songs recited in the mountain villages between Serbia and Bosnia, and their popularity broadened, expanding with the movement for Serbian independence.

The *Kosovo Cycle* is a deeply European story, for the Ottoman threat was faced across the continent, drawing out armies from Russia in the east to Spain in the west. Supplanting the Crusades, the battle between Christendom and the Turk became Europe's primary geopolitical narrative for several centuries, straddling the medieval and modern ages; and amongst its many contests, few have inspired as much creative attention as the 1389 battle at Kosovo Plain. The English playwright Thomas Goffe made it the subject of a drama, performed in Oxford in 1618; one of the battle leaders played a role in Christopher Marlowe's *Tamburlaine the Great*. But for all its continental resonance, this conflict was remembered as a peculiarly national story. For the Serbs, it became their cultural touchstone. Because it was Serbs who led the Christian army in 1389, and it is Serbs who continue to relive this iconic battle.

Jostling against each other, forming unlikely alliances and splinter groups, the people of the Balkans have spent the last millennium in a dance of death defined by unlikely partnerships and new moves nobody could have seen coming. Climbing down at Skopje, the Macedonian capital, I wandered amongst the ubiquitous statuary – from Alexander the Great on a ten-metre-high column to a woman in a bodycon dress, frozen mid-chat on her mobile phone – and ate a sandwich under the mace-wielding Prince Marko, a mighty medieval Serb in a cuirass decorated with jagged lines. Although a Christian hero, still celebrated from Bosnia to Bulgaria, Marko became a Turkish vassal and died fighting against the Christians.

Characters like Marko reflect the mixed and often contradictory storytelling traditions of the Balkans, which filled Ramadan nights with saz-playing Muslims and spun shared heroes between Orthodox Serbs and Catholic Croats. Interweaving around the Balkans, these traditions survived feudal and Ottoman rule, spinning through the nineteenth-century independence movements, tottering through the decades of Communism when Marshall Tito, the so-called 'wily locksmith', kept the Yugoslav Federation together. But with the collapse of Communism at the end of the 1980s, tensions widened around strikes, unemployment and growing corruption, and nationalism broke free. The scholar Marko Živžovic writes:

> With the advent of war boundary reinforcements occurred and each community selected only some from a pool of largely shared traits as markers of identity. It is in this way that epic poetry accompanied by the *gusle* became exclusively associated with the Serbian communities of the Balkans, particularly with the Bosnian Serbs.

The Yugoslav wars spanned the nineties, from the ten-day Slovenian war in 1991 to the ousting of Serbian president Slobodan Milošević in 2000. Journalists reporting on these terrible events often defined them as 'ethnic' battles, misled by the divisive rhetoric of Balkan politicians. But ethnicity is one trait shared across the Balkans – Yugoslavia, the 'land of the south Slavs'. Already, I could hear the buzzing of multiple sibilants, all those Zs and Ss and the cymbal clash of multiple Ts. Macedonian, Bosnian, Croat and Serbian aren't separate languages but dialects from a shared Slavic root. It was on the basis of other differences, such as religion and the historical narratives they followed, that identities were formed. The Serbian guslars sang their songs about Kosovo, and saw themselves fighting a new battle for Kosovo. But whereas the old battle united the peoples of the Balkans against a common enemy, this time they were fighting against each other.

Now, as I crossed three of the nations most scarred by those conflicts – Kosovo, Serbia and Bosnia – I hoped to learn how the old medieval stories had stirred themselves into recent history. If Homer's epics were the amniotic fluid from which Greece was born, then the Serbian epic is more complicated. For the Serbian kingdom had flourished *before* the Ottoman conquest: 1389 marks the date not of its beginning but of its end. The poems of the guslars didn't give birth to Serbia so much as keep the dead living: a cryogenic chamber nurturing the national mythology from which Serbian independence would be spawned, more than four centuries later.

★

After a night on the streets of Skopje, resting against neo-Hellenic statuary and warming up beside the ablutions fountain of a fifteenth-century Ottoman mosque, I climbed into a minivan to Priština, the capital of Kosovo. Spruce and sessile oak thickened around cliffs of limestone and slate, where minerals flashed under the high-altitude blaze and rapids plunged into frothing rivers surging in pleats of blue and gold.

Paradise was short-lived. Low-slung warehouses colonised the flood plain: brick depots, tilers' stores, glaziers and roofers. But the buildings were relentlessly unfinished – unplastered, rebars sticking out of roofless upper storeys, occasionally humbled by marble-fronted examples of 'Gangster Baroque'. Priština was jagged with even more of this kind – brutalist tower blocks raised by unscrupulous developers enjoying the post-war construction boom, permits and protocols shrugged aside in a gangland free-for-all. There had been attempts to clamp down, but public figures who put their heads above the parapet tended to find themselves in ugly encounters with hitmen.

Stumbling out in Priština, I wandered between slapdash multistoreys and glassy mosques with minarets that could easily be mistaken for cooling towers or telecom installations. Concrete slurped off the sides of buildings like the crusting on a pan of porridge, and shifty-looking men wandered out of a darkening park, flicking their cigarettes between the wheels of rusty cars. I climbed up a hill flanked by haphazard constructions, making my way towards an old townhouse where a retired university professor ran a hostel.

He was dozing in his office when I arrived. Rheumy-eyed, with liver-spotted hands and skin so translucent it looked like you could peel it off his skull, he jittered over his paperwork and called up his daughter to show me to my room. Prints of old Priština, showing horse carts and domed mosques, flanked the carpeted stairwell, images from a gentler cityscape where the buildings had space to breathe.

The Professor was Albanian-speaking and Muslim, like most of his neighbours. He represented the Kosovar Albanian culture that Slobodan Milošević's army had tried to erase in the late 1990s (and nearly succeeded – 90 per cent of Kosovar Albanians were displaced in the conflicts). Many Serbs saw the Kosovar Albanians as interlopers, overlooking that the Albanoi tribes predated Slavs in this region, and as a Christianised people they fought beside the Serbs in the battle of 1389 before partially converting to Islam during the Ottoman period. For many Serbs, Kosovo remains their spiritual cradle, too precious to give up their claims. So, on my first morning in Kosovo, I set off to visit the place where this cradle was made.

Only a diehard glory hunter could envy those medieval soldiers. Sun like a blowtorch, flaring off helmets, frying cuirasses. A ferocious June heat, with dust swirling round, stirred by the capricious Kosovar wind. It was a last-gasp bid for autonomy, and the Christians were gambling all their cards. Tvrtko, king of the Bosnians, brought his army; there were Croats, Hungarians, Wallachians, Albanians, Rumanians and, most numerous of all, the Serbs. They must have looked impressive. But not only did the Turks outnumber them, they also had the advantages of less cumbersome armour, the springy mobility of their Mongolian ponies, and their expertise with the bow. Just as Henry V would show at Agincourt twenty-six years later, well-trained archers and lighter gear are formidable assets.

Can you call it a victory when your commander-in-chief's been killed and your casualties number in the tens of thousands? Whichever side you were on, the battle was a disaster: 'the blood of the heroes bled', sings the Serbian standard-bearer in the epic cycle, 'stirrup-iron deep to a high horse'. Both armies lost most of their men (fatalities have been estimated at 20–35,000), including their leaders, Sultan Murad and Prince Lazar; which is why historians are still debating who won the battle. 'Blessed above the rest was he who, running his sword into the throat and skirt of the leader of such a great power, heroically killed him,' reported the Florentine Senate, referencing the assassination ascribed to Miloš Obilić. But killing the sultan wasn't enough. Under the leadership of the sultan's son, Bayazid, the Ottomans launched a counter-attack. Compressing his troops into a single, explosive charge, Bayazid ripped through the heart of the Christian army, capturing Prince Lazar and earning himself the nickname 'the Thunderbolt'.

The outcome may have been indecisive, but history's trajectory was set. Rudderless after the death of Prince Lazar, the Serbs had little to throw against the Turks, and by the 1460s they were firmly under the Turkish yoke. Their consolation was the heroic poems they sang about the battle. In 1497 an Italian court poet watched exiled Slavs 'jumping like goats', singing a form of epic; later observers noted their distinctive single-string gusle. Scholars have speculated that in places like Dubrovnik the original singers were Serb exiles, who may have been inspired by troubadours, Italian poets and the Greek epics. If the *Odyssey* is ambiguous about the rewards of victory, then here is the ambiguity of defeat: loss elevated to heroic celebration.

Over the centuries, Serbian leaders tugged at the tale of Kosovo, like bell chimers calling the faithful. In the early nineteenth century there was 'Black George', a wealthy pig farmer who adopted Prince Lazar's coat of arms and launched a major uprising against the Ottomans. On the outbreak of the First World War, there was King Petar of Serbia, who 'got it into his head', according to his son, 'to die and become a saint, like Lazar at Kosovo'.

But nobody exploited the legend of Kosovo like Slobodan Milošević. After months of rabble-rousing, the Serbian president touched down on the medieval battle site on 28 June 1989, the battle's 600th anniversary, and addressed a million-strong crowd:

> The Kosovo heroism has been inspiring our creativity for six centuries, and has been feeding our pride and does not allow us to forget that at one time we were an army great, brave, and proud, one of the few that remained undefeated when losing. Six centuries later, now, we are being again engaged in battles and are facing battles . . .

With propaganda on overdrive, his face plastered beside Prince Lazar's on public buses, Milošević grabbed history by the neck and shook it at the crowds. Storytelling, in his hands, was a weapon of mass destruction.

Beyond the tower blocks and flyovers, Priština spills its infrastructural sprawl out into the open country. Warmed by the sun, tar steams through the old battlefield, under billboards pasted with the suspect smiles of election candidates. Blackbirds or *kos*, which gave Kosovo its name, are still ubiquitous, sending the lizards on rapid escape routes down the sun-hammered loam.

I was enjoying the walk, enjoying the adrenalin of a new epic, but it was a dog-day afternoon. Between a billboard for 'Election Candidate Number One' and the Oraca Baumit Colour Centre, a dirt track snaked towards a razor-wire fence surmounted by closed-circuit television. A dog whooped up a storm at my arrival, leading out a sleepy-looking guard, who tucked in his shirt and flicked through my passport. Behind him rose a stone tower, lichen-licked and loopholed, twenty-five metres to the top.

Commissioned by Milošević for the 600th anniversary, the Gazimestan tower was a grim medieval pastiche, a propaganda phallus. On one side a broken sword was fixed; on the other, bronze letters snarled verses from the *Kosovo Cycle*, spoken by the beloved Prince Lazar:

> Ко је Србин и Српскога рода
> *Whoever is a Serb and born of Serbs*
> А не дошо на бој на Косово
> *And does not come to fight at Kosovo,*
> Не нмао од срца порода
> *Let such a man receive no loving spawn,*
> Ни мушкога ни девојачкога
> *Let him not sire son, nor daughter too,*
> Од руке му ништа не родило
> *And from his hand that sows let nothing grow,*
> Рујно вино ни пшеница бела
> *Not on the vine nor field's whitest wheat,*
> Рђом капо док му је колена
> *And from his seed let nothing fruitful flow.*

Epic rule number one – fight or be shamed – installed on a monument like an army recruitment poster. Considering the political tensions at the time these words were mounted, it's hard to imagine Milošević choosing a more provocative commemoration.

The sun was puncturing my shoulders, so I was glad of the shade inside the tower. Strips of light snagged on bronze letters mounted on carved tablets: more verses from the *Kosovo Cycle*. A banister twisted rustily and wrenched-out light fittings yawned over the tablets. Chocolate wrappers and condom packets slid under my shoes.

I emerged from the darkness to thorns of heat. Parapets formed a tight square and a bronze map encouraged me to reimagine the flat fields below as the battlefield of 1389. The steam from a nearby thermal power plant became the smoke of the Turkish camp; the peonies splattering the fields became the blood of the fallen soldiers.

Although Sultan Murad's body was taken back to Constantinople, his blood and intestines were buried in the soil of Kosovo, allegedly on the very spot where he was slain. What this gave the Turks, according to the Albanian novelist Ismail Kadaré, was 'both a curse and blessing at the same time'. A mausoleum was built around the sarcophagus, and a local family commissioned to look after it.

The mausoleum is a short walk up the highway. Inside a grassy quadrangle perfumed by roses, the gnarly branch of a fissured blackberry bush gropes at the door, as if to pay homage to the sultan – or stab him anew. A giant turban, wrapped in plastic sheeting like a toffee apple, tilts over a cloth woven with gold thread, and calligraphic pieces display the sultan's *tughra* (royal seal). Honeyed light seeps into the chamber, evoking peaceful serenity, far from the brooding atmosphere of Gazimestan's dark tower.

Next door to the mausoleum was a museum dedicated to Sultan Murad. A student called Emin was skulking about, his angular face lit by narrow brown eyes that seemed to be crushed with secrets. He led me between waxworks of Sultan Murad's turbaned inner circle, a model of the battle formation and photographs of a 2010 visit by Turkey's president (then prime minister), Erdoğan, whose government is the museum's sponsor.

'From Britain, you say? I really love your country! You can say the truth there. You can say, "this king was lazy, this one was greedy, this one was homosexual". But here, everybody has to be a hero.' As far as Emin was concerned, you couldn't trust anything about the Battle of Kosovo. 'Look at Miloš Obilić! Some say he was Serbian, others say he was Albanian, or Hungarian, others say he never even existed. These things have been exploited by politicians, so they become very dangerous.'

In the weapons room, we stood before helmets, shields and swords in glass cases. 'Maybe it is better if we forget about these things,' said Emin. 'Look at the Serbians – they are obsessed with Kosovo! Did you know, whenever there is an election in Serbia, the candidates have to answer three questions. First there is the economy. Then, whether to align with the West. And finally: how they can get back Kosovo.'

Through the reflected glass, I could see us both, superimposed around the curved swords. We looked like soldiers on the eve of battle, anxiously selecting our weapons.

Hundreds of thousands died on every side, and there were no winners: in this respect, the battle of 1389 and the fighting of the 1990s were eerie mirrors of each other. Walking to the Serbian Orthodox monastery of Graçanitsa the next day, to gaze at its macabre Last Judgment, with its snake-tailed devil and sea dragon, I stopped beside a monument to Serbs missing from the war. The giant letters of 'Missing' were clad in hundreds of passport-sized photographs, ranging from a bespectacled woman in her sixties to a youth in a leather jacket, his lips half parted, as if he was in the middle of a wisecrack. Like images of the missing all over the world, they were deeply poignant: their fates undeclared, their stories incomplete.

Over those days in Priština, I wandered around the capital and the sites nearby, often drawn by tips from the Professor, who circled his recommendations on a photocopied map. I browsed the book fair on a concrete esplanade of bo-ho brutalism that reminded me of London's South Bank, chatting to the student vendors and learning about the latest masters of Balkan noir. I treated myself to a slice of millefeuille at the Pianno Cafe and drank Peja beer in the wood-panelled Baron Taverna, where I was approached by teenagers selling roasted chestnuts and young women skilfully balancing themselves on six-inch heels. Some asked about my travel plans, and when I said I was planning to visit Serbia, they leaned in close, warning me to be careful.

The Professor was equally cautious. 'It is better if you do not go to that country,' he said. 'They are . . . not an easy people.' He had a reason for his warning, which he revealed, slowly, while his daughter was counting out the pills in his caddy:

We had to leave, as soon as the Serbian army came. I spent a week on the Albanian border, sleeping under a tree. We didn't know what was going to happen to us and we couldn't get any news from the people who were still here. Two of my daughters got away. One of them reached Macedonia, another made it to America. But one of my daughters was unwell, she wasn't able to travel.

As he continued the narration, he pressed his hands against the edge of the desk, fingertips quivering on the wood. 'When we came back, she was a missing person for many years. Then, at last,' he said, his lips curling in a frail smile, 'they showed us the mass grave.'

I thought of the poems I had been reading from the *Kosovo Cycle*: grief embedded in every line, spiritual victory reckoned out of loss. The Professor had lost what was dearest to him, but he knew how to smile against the sadness. For this is a region where men and women have long learned how to absorb tragedy and weave their own gauzy silver linings.

7

Lazar, Lazar, prince of a noble family,
Which kingdom of the two will be your choice?
Do you prefer the empire of heaven?
Or is your choice the kingdom of the earth?
    The Kosovo Cycle, 'The Downfall of the
                                Serbian Empire'

WINGING OVER THE battlefield, the black crows come, bearing their terrible news to the White Tower of Kruševac:

As God is witness, Princess Militsa,
Today we come from lowly Kosovo
And we have seen two mighty armies clash . . .

The distance from the Kosovo Field to Kruševac is less than eighty miles – for a crow. But earthbound backpackers have border disputes to contend with. As Kosovo's independent status was still contested by Serbia, the Serbian authorities were refusing to admit visitors across this unacknowledged border. Which is why I found myself sleeping on a bench in the bus stop of Niš, the night after leaving Priština.

The Professor had warned me: a Kosovo stamp in my passport was a red rag for the bullish Serbian border guards. Online recommendations agreed with the surprisingly voluble advice dished out at Priština bus station. Reluctantly, I backtracked, boarding a bus towards the Macedonia–Serbia frontier, tripling the distance.

At the Tabanovce crossing, the Serbian guard rattled through my passport, sniffing at some of the more obscure visas. 'Tourist? *Only* tourist?' I showed my most guileless smile. Behind him, his colleagues were disembowelling a long-haul truck with surly zeal.

For all the fractiousness of entry, beyond the steel piping of the border Serbia looked surprisingly harmonious. Meadows rippled under strip plantations; firwoods assembled in neat rows above fields as crisply partitioned as any English shire, green and gold with corn, beans and wheat coming into ear. Starlings fanned out of the woods and sheep stood still, as if they were posing for cereal box designs. Serbia had neither the decrepitude of Macedonia, nor the building frenzy of Kosovo. The fields were fat with bell peppers and bulbous tomatoes, verged by magnolias the size of champagne flutes. Even the road signs were orderly and shiny, behind tidy heaps of rubble.

I had chosen to focus my Balkan journey on the Serbian story partly because the Serbian epic has played such a key historical role; partly, I now realised, because I had always read about the Serbs as the villains of the Yugoslav wars, and isn't it the villains who play the best tunes? I had seen the backdrop to the epic cycle. Now I wanted to meet the people who sing the tunes.

Office blocks and banks, lead-roofed state buildings and sports cafes: at first glance, Kruševac didn't look much like the grand capital city of the epic cycle, where Prince Lazar feasts his knights and Princess Militsa leans out of the White Tower to learn the battle's outcome. But all over the city the medieval battle casts a pall, like a watchful elderly aunt keeping an eye on the youngsters.

You step inside the neoclassical Principality Building, and there in mosaic form is Prince Lazar, gazing beside his heavenly church. Above the stony ruins of his keep, a bronze Lazar rests over his sword, a few paces from a church named after him, where double-headed eagles and knights' helmets conjure the military and royal imagery of his epoch. Go to the Centar Café for a bottle of Lav beer and you're looking at characters from the *Kosovo Cycle*, twisting around an intricately carved totem pole: knights on horseback reaching out their swords, clashing with the scimitars of turbaned Turks, Miloš Obilić on his knees under Lazar's giant head. The same incidents and scenes, scrambled in different patterns, different spokes of the cycle radiating from the same enduring principle.

The most evocative of the memorials, sculpted in the nineteenth century in the wake of Serbian independence, is installed on the very spot where Prince Lazar's army traditionally gathered to march. Underneath an angel with black marble wings, bas-reliefs show Prince Lazar praying with his troops and Miloš Obilić daggering Sultan Murad. More than the reliefs, however, it was the statues sitting either side of the monument that sucked up my attention.

Glowing in the sunlight was a young noblewoman in a medieval bodice. She dangled a victory wreath from her arm, but on her knees was draped a funeral shroud. Known as 'the Kosovo Maiden', she is a beloved character in the epic, associated with the aftermath of the battle:

> And now the heroes red with blood she turns,
> And every hero that she finds alive,
> She washes him with water from her jug . . .

The Kosovo Maiden is a medieval Florence Nightingale, tending to the wounded men, easing their passage to the hereafter. Sponging her identity out of the soldiers' wounds, she symbolises the nurturing, self-denying role of women in the patriarchal world of the epic. She could be the kindly Nausicaa, who helps Odysseus on the island of Scheria; she could be Wealhtheow, who presents the mead goblet to the warriors in *Beowulf*. But what shines a particular significance on the Kosovo Maiden is the clarity of her voice, articulated by 'blind Živana', the female guslar who recited this song around 1817.

'Unhappy! Evil luck has come on me,' she moans, after the prince's standard-bearer sends her back home. 'Were I to touch, just touch, a green pine tree, / Even that leafing pine would wither too.' Her role as a nurse has been cut short, her fiancé is dead and she is confined to the principal role that women play in the *Kosovo Cycle*: mourner. Like Princess Militsa, who begs Prince Lazar to spare just one of her brothers from the battle; or the Mother of the Jugovichi, who breaks into pieces when a raven drops into her lap the hand of her tenth and last remaining son. In the *Kosovo Cycle*, the tears of women serve to measure the worth of men. But compliance doesn't necessarily mean silence, and in the Maiden's protest against her 'evil luck' we hear a voice that is all too often muffled.

If the Maiden's statue drew me into the epic cycle, the statue on the other side of the pedestal symbolised the long arm of its influence. The elderly bard sitting there was Filip Višnjić, a famous blind guslar active during the First Serbian Uprising of 1804–13, when Black George launched his campaign to drive the Turks out of Serbia.

Standing before this mercurial performer who did much to inspire the men fighting for independence, I tried to imagine him sawing his bow. Shoes curled under rugged bindings, trousers sagged under baggy folds and a ropey moustache dangled over his chin like a basket handle of woven hemp. Everything about his appearance resonated with the atmosphere of nineteenth-century Serbia, when epic poetry supplied the soundtrack to the drive for independence.

But where are the Višnjićs of today? The oral traditions of the Balkans were so fertile that in the 1930s they lured the philologists Milman Parry and Albert Lord, who built a ground-breaking investigation of epic composition around them. This was one of the reasons I had chosen to follow the *Kosovo Cycle*: it is a rare European epic that continues to live as an unbroken oral tradition. Across Europe, nowhere has more intense a relationship with its epic literature than the Balkans – because this is the place where they still sing it, as an active part of their lives. At least, so I had read . . .

'We haven't had guslars here for, *ahhhh*, maybe six or seven years,' said the lady at the tourist office. When I asked for more details, she suddenly became terribly busy, as if I'd stumbled on some kind of double entendre, and it wouldn't do to wander around Kruševac asking people to show me their guslars. The receptionist at my hotel, the caretaker of a nineteenth-century museum town house, a restaurateur advertising an evening of 'folk songs' in a wine-stained flytrap – all had the same response. The only guslars I was allowed to peep at were carved.

In the song known as 'The Building of Ravanica', Prince Lazar declares his intention to 'build a great church in Resava by Ravan water'. Miloš Obilić advises him against building it with lead and silver, for 'the Turks will take the kingdom away . . . they will dig the foundations of lead, and they will melt them to make cannon balls'. Instead, Miloš suggests, the church should be built of stone, for 'stone will not go from stone for any man, / And it will stand up for a thousand years'.

Climbing off the bus in the town of Ćuprija, a short ride north of Kruševac, I set off towards the church commemorated in that poem. It was a ramble of ten miles, between groves of bell peppers and firwoods droning with hard-working bees.

The broad stone wall around Ravanica is partially ruined, as if some sky god has been nibbling it from the top. Rising over a trefoil, a trio of golden crosses glows above this jagged parapet, lifted on polygonal lead domes. Stone and brickwork stripe the surface of the church, blending the blind arches with chequerboard panels, a biscuity basilica framed by a steep green cliff of cypress trees.

Painted in the late fourteenth century, the frescoes of Ravanica are prime examples of the Morava School, a late flowering of medieval Serbian art. Warrior saints brandish swords, spears and bows; Lazar, in a beaded crown, his beard hanging from his chin in thick swags, holds a cross-shaped staff; Princess Militsa appears with their sons; a gold-mantled Christ Pantocrator raises a three-fingered Orthodox salute.

This is storytelling by royal sponsorship, for the cult of Prince Lazar wasn't some organic folk outgrowth; it was a matter of public policy. In the turmoil after the Battle of Kosovo, when Turkish authority was still contested, the Serbian court struggled on and Princess Militsa put the church scribes to work. Hagiographies of Lazar were produced, establishing the legend of the 'heavenly kingdom': the belief that Lazar, visited by a heavenly hawk on the night before battle, chose to abandon the 'worldly kingdom' for the 'kingdom of heaven'. Over time this legend would become a key component of the epic cycle, sealing a compact with religion unparalleled in European epic.

Most of the epics draw on older pagan traditions. Part of their appeal is the link to our pre-Christian roots, from the Olympians to the Nordic gods. On the surface, the *Kosovo Cycle* is swaddled in the black robes of Orthodoxy. But underneath is something more complicated, the attempt to drape an old pagan idea in Christian garb: fight for your homeland rather than suffer the indignity of shameful retreat; an idea so enduring we can trace it back to the *Iliad*. Ideologically, Christianity is supposed to transcend tribal or national allegiances. The achievement of the *Kosovo Cycle* is to rebrand the old pagan heroic type with a Christian stamp, from Lazar's heavenly choice to Miloš's vow to 'die for the Christian faith'.

Militsa's propaganda campaign was aimed at shoring up support for her son, Stefan, if and when he was set free from the Turks (which did happen, between 1402 and 1413). In the long run, the Ottoman grip tightened and Lazar's line fizzled out, but the stories set down by the scribes would feed a cult that's still going strong. Which is why possession of the prince's bones became the ultimate prestige for Serbian churches.

Brought to the monastery soon after his death, Prince Lazar's remains stayed put until 1690, when Turkish attacks emptied Ravanica. Hidden away in remote bolt-holes such as the mountain monasteries of Szentendre and Srem, Lazar was kept out of harm's way until his golden rings were stolen by Ustašes (members of the Croatian fascist movement) in 1942 and he was relocated again, this time to Belgrade. Half a century later, in the run up to the 600th anniversary of the Battle of Kosovo, the gravitational pull of the past dragged the prince back towards Ravanica. At a time when Slobodan Milošević and his supporters were determined to bring the past into sharper focus, its physical manifestations had a special currency. And in Serbia there are few manifestations more powerful than the body of the prince-martyr of the *Kosovo Cycle*. So a long-winded procession bore Prince Lazar around the region, from monastery to monastery, including a visit to the old battlefield at Kosovo Polje in time for Milosević's provocative speech. Shortly afterwards, the prince at last completed his return.

Now, he lies in front of the brightly painted iconostasis, sealed inside a wooden casket with beaten silver edges. On one side, a carved panel records the triumphant homecoming of 1989 – Lazar borne through the gates of Ravanica by elaborately bearded priests. On the long side of the casket, facing the worshippers, appears Miloš Obilić, wielding a curved sword and a round shield, his ribbed cape floating behind him; a rare visual example of the Church acknowledging the cult of this ahistorical hero. Here is epic aligning with ecclesiastical – the two forces that together held up Serbian identity through the long centuries of Turkish dominion.

I had timed my visit to Ravanica deliberately, for I had heard about a regular Sunday ritual. The nuns were bustling and you could sense the anticipation as they hauled down candles on pulleys, wiped the casket with an oiled cloth and filled the nave with a heady smell of beeswax. When all was done, they gave themselves a breather and stood over a lectern, taking turns to read out the Psalms.

The buzz intensified with the arrival of an icy-bearded monk, helped forward by a novice. Incense was sprinkled and prayers chanted, cowling us in the atmosphere of an evening vigil. One of the nuns gave the casket a last wipe and pulled back the lid. The old monk tottered forward, eyes inflamed with pious hunger. He leaned over the casket, held steady by the novice, and planted a kiss on the pane of glass protecting the prince.

This was my cue. Edging forward, I stood over the casket, looking down on double-headed eagles and dragons, the embroidered decorations of the velvet shroud. Poking out of the red sleeves were the visible remains of Prince Lazar. Dark brown and dry, like huge, moulded gobbets of earwax: not bad for the flesh of a 688-year-old. I looked up, catching the expectant eyes of a nun, and pressed my lips to the glass.

In Greece, I had tracked a few physical connections to the *Odyssey*, but they always remained opaque. Here was something I had never anticipated when I started my journey: to be looking at a character from epic *in the flesh*. A Serbian speciality, for it could only happen here, where poetry and faith are twin life-support machines keeping the dead amongst the living.

There was heat behind me and the drumming of footsteps. More than a hundred worshippers were packing into the church, snaking all the way out to the forecourt: a convoy of school groups lining up like mourners at an open-casket funeral. There was a little jostling, the odd student spitting chewing gum into a palm. But mostly they were intent on the casket, their faces reflected as placid moons in the illuminated gilt of the icons.

I met one of them outside. He told me this was his fourth visit.

Whilst a few of his friends were putting on their headphones, we stood around chatting, and I asked what he saw.

'What do we see?' He jerked his thumb at the church. 'Didn't you look?'

'No, I mean . . .'

The old monk was tottering behind us, so the teenager called to the novice who was helping him along. They came over, and the monk carefully considered my question:

'For us, the Orthodox, we believe . . . that Prince Lazar was very holy, he did many great things, and through the power of the Holy Spirit, he continues to do these things.'

'Were you here when the coffin came back to Ravanica?' I asked.

The monk tipped his head. 'Many people attacked our church. The Turks . . . the Germans . . . the Albanians . . . But on that day, the glory of Christ shone down. Prince Lazar came back to us.'

8

Then Miloš saw before him many Turks
And bore his sword against them, fearlessly,
And with his strokes the hero cut them down.
                    The Kosovo Cycle, 'Song of
                         the Battle of Kosovo'

S LIDING BASSLINES, LOOPING beats and lurid images flashing on
a row of television screens: angel-winged go-go boys and flashy
nipple jewellery; oiled, ripped chests carved with lines you could
play a game of noughts and crosses on. I was a few hours and several
drinks into my first night in the Serbian capital, Belgrade, after a
long bus ride from Kruševac. Tactical error: I'd booked a room with
a professional DJ, which meant instead of spending the night in
tranquil repose, I was elbowed around a place as dark, smoky and
packed with miserable souls as any epic underworld.

The next morning, I had a light hangover to shake off. I stepped
out of the DJ's two-bed walk-up and followed the main road to the
centre, past billboards showing female soldiers in chic red berets.
Towering over the hoardings, the victims of NATO's 1999 bombing
campaign stood against the skyline in their jagged glory. Cables and
girders dangled from the skeleton of the Radio Building, like the
relics of a martyr, hung up to inspire the faithful. Belgrade is a hilly,
highly strung city, teetering between grand nineteenth-century
palaces and the concrete tower blocks raised under Marshal Tito,
collapsing around the Danube in seedy tunnels groggy with graffiti.

I was feeling a little highly strung myself. A couple of weeks since
Cape Tanairon, I was struggling with my own chemical imbalance,
the occasional headache, a feeling of airy inflation behind the temples.

I hated being dependent on medication, but I knew these were classic withdrawal symptoms. Over the years, I'd learned a few tricks, but what helped most of all was excitement about what lay ahead: a week in Bosnia, iconic cities like Sarajevo and Dubrovnik, the ferry to Italy . . . I had arranged for medication to be sent to Sarajevo in a week's time. With four days there, it would be my longest stop in the Balkans, so the best chance to pick something up. But I was frustrated by this proof of my dependency. And at the same time, I was grateful for the reality check: a warning not to confuse my own journey with the tales I was reading about.

So far, I had explored places associated with the events and characters of the *Kosovo Cycle*. Here in Belgrade, I was hoping to learn about their legacy. In particular, I was curious about two iconic Serb 'heroes' who share the same surname: one from the nineteenth century, the other still alive. One of them did more than anybody else to organise the *Kosovo Cycle*; the other arguably did more than anybody else to exploit it.

'I was born and brought up,' wrote Vuk Karadžić, 'in a house where sometimes my grandfather and uncle, sometimes men from Hercegovina . . . would sing and recite songs the whole winter through . . .'

Raised in the hill country between Serbia and Bosnia, this towering nineteenth-century intellectual was schooled in Belgrade, and the building where he studied not only survives — a bay-windowed town house on a street full of hipster bars — but has been turned into a museum in his honour, giving you Vuk piece by piece. Between his peg leg, crutch and ebony-handled cane, you can tease out his turbulent biography: the letters of safe conduct he carried into exile, his snuffbox, travelling inkpot and ceramic blotter, the grammars and translations they helped him to write, in between scribing stints for the anti-Ottoman rebels and a role on the fledgling Serbian Governing Council. His continuing popularity is illustrated, literally, by schoolchildren's drawings, hanging on pegs beside his old smoking room: crayoned portraits of a fez-wearing Vuk alongside coloured-in templates of Orthodox churches and an eerily detailed battle drawing.

Vuk didn't write the *Kosovo Cycle*, but he did more than anybody else to formalise it, identifying the guslars who roamed the mountain villages, as well as the poets, priests and fellow folklorists in contact with them. Fusing these tales with his reform of the Serbian language, he transformed the songs of the guslars from backwater entertainments into the pith of an awakening national culture. Admirers quickly gathered, not only in the Balkans. Jacob Grimm (one half of the famous fairy-tale-collecting fraternity) became an enthusiastic correspondent, teaching himself Serbo-Croat so he could translate the poems, and many other European luminaries joined the fad. Goethe wrote about them and the great Polish poet Adam Mickiewicz lectured on them at the Collège de France. Strange to think that for a brief period in the early nineteenth century Serbian epic had a readership more cosmopolitan than *Beowulf* or the *Song of Roland*.

It was a great time for the rediscovery of epic literature, and the *Kosovo Cycle* fitted into a broader, pan-continental tapestry. The Serbian songs may lack the psychological nuance of Homer, the evocative poetry of *Beowulf*, the propulsive drama of the *Nibelungenlied*. But in the range of episodes and the voices behind them, they communicate the full scale of war wrack. One episode focuses on Prince Lazar's encounter with the heavenly hawk, another on the Kosovo Maiden's lament, another shows us Sultan Murad marching with his army, another mourns the losses of the soldiers' mothers. You can hear the war leaders and the men who throw down their lives for them, but you can also hear the anguished wives and daughters. This polyphony lends itself to multiple interpretations, so it should be no surprise the cycle has been understood in radically different ways. These are stories to console the grief-stricken and tend the lonely, but they can also stir and provoke, voicing the different impulses lying behind the compositions.

Although they weren't authored by a single sensibility, they were curated by one – which is why it's important to remember the turbulent context in which Vuk was compiling these songs. Black George's uprising was under way, slowly unfastening the Turkish yoke, and many of the guslars who supplied Vuk's material took part in the fighting. Teshan Podrugovich, for example: an outlaw with a formidable scowl, who swung from guerrilla assaults on Turkish positions to singing charming ballads about the adventures of Prince Marko.

'On this threshold of national independence,' writes the Serbian scholar Svetozar Koljevic, 'all previous history seemed to matter much more than ever before, and the old heroic formulas were invoked as a challenge to contemporary historical ordeals.' The heroism and sacrifice of Prince Lazar's knights chimed with the trauma of the independence struggle. Men were roasted alive, hanged by their feet over smoking straw, castrated and stoned to death, the flesh stripped from their bodies with pliers; women and children were raped. In this tumultuous atmosphere, epic provided motivation and scale, a context in which every wound was knotted into the never-ending narrative. The Greek War of Independence had sucked in epic as a mild inspiration, but the Serbian epic was on another level. Miloš Obilić and the heroes of Kosovo were in men's ears and minds as they swung around the battlefields and plunged down mountain slopes, the verses on their lips as they bayoneted and loaded their cannons, spilling their guts on the long crawl towards independence.

A century and a half later, there was no Turkish occupation to fight, and the stories collected by Vuk Karadžić mapped less directly on to contemporary reality. But emotions still pulsed under the weight of these stories. And none used their power more viciously than Vuk's namesake: the Bosnian warlord, Radovan Karadžić.

A flyover swoops over the grey swirling snake of the River Sava: a giant tongue gorging on the rust-smeared grime of construction cranes and warehouses. Gigantic slabs of concrete rise and hover, crowding together as tightly as pine trees on the mountain-tops. Here is the brutalist Blok architecture of Marshall Tito's Yugoslavia, sucking people out of the villages and crushing individuality to tiny specks of grit. And here, in a quirk of history, lived one of the most destructive but stubbornly individual figures of recent Balkan history.

Radovan Karadžić was an odd candidate for warmongering. A poet and sports psychiatrist, he founded Bosnia's first ever Green Party, but failed to inspire much environmental engagement. Vicious sectarianism, it turned out, was a more effective route to power. Aligning himself with General Ratko Mladić, the most ruthless of the Bosnian Serb warlords, he carved a path to the Serbian motherland through a policy of 'ethnic cleansing' that killed around 100,000 people between 1992 and 1995. Not that there was anything truly 'ethnic' about this 'cleansing': nearly all Mladić's victims were Slavs, just like their killers, speaking similar languages and descended from the tribes who filled these mountain valleys in the first millennium AD.

Literary interests, in the Balkans, have often dovetailed with politics. But the men who led the region into war in the 1990s were a particularly literary lot – from Croatian President Franjo Tudjman (a historian) to Kosovan President Ibrahim Rugova (a professor of Albanian literature who had studied under Roland Barthes in Paris) to Karadžić's own Serbian Democratic Party comrade Nikolai Koljevic (the foremost Shakespeare scholar in the former Yugoslavia). The notion that literary interests are a safeguard against genocidal violence is a naivety that Karadžić and his contemporaries went a long way to disproving. Karadžić wasn't a warmonger *in spite* of his poetic inclinations; he was a warmonger, at least in part, *because* of them.

In a region where storytelling has so much currency, the people who know the stories and how to spin them have the best chance of wielding power. For Karadžić, singing gusle poems, framing his own biography as an epic tale – with its climax as a heroic martyr for the Serbs – was a deeply rooted part of his psychosis.

> *Oh Radovan, you steel man, the greatest since Black George,*
> *Defend our freedom and our faith on Lake Geneva's shores.*

So sang a guslar when Karadžić set off for peace talks in 1993. He didn't simply use epic to push forward his goals, 'he saw himself as the hero in an epic poem', as Aleksander Hemon has written, 'that would be sung by a distant future generation'.

So, when the Dayton Accords brought the Bosnian conflict officially to an end in 1995, Karadžić decided to launch a new dramatic layer to his tale. Rather than hand himself over, he went into hiding, casting himself as the 'Serb Pimpernel'.

If you were living in New Belgrade in the early years of the twenty-first century, suffering back pains or respiratory troubles, or maybe lacking oomph in the marriage bed, a walk to one of the tower blocks on Yuri Gagarin Street could be the answer. For there lived a New Age health guru known as 'Dragan Dabić', an expert in the healing arts with a regular column in *Healthy Living* magazine. Whilst a billion-dollar manhunt was picking through the Balkans in search of the former Bosnian Serb president, Karadžić pulled off his extraordinary disguise – so proficiently that even his neighbours didn't guess his true identity (not even an Interpol agent living in the next block), and so confidently that he was able to publish a new volume of poetry, entitled *Under the Left Breast of History*.

It was only in 2008, after his brother's phone was tapped, that Dabić the thickly bearded health guru was unmasked as Karadžić the warmonger. It would take another eight years before the International Criminal Tribunal convicted him (on ten out of eleven charges, including responsibility for the shelling of Sarajevo and using 284 UN peacemakers as human shields). That was a year before my visit, so for all the passing of time, Karadžić was still a hot topic.

'The Luda Kuća (Madhouse)?' says a cafe waitress. 'Just go left at the parking lot, it's next to the mini-market.'

The tiny roadside kiosk looks too small for a bar, but they've certainly made the most of the space. Light ricochets between metal tankards and bottles of rakija, pooling around the frames of portraits on the wall. The faces in the portraits are strangely familiar. Standing under a row of shot glasses and a pair of antlers, I'm looking into the eyes of some of the West's most dreaded bogeymen.

One portrait shows Karadžić in his trademark black-and-white pompadour; beside it is the disguised Dragan Dabić, peering under his topknot. Slobodan Milošević glowers to his right, while Vladimir Putin watches the room in poker-faced serenity, next to a bizarre depiction of Colonel Gaddafi. Hanging above them all is a beautiful elm-wood gusle. The faces of Vuk Karadžić and the Montenegrin poet-prince Petar Petrovic-Njegosh are sculpted to the tailpiece, and carved eagle wings fan over the peg box. The gusle is intricately fashioned, but it looks too decorative to play: a museum piece rather than a practical instrument. Which, I suppose, is why Radovan Karadžić relished playing it.

'You want to join us?' asks Mirjana, a husky-voiced, grey-haired woman in a red fleece, who's running the bar tonight. 'I don't like the gusle,' she tells me. 'It reminds me of old women crying over graves.' But she's still tickled by Karadžić's disguise. She lived through the NATO bombing of 1999, and some memory of those days lights a spark in her eyes.

'He played well,' she says. 'He knew a lot of songs and he could play them without any difficulty. But he didn't sing very often. You see, he didn't want people to recognise his voice.'

We sit around a table outside, the air so warm I'm able to sit in just my T-shirt, stoked a few degrees every time another shot of rakija arrives. We balloon to a group of half a dozen, voices volleying back and forth, along with the rustle of crisp packets and sizzling lighters. My foreignness makes me a conduit to the outside world, and they take it in turns to lean towards me, grabbing my arm, pouring another shot.

'The West ordered us to stop fighting – then they bombed us for three months!' recalls a short-haired blonde called Annika.

'But it was a good time,' adds Tomas, a homburg-wearing old-timer. 'Don't you remember the meat parties? When the power cuts happened, we ate everything up before it went off.'

Somehow, almost certainly my fault, the subject of refugees comes up, which sets off a rally of tirades.

'Haven't we already got the gypsies?' says Danny (short for Danilo), a curly-haired Montenegrin whose voice rings louder than anyone else's. 'Why should the Germans tell us to look after all these Muslims?'

I have put my foot in it, and now I'm in urgent need of validation.

'What are you here for anyway?' Mirjana points her cigarette accusingly. 'I thought you said you were interested in music.'

'Are you a spy?' asks Danny.

Uh-oh. I'm starting to wonder if I should be thinking about doing a runner, when a casual mention of my half-Irish background spins the whole thing round.

'You are a Celt!' declares Danny. 'So you are like us! Serbs and Celts are the same – we both like drinking and fighting!'

He refills my glass and jams my mouth with a Victory cigarette.

It's that kind of evening: rapid descents and equally rapid swoops. Celts flourished in this region long before the Slavs, founding a forerunner of Belgrade in the third century BC; so in the ethno-centric atmosphere around the table, my Irish grandparentage anoints me as an honorary Belgrader. Now I'm in deep – so deep I'm even allowed to give the gusle a try.

'No! You hold it like this, under the chin,' says Danny, sitting inside with me, under the ghoulish portraits. 'And pull the bow this way . . . okay, you've nearly got it!'

Holding that famous gusle, I feel a surreal telescoping of time: Vuk Karadžić's stern face watching from the neck; Radovan looking down from the wall, doubled by his disguise, quadrupled by the drink. For my first gusle performance, I grace my audience of one with an imitation of the dying gasps of a slowly strangled rodent. Only when Danny eases the instrument out of my arms, adjusting the tuning pegs and checking the bridge, do I realise it doesn't have to sound quite so god-awful.

'You have to play it with pride,' he says. 'This is the important thing. When Serbs play the gusle, we remember the battles of our ancestors and the sacrifices they made. We say we prefer graves to shame! This is why I have no respect for those refugees. What kind of man deserts his homeland? If Assad is their enemy, they must stay there and fight him!'

But is it really remembering, I ask. When no scholar has ever proven that Miloš Obilić existed? When Vuk Branković, the epic's arch-traitor, was in reality one of the key fighters against the Ottomans who ended his life in a Turkish prison?

'But that is the story!' says Danny. 'It isn't about history, it's about . . . culture . . . identity!'

And with those words he's nailed it. The story doesn't have to be true – because it isn't about the events of 1389. It's about the wheel that keeps turning. The cycle revolving, on spokes of romance greased by history's oil.

9

He leaves a fame immortal to the Serbs
To tell in song and story evermore,
As long as man and Kosovo endure.
The Kosovo Cycle, 'Song of Prince
Lazar and Princess Militsa'

BELGRADE OFFERED GLIMPSES, but in order to experience the deepest resonances of the epic cycle's legacy, I needed to head for the mountains. Living epic retains a link to its oral origins: not stories browsed in some bibliophile's study, not even tales absorbed in readers' bedrooms (which is where I've done most of my epic-digesting), but booming out loud in public spaces. Now, on a tip from the guys at the Madhouse, I was on my way to the Republika Srpska (Serbian Republic), a canton torn out of the fragile peace of the 1995 Dayton Accords.

A relay of buses carried me south and west of Belgrade. At the monastery of Studenica, I marvelled at the bestial sculpture (a dragon! a basilisk!), and when the monks beat the semantron, I joined them for incensed prayer under the beautiful, fragmented frescoes. After a night in the monastery lodging, I was setting off for another border, joining a dozen villagers in a rackety minivan. Fast-moving streams played glissandos on the shallow beds and precipitous meadows dangled above us, like rugs pinned to the sky by their sheep. We stopped by a bridge so a haywain could cross, pulled by two mangy-looking horses, while two boys with fishing rods and buckets ambled past. The metropolitan buzz of Belgrade already felt very distant.

The yellow–blue barrier looked like it had been rammed by a

tank (which, round here, wouldn't be unlikely). Officially, I was entering Bosnia and Herzegovina, but this is where Balkan borders get iffy. The Republika Srpska is a limbo place, neither fully part of Bosnia nor of Serbia, its status undecided as long as post-war tensions continue to simmer. If anywhere demonstrates the insolubility of the Balkan conflict, here it is: peace installed like dodgy tech that could fizzle out at any moment.

Green as bottle glass, the chalk-chewing Drina pulses under towering pinewoods and karst hills, running for 300 miles from its headwater in Montenegro, tracing the border between Bosnia and Serbia. A few miles from the checkpoint, it winds under an eleven-arched bridge raised in the sixteenth century by the Bosnian-born Ottoman vizier, Mehmed Sokollu. One of Bosnia's most iconic structures, this bridge was immortalised by the Nobel laureate Ivo Andrić's 1945 novel, *The Bridge over the Drina*.

You see the bridge – and Andrić – all over the town of Višegrad: printed on menus, on the canopies of restaurants, in the model bridges sold in the souvenir stalls clustering around Andrićgrad (a fantasia of architectural styles conceived in homage to Andrić).

The novelist's humanist vision represents the best of the Balkans, even as the events of his most famous work describe the worst. In *The Bridge over the Drina*, a halfwit is beheaded for singing a revolutionary song about Black George. A bride, married against her will, hurls herself from the parapet to drown in the Drina. Men and horses are killed by incendiary shells in the opening salvoes of the First World War. Everybody suffers, regardless of background, in a blood-soaked equivalence centred on the turbulent beauty of the bridge.

Andrić ends his novel in 1914, with the early blasts of the war. But the cycle of violence, the pattern of ordinary lives crushed between history's revolving spokes, never stops. It's all too easy to imagine the chronicle's melancholy continuation. Take the story of Ševal Tabaković: a real-life example of history repeating itself in the deadliest fashion. A Bosnian Muslim who lived his life in Višegrad, Tabaković was seized by Serb Chetniks during the Second World War. They brought him to the bridge, cut his throat and threw him into the Drina. Somehow he survived, and went on to live another five decades until May 1992, when soldiers of Radovan Karadžić's

Republika Srpska repeated the fifty-year-old murder attempt, throwing him off the bridge. This time, they were successful.

Early in *The Bridge over the Drina*, a guslar entertains a group of peasants resting in a stable: 'his sharp profile was outlined in the firelight,' writes Andrić, and he 'sang in a strangled and constrained voice'. Guslars reappear at different stages of Andrić's novel, which isn't surprising: as the British archaeologist Arthur Evans noted in 1875,

> Epic lays of the fatal days of Kosovo are still sung every day to throngs of peasant listeners by minstrels of the people, whose rhapsodies, set to the dolorous strains of the gusla, resound in a great national dirge along the walled banks of Sava and Danube, through the beechwood glens of Bosnia . . .

In the early twentieth century, the Austrian statesman Joseph Maria Baernreither reported, 'there are minstrels with their guslas, putting pictures of the glories of the Serbian past into folks' heads'; and in the middle of the century, Rebecca West heard guslars in homes and cafes all over Bosnia, as well as soldiers playing gusle at a military barracks and even a gypsy guslar in a nightclub in Skopje.

Ever since arriving in Serbia, I had been asking where I might find guslars. I was wary of the trap, reducing local culture to some folksy fossil. But how could I begin to understand the Serbian epic without meeting the people who perform it? It is the *Kosovo Cycle*'s oral longevity that best explains its power – because the poems continue to be sung aloud, as shown by Radovan Karadžić's fondness for gusle-playing at the Madhouse. The people I met there had given me fresh encouragement: the way they talked, it was clear this story still mattered to people. And Danny had also given me a tip: 'If you go to Višegrad, there is a 95 per cent chance you will meet guslars.'

But for three days in Višegrad, I was stuck in the other 5 per cent. The closest I'd come was in a wood-beamed restaurant on one of the old town's plunging alleys, where a gusle hung beside a mounted stag's head. Looking up from a plate of marinated sow's ears, I asked the waiter if he knew anyone who could play it, but he shook his head: 'No guslars in these days.'

Was there some kind of local *omerta*, a code of silence to keep this controversial art form from foreigners' ears? Dejan, who was renting me a room in an apartment block near the bridge, was no more positive: 'Guslars? No, that is from old times!'

But a flick through a telephone directory revealed a number for the 'Višegrad Guslar Society', and I persuaded Dejan to call them up.

'This man,' he explained, after a minute's respectful whispering, 'says he doesn't work with the society any more.' Foiled once again! But . . . 'He says there is a place . . .'

A clue, at last! I was directed towards a mechanic's workshop and a mini-market in the hills above the old town. Old election posters clung to walls that dribbled cement like wax on church candles. Next to the mini-market was a one-floor cafe with 'Guslar' in peeling red Cyrillic over the windows. Inside, an elderly woman in a floral-print housecoat was sitting between walls painted pale green, striped with shadow by the blinds. A few herbs were scattered beside a stove, next to a fridge stocking bottles of Jelen beer and peach juice. Behind this was the bar, where a maple-wood gusle rested on a ledge. After the ornamented gusle I'd played in Belgrade, this one looked pale and humble, reassuringly practical.

The woman gestured for me to sit and bustled outside. A few minutes later, in walked her husband, Mr Tomić – a bull of a man in mechanic's overalls, arms tattooed with grease. He scrubbed his hands in the sink beside the bar, took a bottle of juice out of the fridge and set it down on the table.

'Gusle?' I asked.

His jowls sagged under dark brows and a back-combed sweep of grey hair. I offered to pay for the juice, but he wouldn't hear of it. I mentioned trying to bring a translator, and he nodded, tapping out the number seven and pointing to his wrist.

'Tonight!' he said.

I returned to the Guslar bar that evening, accompanied by Aleksander, an English-speaking hotel clerk recommended by the Andrić Institute as a translator. Over the course of the evening, more than a dozen men gathered around us: mechanics, bricklayers, electricians, an accountant, a few who were officially unemployed. They curled their fists around bottles of Jelen beer and flicked their cigarette lighters across the table, blanketing the room with the atmosphere of a working men's club – a sanctuary of relaxation after the daily grind.

'There are gusle songs,' said a bull-necked accountant called Djordjo with a gold Orthodox cross hanging over his polo shirt, 'about all periods in our history. The gusle was the soul of our people, and the songs were important for Serbian morale. Beside the Church, the gusle gave the people the strength to fight.'

Amongst the players, the one pushed forward was Slavko: striped polo shirt, dusky eyes under a mop of grey hair, looking like any ordinary bloke winding down in his neighbourhood bar. I asked him to tell me how he'd started playing, and Aleksander translated his answers.

We had a gusle hanging on the wall of my home, but for many years I was too small to reach it. So I made my own gusle and that's how I started. I was fifteen when I first played for the public. To be a guslar, all you need is will and pride. The first time I performed, the people gave me a big applause, and after that my will to play was even stronger.

During the fighting of 1992–5, he joined the Republika Srpska army, under the leadership of General Mladić. It was a brutally uncomfortable life: patrols in the mountains, sleeping in stables and abandoned farmsteads. But his gusle brought relief and encouragement to his fellow soldiers.

We sang and played gusle in the trenches, in the mountains when we were resting, and just before the fighting. Whenever we knew we would have to fight the Bosniaks, or the Croats, we sang with the gusle. It made me stronger from playing it, and it made the other men stronger from listening.

'What stories did you sing?' I asked.

> We sang the Kosovo songs, about Prince Lazar and Miloš Obilić, all
> the heroes who fought against the Turks. These are our greatest
> heroes and they make us proud to be Serbs. But we sang many other
> songs. Some people made up new songs, and I learned to sing them
> too. There were songs about General Mladić. About his victories
> and how he is a great leader for us. How we feel proud to fight
> behind him.

I could sense their eyes scrutinising me. Slavko broke off to discuss
something with Tomić, and Djordjo leaned towards them. 'They
are thinking,' whispered Aleksander, 'because you are British, maybe
you have the wrong idea about General Mladić. Because the
International Criminal Tribunal has made accusations against him.
But he is not a war criminal, he is a soldier. He was fighting for
our independence.'

This elastic approach to history left me reeling. They rushed from
medieval battles to events so recent I could almost hear the rattling
artillery on BBC bulletins. At the time of my visit, Mladić's trial in
The Hague was ongoing. Five months later, he would be convicted
on ten charges (one of genocide, five of crimes against humanity,
four of violation of the laws of warfare), including responsibility for
the Srebrenica massacre and the siege of Sarajevo.

They talked of many other songs, spanning the ages. Djordjo was
particularly keen on the songs about the Second World War battle
of Mitrovdan, 'when Serbs were attacked from the air by Croats and
from the land by Muslims'; and he mentioned poems in praise of
Gavrilo Princip, the Bosnian Serb who assassinated Archduke Franz
Ferdinand in 1914, lighting the spark of the First World War.

'The Austrians took our land,' he said, 'so Gavrilo was fighting
against that. He was fighting for our freedom.'

When Mrs Tomić had filled our glasses, her husband pulled the
maple-wood gusle down from the bar and placed it in Slavko's hands.
With a workman's briskness, the ex-soldier tucked the bridge under
the string. The first notes were practice, harmonising his voice to
the gusle. Only then did he begin to sing.

I never have been faithless, nor can so be called,
And when the battle's joined tomorrow, so I'll prove,
Tomorrow, on the day Saint Vitus is recalled,
Tomorrow, hark me, with my blood I'll show my love,
Tomorrow, when we meet on Kosovo's broad plain,
Who's faithful and a traitor will be clear to all.

I can't pretend I found it especially musical: Slavko's voice rolled in a deathly monotone, the gusle humming underneath, at times like a mournful accompaniment, at times like a vicious mosquito that's determined to bite everybody in the room. But for the regulars, this was the business. When I turned to Djordjo, I saw him nodding, his face softened to a look of deep contentment, tapping out the metre with his fingers.

The verses were decasyllabic and trochaic: ten-syllabled with the stress at the beginning of the foot; a growling, relentless tempo. They made Homer sound like the tripping sing-song of an undisciplined freewheeler. Later, Tomić played a grizzly dirge, a song by soldiers appealing for Miloš Obilić to rise from the dead. While they were singing, Djordjo called over to Mrs Tomić, who brought a bottle of rakija to the table.

'Serbs always do things in three,' said Djordjo. 'We kiss three times, we drink three glasses of rakija. The first glass, you sip, the second as well – but the third glass, you must drink it in one.' A steely look fixed me in challenge. 'You must not betray me!'

Heat split my back as I slammed down the glass; my shoulders twitched in involuntary convulsion. 'This is no Vuk Branković!' Djordjo declared, recalling the epic's chief traitor. It felt like a door was unlocking, allowing me into the next chamber in the labyrinth. Breathing out slowly, I sat back, exchanging smiles with Djordjo and Tomić, as Slavko took hold of the gusle and tuned his voice for another song.

When Albert Lord and Milman Parry did their ground-breaking research into oral epic in the 1930s, they focused on 'the laboratory of the living epic tradition of the Yugoslavs'. Here, in the mountains and valleys of Bosnia, they met guslars who could recite thousands of verses by heart; not only pouring the stories out of their memories but actively reshaping them with every telling. In the process, Lord and Parry challenged structural ideas about textual purity, reconfiguring epic tales as stories in perpetual flux.

The guslars I met were a few generations further down the line from the epic prime. According to Djordjo, Slavko's recitals were based on texts he had learned. But as Slavko pointed out, new gusle poems are still being composed, and he had recited some of these during the war.

I didn't have the expertise to analyse the Višegrad guslars' recitals like Lord and Parry had done. What I was looking for was experiences. Sitting among the regulars of the Guslar bar, I felt privileged to be part of this communal gathering: a combination of storytelling, a seance conjuring the ghosts of the dead, and an excuse for drinking an awful lot of rakija.

Djordjo was keen to show me more of the guslars' world, and over the coming days I spent a lot of time with him. He played me gusle CDs (on many of the cover sleeves, men wore bullet bandoliers around their necks and carried rifles in their arms) and passed me magazines containing reports of guslar gatherings around the region, in Montenegro, Herzegovina and here in Bosnia. The photos showed dozens of performers, wearing traditional guslar outfits of red waistcoats and frogged gold buttons.

I warmed to his enthusiasm for this active body of epic literature, although some of his opinions were a little harder to stomach: his insistence on Serbian victimhood and the 'betrayal' of Western powers; his unstinting admiration for the Chetniks, ignoring the tens of thousands of killings they dealt out. But travelling is about breaking out of your own bubble, listening to other viewpoints. I wanted to hear the Serbs' perspective, to learn how differently they interpreted history. The more we talked, the more I sensed Djordjo was keen for me to understand, to make up for the disappointments he'd experienced from other 'Children of NATO'.

One morning we climbed into Aleksander's car for a drive into the mountains. In a secluded grove of silver fir and cypresses, a statue of the Chetnik commander Draza Mikhailović had been mounted, in the glade where he was dragged out of hiding in 1946, before he was executed by Tito's Communists. A monastery had been built in the glade, and one of the monks, Brother Gavril, invited us to take some refreshments on the porch.

'We have many Miloš Obilićs in our history,' said Djordjo, while Brother Gavril was passing round tulip-shaped glasses of coffee and a bowl of raspberries picked from the monastery garden. 'For example, Gavrilo Princip who killed the Austrian duke, and of course Mikhailović. You know he was supported by the West? Then they betrayed him and sided with Tito.'

'This happened a lot in our history,' added Brother Gavril. 'Our history is a pattern of betrayal by the West. The people in Hollywood even made a movie about the Chetniks – then they changed their minds and supported the Communists!'

For Gavril and Djordjo, these were examples of the never-ending cycle: the Western failure to support Prince Lazar, the Austro-Hungarian occupation, the realpolitik of the Second World War. Serbia as the border guard for Christian Europe, keeping the rest of the continent safe while they fell under and took the brunt of the suffering.

'So you wouldn't want Serbia to join the EU?' I asked.

Djordjo swallowed his coffee, slamming down the glass in his rush to get the words out. 'Why would we put ourselves under the power of the Austrians all over again? No, you can call me a Eurosceptic, for certain!'

The cycle of conspiracy theories did the round of the table. Brother Gavril launched into a denunciation of the 'British agents who betrayed Mikhailović', followed by a diatribe against NATO. Djordjo mentioned the 'Western assassins' who, he believed, killed Black George in 1817, and the allied bombing campaign on Belgrade in the 1940s, 'even though the Germans weren't there'. When they had sufficiently excoriated the West, they turned on their neighbours, reeling off atrocities by Bosniaks and Croats, Albanians and Slovenes, nodding contentedly, like any group of old men indulging in their favourite pastime.

It made for unsettling listening. Even on the subject of Srebrenica – where around 7,500 men and boys were murdered on General Mladić's orders – they turned it round to Serbian victimhood: 'Why should we not fight,' Brother Gavril insisted, 'against the Greater Albanian project? Are we animals, that we should let them destroy us?'

Their conviction was troubling. (I would think of them all again, months later, reading about General Mladić's war crimes trial in The Hague – when his lawyer claimed his client was suffering from a 'memory disorder'.) But I was intrigued to hear them talking so openly. As an outsider, it was easy for me to view all these deaths with cold detachment, forgetting that everybody I met in the Balkans had been deeply touched by the conflict. It was they, not I, who had lived through this war, and who would spend their remaining days in its shadow.

'Why,' I asked, sitting in the Guslar bar on my last night in Višegrad, 'do you sing so often about Kosovo?'

Tomić laid down the gusle and ripped open a fresh packet of cigarettes. Smoke mushroomed between us, mixing with the plummy scent of rakija.

'Kosovo is our cradle,' he said. 'We are celebrating the heroism of that battle for Serbs. We are singing about Kosovo because in 1389 we fought against the Turks and then NATO took that place away from us. So we are reminding ourselves we have to fight for Kosovo.'

Beside me, Djordjo pushed his glass across the table.

'There is a long fight for Kosovo,' he said. 'That is why the most popular songs are the Kosovo songs, and at festivals and competitions, these are the ones that receive the greatest applause. The attitude of the world towards us makes Serbs love to fight even more for Kosovo. What they are doing is putting salt on an open wound!'

IO

This army is not packed with warriors,
It's made of aged pilgrims, crippled hodjas,
Untested artisans, apprentices,
Who've never even tasted battle's blood,
Who've come to Kosovo to earn some bread.
          Miloš Obilić, *The Kosovo Cycle*,
          'Captain Miloš and Ivan Kosančić'

R AIN WAS MIZZLING over the mountains, running beads down
the windows of the bus to Sarajevo. Submarine light glowed
among stooping willows and silver fir, which lined the cliffs of the
gorge and reappeared in the chalky waters of the Drina. Sitting
across the aisle was Militsa, a Bosnian Serb who had spent the last
two decades in Australia, working as a taxi driver. Now she was
back visiting family.

'I forgot how beautiful it is,' she said. 'Because of everything that
happened. When you've been through so much, it's hard to see the
beauty any more.'

Before the Bosnian War broke out, she had been working in a
bank, with Croat and Bosniak colleagues.

'We never had any problems,' she said, 'but when the politicians
stirred things up, we knew we'd have to go our separate ways. A
Croat friend said to me, "I'll be on this side of the hill, you'll be
on that side, we'll have to wait it out."'

But with two small children to raise, Militsa and her husband
couldn't afford to wait. After scrambling round different family
members, struggling for space and dealing with unfriendly in-laws,
Militsa took a friend's invitation and flew her family to Australia.

'People forget,' she said. 'Now refugees are pariahs. But as a Bosnian in those days, you were welcome anywhere.'

We were riding the karst canyons moulded by the Drina through the Dinaric Alps – the long necklaces of parallel ranges strung from Italy to Kosovo. Lush hillsides teetered over the rapids, snapped out by tunnel black; a green river ribboned below, frilled by the looping branches of willows. Rain crackled over the face of a last tunnel, like scratch marks on old film. Jettisoned on to the rimrock, we rolled over the valley of the Miljacka.

Domes, spires, glassy turrets, the yellow Lego block of the Hotel Holiday, the 577-feet twisted spear of the Avaz Tower: Sarajevo bristles from the valley like a secret base in a crater, probing the sky with fingers of metal and glass. Here was the Bosnian capital, the most resilient city on earth: the defiant survivor of the longest siege in modern history (from 5 April 1992 to 29 February 1996).

Back in the 1970s, in his poem 'Sarajevo', Radovan Karadžić imagined the city burning 'like a stick of incense'. For forty-four months he tried to realise his simile, defying human rights, international outrage and the signing of the Dayton Accords. He even recited his poem for the cameras, while General Mladić was pounding Sarajevo at a rate of 329 shell impacts a day. Now I was descending the hills where Mladić and Karadžić launched their attacks. As the road plunged between shell-spattered tower blocks and parks adorned with marble lists of the fallen, I thought of a verse from the *Kosovo Cycle*: 'the nine widows are lamenting, / the nine orphan children are weeping'. And I wondered if Karadžić and Mladić, who loved those poems, had ever really listened to them.

Sarajevo is where the *Kosovo Cycle* runs out. From 40 per cent of the population in 1914, the Serbs now represent less than 5 per cent, and the city plays no role in the medieval narrative. Conquered by the Ottomans in 1463, a majority of Bosnians converted to Islam (although a third of the population was killed or enslaved), leading them down a very different historical path from the Serbs. But Sarajevo is a city as deeply affected by the Serbian epic as any other. Two key events have defined its modern history, and they are both steeped in the legacy of the *Kosovo Cycle*.

Strolling around Sarajevo, memories of the siege murmur around you: as you step over the red waxy spray of 'Sarajevo roses' on the pavements, commemorating civilian casualties; crossing the 'Romeo and Juliet' bridge, where a Bosniak woman died clasping the body of her Serb lover; as you climb up the hill towards the Yellow Fort, past the hundreds of white marble headstones glittering in the Martyrs' Memorial Cemetery. There are museums that suck out your tears and spit you on to the high street, curdled in shame: exhibitions on Srebrenica and 'Crimes Against Humanity'; poignant photographs (a mother wearing a tunic sewn with the names of her missing children; a doll left in secret above a mass grave); billboards tasselled in damning Post-it notes: 'We will never forget!' 'Shame on you Serbia! Why!!' 'The same thing is happening in Syria. Will we ever learn? UN – act.'

I was staying in a stucco-clad, *fin de siècle* apartment block thanks, once again, to Airbnb: a wood-panelled flat with a claw-foot bathtub and brass bedsteads. On the surface, it looked inoculated against the impact of the siege, too 1890s to be touched by the 1990s. But on closer inspection, there was shell spray under the stucco and bullet holes in the corbelling – for this was the old 'Sniper's Alley', one of the most dangerous places in the siege.

'It was a miracle we survived,' said my host, Hasnija, who had lived here as a child. She continued:

> We used to sit in the basement for days. We had nothing to eat except the tin cans sent by the UN, and packets of dried meat. It was so exciting when the UN brought the food supplies – it meant you'd get something to eat, but it also meant no shooting. We'd empty the cans on our plates. It was like meat jello, you could see it wriggle. Somehow we liked it, but I couldn't eat it now! My mother would boil stinging nettles and tell us she was making spinach pie. We used to joke, 'We're getting the left-over rations from World War Two!'

Gallows humour runs through Sarajevo like the waters of the Miljacka: defanging the bitterness of life in hell, sucking out the poison with jokes. Pouring the coffee from a skillet, Hasnija filled a couple of small china cups and set down a saucer of pistachio-flavoured Turkish Delight.

> We used to play games like, 'Who can find the biggest piece of shrapnel?' As you can imagine, games of hide-and-seek would get pretty dangerous. Most of the time, we sat around, our parents wouldn't let us out. I read so many stories in the newspaper supplements – all those terrible romances! But I enjoyed them at the time.

★

Epic doesn't pull the trigger or launch the missile, it doesn't rape the prisoners or gouge out their eyes: it's an instrument in men's hands, but the men have to choose what to do with it. Still, the influence of epic can sometimes be overlooked. When historians talk about the assassination of 28 June 1914, the most seismic event to come out of Sarajevo, they pay little attention to the mythology that played such a key part. But without it, this world-shattering event would not have occurred in the way it did.

Walking away from Hasnija's block, I followed the Miljacka along the old Appel Quay. Snipers' bullets and shell splatter inscribed *fin de siècle* town houses, like the diacritical markings to a message from the Grim Reaper. I stopped beside the stone arches of the Latin Bridge, looking into the shallow river. A plaque commemorated the fatal encounter between the magnificently dressed Archduke, heir to the Austro-Hungarian throne, and the scruffy revolutionary with his shaking Browning. Gavrilo Princip's assassination of Franz Ferdinand was a famously obscure origin for such a global catastrophe. But that's geopolitical snobbery: one end of the same wedge, Serbs might argue, that fails to recognise their role in holding off the Ottoman advance for so many centuries. After wallowing in decades of Western meddling, this was the moment when the Balkans repaid the compliment, sending a shock wave of destruction that changed the world, but especially Europe, forever. Four empires were brought down, European maps radically redrawn and the continent lost its long-held supremacy over the rest of the globe.

Princip and his comrades were responding to a specific fear: having so recently shaken off the hated Ottoman hegemony, the Serbs were going to be shackled by the equally oppressive chains of Catholic Austria. Or, as Djordjo in Višegrad described it: 'one invader followed another'. In parading through Sarajevo in his open-top *Graef und Stift*, Franz Ferdinand was asserting Austrian power; but in choosing 28 June, he aligned his imperium with the one recently discarded. For Franz Ferdinand chose to visit Sarajevo on Saint Vitus's Day (or Vidovdan), the anniversary of the medieval Battle of Kosovo.

This date was critical to the conspirators. 'Tomorrow is Vidovdan,' wrote one of them, Nedeljko Čabrinović, on the eve of the assassination, 'and we shall see who is faithful and who is unfaithful. Do you remember the great oath of Miloš Obilić?' When Čabrinović threw a hand-grenade at the archduke's car, he was carrying a copy of the Serb daily *Narod*, which contained a lengthy editorial about the 1389 battle as well as poems commemorating it. He saw himself in the line of Miloš Obilić, who, he told his interrogators, 'became the first assassin who went into the enemy camp and murdered Sultan Murad'.

Čabrinović and his fellow conspirators weren't especially radical – in their obsession with the medieval warriors, they were simply following local convention. As Vladimir Dedijer argues in *The Road to Sarajevo*, 'The historic circumstances under which the South Slavs lived, in an uninterrupted state of rebellion against foreign occupiers, facilitated the preservation of the ancient idea, expressed in the folklore epic of Kosovo, that the assassination of a tyrannical foreign ruler is one of the noblest aims in life.' For Princip, a bibliophile who read Serbian epic as a youngster, who scribbled verses in heroic metre on the walls of his prison cell and scratched them on to his metal dinner plate, the heroes of the medieval battle were a powerful influence.

The war would have broken out anyway, as Princip pointed out to his prison psychiatrist: the conflict between the Great Powers was waiting for somebody to light its spark. Still, it's a troubling thought that Serbian epic played an inspirational role in its conception. If ever there was an example of the macabre reach of epic, its ability to twist itself around the rigging from which history is built, here it is.

History and travel can be powerful sources of mindfulness. Roam this blood-soaked region and you soon realise how lucky you are. Still, I was struggling. Headaches, hot flushes. Waiting for my package, I was like a junkie itching for the dealer to arrive. I got tetchy about transport delays or the cost of museum tickets or people misunderstanding my guidebook Bosnian, but it was only later I realised why I'd been snappy. When you're deep in it, it can be hard to recognise what's obvious from the outside.

But you cling to what's available. I may not have my serotonin regulator, but I did at least have the epics. So I turned their verses in my head as I grappled with issues I'd never fully managed to suppress. Grief or guilt . . . The sight of my father, all those years ago, lifeless on the hospital bed, or the wish I'd come back sooner . . . Those hands like nubs of stone, the calmly pale face, a trail of freckles running to his few remaining hairs; the breathing so regular it was hard to dissociate from the machine that was enabling it.

Grief pours through the epics, and especially the multi-voiced Serbian epic, which deals so much with the aftermath of war. An epic, after all, that was composed *to deal with the aftermath of war.* The epics have great political power, but they have something more than that, and it was in the Balkans that I started to recognise this. These stories can offer us empathy, they can nudge us with the emotions we've tried to suppress in ourselves. Who has lost as much as the Mother of the Jugovichi? Nine of her sons have fallen, but she retains a stoical smile until the hand of her tenth son is dropped into her lap. Now she has no children left, no one to stay strong for, and she breaks into pieces. You don't need to lose ten children to recognise the power of that image.

During my Balkan journey, I had caught glimpses of epic's dark side. Standing in Sarajevo's unambiguously named Museum of Crimes against Humanity, I felt my heart sink as I watched a video of General Mladić. 'Time has finally come,' he growled, 'for us to take revenge against the Turks', his knife-edge baritone invoking the centuries of conflict, the verses sung by Radovan Karadžić and his fellow guslars. But in the same museum where this video was installed, I saw some very different verses, composed by a Bosnian poet called Eset Muračević. Before leaving the Balkans, I hoped it would be possible to hear a less combative angle on poetry. So, on my last morning in Sarajevo, I met Eset in a back room at the museum, to learn how poetry had saved his life.

Wearing a chequered shirt and jeans, Eset looks out from under a thatch of strawlike hair. Sunken, bony cheeks compress his calm blue eyes, so they shine like precious stones in deep fissures of rock. He has lived through hell – a hell so intense he titled one of his anthologies *The Last Circle*, because Dante's *Inferno* couldn't match his own experiences.

Before the war, he was an up-and-coming provincial writer in his mid-thirties, with a small family, secretary of his local community, Svrake. His nightmare began on 4 May 1992, when the forces opposing Bosnian independence – the fledgling army of the Republika Srpska – took over Svrake after a two-day battle.

'I managed to get away from the town, but I was captured along with seven others,' he says.

> They divided us up and I was taken to a concentration camp called the 'Bunker'. It was a house with two floors, about forty people on average, sometimes as many as eighty. They did terrible things. They raped the women, forced men to have sex with each other, stubbed out their cigarettes on people's skin. Sometimes they made people jump from the second floor, just to see what would happen. They set their dogs on us and pepper-sprayed us. We went days without eating, and there was no water during the day. Our meals were the soldiers' leftovers, and if they found any meat in it, they would give it to the dogs.

All through this ordeal, Eset had one source of strength.

> I wrote poems. It was necessary, to keep me calm. What gave me strength was the thought I could get those poems out and some-body might read them. Whenever there was an exchange of

prisoners, I would give my poems to the people whose names had been read out, hoping they could show them to people. Sometimes, I encrypted the names of prisoners and guards in my verses. I was hoping they would be useful. But I didn't realise, most of the people who left were not being exchanged. They were being executed.

> Sloboda je
> *Freedom is*
> Kad listaju šume
> *Spring in the forest*
> I vjetar blagi
> *And the faint wind*
> Kada krošnje njiše
> *In the treetops*
> Sloboda je
> *Freedom is*
> Kad srce šuti
> *When the heart is silent*
> I kad pjesme piše
> *And when it writes poems.*

What a contrast to the songs of the guslars. For Eset, there's no doubt about it: it's the poems that helped him survive.

> So many times, the guards said, 'You won't get out of this place alive.' So I thought, maybe my poems will get out. I didn't know where my wife and daughter were, but they had been visiting relatives in the Free Territory, so I hoped they were safe. I hoped my poems might reach them.

After seven months, Eset was taken as a human shield to a battle on the Žuč hill near Sarajevo. He says: 'We were eleven, but only two of us managed to escape. We ran in the chaos and reached the Bosnian side. Later, when we went back to the battlefield, we found the bodies of the other nine. Their faces had been mutilated with knives.'

Eset's experience tied him even tighter to Bosnia, and he spent the rest of the war in the army, collecting names of the missing and dead. But the personal toll was high. His wife took their daughter to safety in Germany, and when he talked to her on the phone, she wasn't able to understand him. 'She had forgotten all her Bosnian,' he says, with a stoical shrug. He's rebuilt his life in Svrake, working as Community Secretary, and has even helped Serbs to reclaim their property.

'I would joke to them, "How are the Chetniks?" But I didn't hate them. No amount of hate could make up for what I suffered,' he says. 'There's a Serb in my building, his son was one of the guards at the Bunker. But we are friends.'

He rubs a hand across his chin and looks at me, eyes gently melancholy in their haunted sockets: 'You know, it was Serbs who helped us find the mass graves, they gave us the information even though it put their lives in danger. I think that is how many of them showed their regret. It was their only way to relieve their consciences.'

Acts like these are the foundations on which the future of the Balkans could be built, bridges across the sectarian divide. They were neighbours before, as Militsa pointed out on the bus, and they can be neighbours again.

Magic potions only happen in fairy tales and epic stories (like the drug Helen of Troy deals out to numb men's grief in the *Odyssey*). But after several weeks cold turkey, my first pill was a dose of sorcery. For the last few weeks, it had felt as if my skin was back to front; now it was the right way round again. I was leaving the Balkans behind, but also the after-effects of my venture to the underworld in Greece. I had confirmed (in case I needed reminding) that I was nothing like the epic heroes; but also that my responses to the epics were grounded in my own experiences. It is because we can read epic through the prism of our own lives that we are able to connect to them. We don't have to *be like* these characters to *feel like* them.

I had come to the Balkans to learn about one of the least familiar of European epics, and had found myself drawn to many of its characters. In Miloš Obilić, I recognised traits of Greek heroes like Achilles and Odysseus (the former's pride, the latter's resourcefulness); in the Kosovo Maiden I recognised grief and other emotions I had struggled with in my own life. It had thrilled me to meet people still reciting these stories, to hear the characters and events discussed with such passion, in places like the Guslar bar in Višegrad and the Madhouse in Belgrade. But their continuing entanglement in the political quagmire kept these stories at a distance, like radioactive materials behind danger signs. Now it was time to head west, towards a story that shares many parallels with the Serbian epic.

A train poured through tunnels of limestone and slid over the banks of the Neretva, which flows under the arched bridge at Mostar. I wandered the old town, climbing the stone steps to the Tolkienesque towers, where shirtless divers perched on the bridge's parapet and artisans hawked flicker pens made out of spent bullet casings. Rapids tongued the bottle-glass green of the river; willows and fir trees quivered on the banks, under the grey stone of the renovated old town. I watched it all in a state of wonder.

There wasn't much sleep to be had that night. I'd missed the last direct bus to Dubrovnik, so I took one up the coast and another back the other way, crossing three borders in the space of twelve hours, falling into a drowsy half-sleep on the last eastward leg.

Tongs of sunlight prised my eyes open and I peered, woozily awakening, as dawn buttered the isles of the Adriatic with golden dabs of light. Ahead rose the huge walls of Dubrovnik, soaring among bastions and quadrangular towers: a marvel of medieval construction, glaring down on all the besiegers who've tried to pull it down, from Saracens in the ninth century to the Yugoslav People's Army in 1991. Over the drawbridge, a dark stone stairwell plunged to the Pile Gate. I had been immersed in the medieval world for the last few weeks; now at last the architecture matched the stories I'd been reading.

There was only one person I was planning to meet in Dubrovnik, and I knew he'd be waiting. After all, he's been standing there, with only a few breaks for repairs, since the fifteenth century.

It was so early, I had the place to myself. I shuffled over the polished limestone, past the chained-up cafe chairs. He was poised on his pedestal under the bell tower, wielding an iron broadsword over greaves as big as cricket pads. He could have been one of Prince Lazar's knights from the *Kosovo Cycle*. But the Latin inscription was a give-away. Here, at the western edge of eastern Europe, the world of Roland began – and here the page turned on another story.

PART THREE

A Song for Europe

The Song of Roland

After seven years of unrelenting siege, King Marsile, the Saracen ruler of Saragossa, sues for peace. Charlemagne, King of the Franks, has won his war against the Saracens.

But Marsile's overtures, and his promise to convert to Christianity, are part of a ruse. He has struck a deal with Charlemagne's treacherous baron, Ganelon, and is gathering a force to ambush the rearguard of the withdrawing Frankish army.

Leading the rearguard is Ganelon's sworn enemy, Roland. Hordes of Saracens sweep across the mountains, falling upon Roland and his fellow paladins. So numerous are they that Roland's companion-in-arms, Oliver, insists their only chance of survival is to recall the rest of the army. But Roland refuses to blow his war horn, his oliphant (not actually an elephant, just a part of it – the tusk).

He only relents when the possibility of being saved has passed and shame is no longer at stake. The exertion of blowing the war horn bursts the veins in his temples and he dies, although not before inflicting a mortal wound on King Marsile and frightening away the remaining Saracens.

Hearing the oliphant's call, Charlemagne turns his army around. Discovering the corpses of his bravest knights, he vows revenge. In a mighty battle, he splits the skull of the Emir of the Muslims and dashes out his brains, before leading his victorious army into Saragossa. The gate is levelled, the mosques ransacked; and Marsile's widow, Queen Bramimonde, is carried back to Charlemagne's capital, a token of his triumph.

II

Whoever is the cause of Roland's death
Will wrench from Charlemagne his mighty fist,
So that his army's power will desist.
                    Ganelon, *Song of Roland*, Laisse 45

L OST FOR CENTURIES, three of the greatest European epics were
disinterred from obscurity in surprising circumstances between
the second half of the eighteenth century and the first half of the
nineteenth. First was the *Nibelungenlied*, the national epic of
the Germans, dug out of a ducal library in the Austrian Alps by a
Swiss doctor in 1755. *Beowulf* followed in 1787, transcribed by an
Icelandic scholar in the British Museum. And finally, in 1835, the
French national epic, the *Song of Roland* (an eleventh-century manuscript written in the Anglo-Norman dialect, later recognised as the
earliest masterpiece of French literature) was discovered by a French
scholar in the Bodleian library in Oxford, inspired by a passing
mention in an edition of Chaucer. It was too late for the French
Revolution or the Napoleonic wars, but just in time to play a
significant role in the tumultuous French struggles of the middle to
late nineteenth century. But it's not quite the truth to say the *Song
of Roland* had been lost: its impact was too strong for it to wither.

Composed around the mid-eleventh century (possibly by a Norman
poet called Turold, who is mentioned in the epic's closing line), this
roaring masterpiece was recited by pilgrims walking to Santiago de
Compostela and chanted by Crusaders on their way to the Holy
Land. It became the great epic of Christians against Muslims – finessing
centuries of conflict into a single storyline (although this involved
some mental acrobatics, ignoring the telling fact the historical Roland

didn't fall in a battle against Muslims). So popular did it prove that nine medieval manuscripts have been discovered so far, along with fragments and other poems inspired by the story, including versions in Middle High German, medieval Dutch, Old Norse, Castilian and Welsh. Later in my journey, I would hear about the *Rolandsrímur*, a rhymed Icelandic take on the story.

On the eastern Adriatic, a legend of Roland turned him into a defender of Dubrovnik against the Saracens, inspiring the statue I saw under the bell tower; and cities of the Hanseatic League raised similar statues in the fifteenth century, celebrating Roland as a defender of civic freedom. Norman warriors took the *Song of Roland* as an anthem, reciting it at the Battle of Hastings; another branch of the Normans carried it to Sicily, where it mingled with local folk traditions, re-emerging in the nineteenth-century *opera dei pupi* (or puppet operas). Fantastical romances embellished the story (most famously, Ludovico Ariosto's Renaissance masterpiece, *Orlando Furioso*) before the Franco-Prussian wars repositioned it as a bastion of French national pride.

Even in more recent times, the *Roland* has retained its pull. Graham Greene, that most English of novelists, built a novel around the manuscript's discovery (*The Confidential Agent*); it inspired a poem by the Nazi troubadour Hans Baumann on the theme of loyalty; and it was made into a successful movie in the 1970s, *La Chanson de Roland*, starring that most German of actors, Klaus Kinski. If there's such a thing as a 'Song for Europe', surely it is this tale of Roland's ill-fated stand on the Spanish pass.

I was planning to explore the *Song of Roland* in three stages, spanning four countries – sandwiching its historical setting between encounters with its legacy. First would be Sicily to learn about its cultural impact in the much-loved *opera dei pupi*. Next, I would travel across northern Spain, visiting Saragossa, the capital of the Muslim Saracens in the tale, and Roncesvalles (Roncevaux in French), the mountain pass where Roland meets his death. Later, in the German city of Aachen, I would visit the court of Charlemagne, the first Holy Roman Emperor and a leading character in the story. In France, I hoped to catch a glimpse of Roland's favourite prop; and I had heard about an event due to take place later in the summer, joining Europe's most ancient people to the historical source of the tale.

So much ground to cover. But that was inevitable, for the *Song of Roland* has branches all over western Europe. If I could swing between enough of them, I might be able to answer the principle question this epic had stirred: why did a prickly Frankish knight from Charlemagne's most ignominious setback become a hero for such a vast span of the continent?

Riding the ferry across the Adriatic, leaving the furred Balkan mountains for the steel alps of tower blocks and customs depots, I was crossing a faultline: from East to West, from Slavic to Latin, from nations still negotiating EU membership to the leading members of the club. But in storytelling terms, the change didn't feel so stark. Both the *Kosovo Cycle* and the *Song of Roland* tell of Christian warriors outnumbered by a massive Muslim army. Feudal overlords surrounded by faithful knights and a lone traitor (mirroring Christ and the Apostles). Heroic last stands, a touchiness in matters of honour, a deep concern for worldly reputation. Information about the *Kosovo Cycle*'s composition is too patchy to know if there was any influence. What is more likely is that both the medieval French poet and the Serbian guslars were responding to a parallel belief: in the battle against Islam, Christendom was facing its greatest challenge – the 'clash of civilisations', as the more bombastic historians like to label it.

But as much as the parallels, the contrasts are equally telling, and none more so than the ending. Whereas the *Kosovo Cycle* fragments into the mourning songs of the bereaved, the last part of the *Song of Roland* charts a fictionalised triumph for the Christians. Charlemagne slays the Muslim ruler and seizes Saragossa, returning home in glory. It didn't happen like that historically, but in its own boastful way, the *Song of Roland* articulates a broader truth: the triumph of the West.

The ferry brought me to Bari and a colourful reminder I was now in the West: the city was celebrating Gay Pride, a polychrome pageant on the evening *passeggiata*, with rainbows striped across bare midriffs, tattooed arms and cheeks. At the back of the station, a transvestite in an empire line dress was doing his mascara, tilting towards a compact balanced on a junction box. I waited beside him until the bus to Sicily swallowed me up.

Through the Italian night, from the Apulian heel to the Calabrian toe, and over the Strait of Messina. On the eastern side of Sicily, I climbed off the bus and staggered through greasy dawn light, along black streets hewn out of the lava from Mount Etna. I was groggy with all the travel, eager for a pick-me-up. But all journeys are relative: compared with the crowd gathered beside the train station of Catania, mine was Snakes and Ladders without the snakes.

They were Africans: Moroccans, Libyans, Eritreans, Nigerians. Many had only been in Europe for a few days, others had escaped from government-run migration centres on the coast. With its proximity to Libya, Sicily was receiving refugees and migrants on a nearly daily basis. Many were sucked into the underworld, valued only for the cheapness of their labour. As I approached the station, a few of them were washing their feet in a marble fountain, brushing their teeth, wringing out their underpants and T-shirts. Above them, a naked Hades was dragging an equally naked Persephone (commemorating a tradition that located the entrance to the underworld at nearby Lake Pergusa) above a riot of horses and bare-breasted mermaids. It looked like a cross between a swingers' party and a day at the races, and it struck me as an astonishing sight to greet you fresh off the boat from Libya. But none of the refugees were paying the sculpture any attention.

'Look! I lost my shoes on the boat,' said a curly haired Moroccan. 'It was terrible. The boat captain takes so much money, and there are so many people.'

Inside the station, a crowd of Arabs and black Africans was struggling with the ticket machine. An Eritrean teenager hobbled on a bandaged foot, and asked my help with the train map.

'Where do you want to go?'

'Milan. There is work in Milan.'

'How do you know?'

'Because,' he said, a shrill desperation knotting his voice, 'I put my trust in God.'

Behind us, a young Arab was rattling the ticket machine. His eyes were hollowed by drink and he took defiant glugs from a beer bottle. One of the Eritreans nudged him to get on with it. Inevitably, the bottle slipped from his fingers; a hoppy aroma wafted around the machine and a couple of barefoot refugees tiptoed between brown-bottle shards. He slammed a fist against the machine, conceding defeat to the subtleties of ticket purchase, and ran for the platform.

Later that day I saw a different kind of African. They had haughty expressions, dark eyes glowering over thick black beards. They exhibited none of the anxieties of the refugees, unsurprisingly given their clothes were so much brighter and better tailored: silk tunics and velveteen capes, turbans wound in creamy swirls, clasped with shiny gewgaws, gold thread shimmering down chests of oak and mimosa, bound in jute. But their limbs were leaking strings, impaled by rods, for they were Saracen puppets: the four-foot-tall bad guys of the *opera dei pupi*.

'This is our tradition,' said Giuseppe Grasso.

The puppet theatre had been established, back in the 1970s, by his late father, Turi, who appeared, hard at work painting a puppet, on Giuseppe's T-shirt.

'It's important to keep it in the family,' he said. 'We perform just as my father did. We never use computers or recordings, everything is live.'

Which meant there were a lot of props. Trawling backstage, Giuseppe handed me the conch shell that makes the sound of Roland's oliphant, rattled the metal sheet used to mimic storms and let me try on the clogs that replicate the beating of knights' boots.

The story unfolded above the auditorium in brightly painted murals. One scene showed Roland blowing his oliphant over baggy-trousered corpses and decapitated turbaned heads. Standing under this gaudy massacre, I wondered how Giuseppe felt about the binary divisions of the story, the moral split between Christians and Saracens, echoed in the *Song of Roland*'s most notorious line: 'pagans are wrong, and Christians are right'.

He looked a little stung by the question, his brow pinched. 'Our stories are not always black and white,' he said, stroking his neat silver beard:

This is what happened, the wars between Christians and Muslims, and we are telling our history. But in our stories, the characters are not simply good and evil. Take Rinaldo, for example. He is a Christian knight, a brave paladin, but he is also a very complicated character. He doesn't always obey Charlemagne's commands, and he argues with Roland a lot. He is like Robin Hood!

I knelt beside Giuseppe to meet the Roland puppet – gently, as if he was introducing me to a beloved pet. Roland glowed in his eagle helmet and red-chested cuirass, cross-eyed in the Sicilian fashion, reflecting a doomed love affair that drives him crazy (which isn't a part of the original epic: it's the Italians, not the French, who turned Roland into a chivalric Romeo). The traitor Ganelon was identified by the black feather on his helmet, and Charlemagne sported the fleur-de-lis of France. For Giuseppe, Roland was the archetypal hero, 'strong and brave and honourable', which is why Sicilians revere him:

> In the nineteenth century, they put Roland on playing cards and cigarette packets. All over Italy you could find this picture, so he became a symbol of our unification. And remember, Charlemagne was the Holy Roman Emperor. He was a king not only of the French but all of Europe.

This was the first of many explanations I would hear for the French epic's reach, mapping itself with the breadth of Charlemagne's imperial conquests.

Poking around backstage, I was like a child who gets to meet the cast at a pantomime. I crouched on the wooden bridge where the puppets are held, and had a go with Roland, knocking his oliphant against his lips, thrilling at the rustle of his shaking armour. Would, Giuseppe asked, I like to watch a scene? You bet I would! He even let me choose, and I gave my request in an instant: could I have the death of Roland, please?

> My good sword Durandal, your fate I mourn,
> For now that death arrives, there will not dawn
> Another like the many fights you've won,
> In conquest of such lands beneath the sun.

I was mesmerised by the hero's moon-walking steps, the rods yanking his sword and shield in Thunderbird jerks. The light sparkled off Roland's golden greaves and solar-patterned shoulder brooches. He seemed to tingle with it, doubly alive. When his legs buckled and his head lolled against his cuirass, there was dimness as well as stillness, underlining the inertia of death.

It was only when the scene was over that I remembered: there was nobody else in the audience. For all its splendour, the Grasso Theatre had no regular performances – the puppets only strutted their stuff when a group came with a booking. Is a tradition without an audience truly a 'living tradition'? I had heard there was more going on, puppet-wise, in Palermo. I looked forward to finding out if that was true.

The puppet theatre was near the coast, and that night I slept on a ledge of basalt near a fishing hut, lullabied by the sneeze and murmur of the sea. It was like sleeping in a hostel dorm with a crowd of phlegmy backpackers. But it was worth it for the sight that greeted me in the morning.

Roused by the stench of the early haul and the salty smell rising off the surface, I lifted myself to the sight of dawn light pouring around a crowd of prismatic columns. Formed by hundreds of thousands of years of sea carving into horns and frills, they looked like the mouldering forms of prehistoric sea beasts. They are locally known as the rocks hurled by the Cyclops Polyphemus against Odysseus' ship, fitting the beliefs of ancient mythologists who associated those one-eyed giants with nearby Mount Etna: for it was the Cyclops, they believed, who manufactured Zeus' thunderbolts from their volcanic forge.

What an island of epic! That day, I swam in the *Odyssey*, picnicked in the Arthurian legends (amongst the lush foothills of Mount Etna, where Morgan Le Fey queened over her fairies and the Bishop of Catania's groom once claimed he'd spotted a sleeping King Arthur) and snoozed on the beach at Capo d'Orlando, or 'Roland's Cape', where knightly feats were painted on motorised *carretti* – pick-up trade carts parked near the station.

Light and sea trembled in the windows of the early morning train to Palermo, cloud drifting in banks of gold and salmon-pink above the Golden Shell. Sun rays plunged towards towers and steeples, which rose like lines on a graph, the spaces between them filled by glassy courthouses and apartment blocks, built on the cheap by Mafia construction goons. Descending into the muggy heat of Palermo, I made my way down the thoroughfare of Vittorio Emanuele, stopping under a battered alley sign depicting a cross-eyed, sword-wielding paladin. If this was anything to go by, traces of the *Song of Roland* should be rife.

12

In many lands he's vanquished many foes,
From good sharp spears he's taken many blows,
He's slain many kings in battle's fray,
When will this warring reach its final day?
King Marsile, *Song of Roland*, Laisse 42

T HE PALAZZO HAD a wooden gateway wide enough for a horse
and a broad stairwell of cracked marble winding up to a scat-
tering of poky apartments. 'Beware of the Lion!' warned the sign
on one of the doors, maintaining the chutzpah of a palace. Next
door was Pietro's place: a narrow maisonette with majolica flooring
and the odd patch of silk wallpaper. 'I am ashamed,' said my host,
apologising for the webbed ceiling and the hazardous gaps on the
stairs up to my room. But I was thrilled: I had a space of my own
for a few days, and a terrace rooftop where I could dine al fresco,
on cantaloupes and grilled octopus from the nearby Vucciria market.

It was perfectly located. Ten minutes' walk brought me to the
towering gateway of the Porta Nuova. Amongst pillars and winged
cherubs appeared four bare-chested Saracen giants carved in the
sixteenth century. Their expressions were abject, lines pinched tight
above their noses. It's said their winding turbans inspired the designers
of the *opera dei pupi*, but they are sadder, more desolate than the
puppets.

Another influence on *pupi* costumery was the Steri Palace, another
ten-minute walk from the palazzo, heading towards the port. Here,
the Chiaramonte family, one of the wealthiest clans in medieval
Sicily who claimed to come from French stock, commissioned a
Norman-Catalan painted ceiling – a long coffered hallway decorated

with mythical scenes. Tristan slays a dragon and embraces Isolde, Charlemagne presides over his paladins, Greek ships arrive at Troy and (in a bowdlerisation to make Homerists weep) the battle ends in a truce and the happy wedding of Paris and Helen.

The Steri Palace illustrated the prestige of the Normans (which is why the Chiaramontes wanted to publicise their Norman ancestry) as well as their association with the rich Sicilian traditions of story-telling. For the era of the Normans – who conquered England and Sicily around the same time – provided the island with some of its greatest heroes: from the conqueror Roger I to Palermo's patron saint, Rosalia.

The Normans who ruled Sicily were a branch from the same trunk as the Anglo-Normans, with roots, via northern France, in Scandinavia – hence 'Norman', the 'North-men'. Hardy, disciplined warriors, they beat down most of the armies they came up against and implemented well-organised, monarchical bureaucracies in the countries they settled. In England, they crushed the Anglo-Saxons and in Sicily they saw off the island's Arab rulers. In both cases, papal blessings swelled the self-belief of these militant Christians. So it's no wonder they had such a fondness for the tale of a Christian knight fighting for king and faith. All the more so, given the oldest extant version of the *Song of Roland* was written in Anglo-Norman French.

It's a little-known footnote in English history that its most famous battle was preceded by a *Song of Roland*. According to the Norman poet Master Wace, a jongleur called Taillefer 'rode before the Duke [William of Normandy] singing of Charlemagne and Roland and Oliver and the vassals who died at Roncevaux'. So fond of the tale was William that when his attendants undressed him after the battle, they declared 'there had not been such a knight since the days of Roland and Oliver'. In Sicily, a similar enthusiasm manifests in geographical names such as Capo d'Orlando and the stories about Roland that percolated into the *opera dei pupi*.

Norman iconography is all over Palermo, mixed with the char-acters from the old French epic. On wine-bar billboards and miniature *carretti* in butchers' shops, hanging over lemon juice stalls, I would see Norman kings like the mercurial cultural patron, Roger

II, alongside Roland and his fellow paladin, Rinaldo. Amongst these images were many puppets – displayed on the pavements outside shop windows or peering from cluttered workshops where greasy-armed craftsmen sat amongst eerie-looking body parts: a row of wooden hands waiting to be coated in paint; a pile of Saracen heads, black eyes staring like dead fish in the Vucciria market.

One of these workshops belonged to Vincenzo Argento, a veteran who had been working with puppets for more than six decades. He was a *puparo,* a puppet-maker but also a puppeteer, the fifth generation in a line stretching back to the nineteenth century.

'We do all the stories,' said Vincenzo, knocking his hammer into a newly minted Saracen's shield. High-browed, with the defiant look that I came to recognise among the *pupari,* he had strangely youthful eyes under frown lines so neatly gathered they looked as if he'd painted them himself, with the same brush he used for his puppets. 'We do the Santa Rosalia story, Roland and the Paladins, Tasso's *Jerusalem Liberated*, the tale of Astolfo. These are the traditional stories – and we are keeping the tradition.'

This was reflected by a photograph of his father, hanging on the wall over tubes of glue, drill bits and strips of sheet metal. Like most of the pupari I met, Vincenzo was running a family business. He'd learned the craft from his father, the puppet making as well as the stories; and he was handing it down to the next generation: his sons worked the puppets with him, while his daughter Anna voiced the female characters.

'You know how long he's been doing this?' she said. 'Sixty-six years!' We were standing in the Argento family's barrel-vaulted theatre, across the road from the lava-block cathedral with its fish-scale tiling and zigzagging arches. While her father was installing the puppets in the wings, Anna added, with a mischievous, affectionate smile: 'He's crazy – like Roland!'

That evening, I sat on a narrow bench in front of a puppet-size proscenium-arched stage. We were an audience of twenty-six – mostly tourists and out-of-towners. Vincenzo made an introductory speech about the art of the pupi, then the curtain lifted on a woodland scene, where Roland, in a green-plumed helmet, raised his sword against his red-feathered rival, Rinaldo.

Sometimes the scene changes were slow, sometimes the puppets were static. But the ambition was dizzying: a plunge into hell to meet a horned devil with eyes in his chest; the battle tent of Charlemagne, where the monarch brokers peace between his squabbling knights; the camp of the Saracens, seething with sharp-toothed dwarves and gigantic freaks trailing manes of terrifying hair. Not so much an ethnically identifiable army as a horde of generic Antichrists.

Much of puppetry's charm is in the mechanics. You marvel not only at *what* they do, but also *how on earth* they manage to pull it off. Rattling towards the climactic battle scene, Saracens and Christians entered from their preordained sides (Christians from stage-left, Saracens stage-right), taunting each other like boxers at a weigh-in. Visors were lowered, swords unsheathed. Assuming the *en garde* position, the warriors threw themselves full-tilt into the fray. Clever designs split the Saracens in half, or popped their heads off their necks; bodies crumpled to the stage. The leading knights rallied to the *battaglia* and the *squadrone* – specific manoeuvres as elaborate as dance steps, see-sawing around each other's swords before they lunged.

So this was the story of Roland, Sicilian style: a pastiche, with oriental princesses and snappy serpents. But it hasn't run all that far from the source. In the *Song of Roland* the poet lists a pick-and-mix of antagonists, including Siglorel, 'the sorcerer who'd once been down to hell', and the mighty Chernubles, whose 'hair sweeps down to the ground'. When Roland faces Chernubles, he 'Slices off his coif and his scalp, / As well as slicing through his eyes and his face . . . His whole body right down to his crotch', and damns his fallen foe: 'A wretch like you will not win today's battle!'

Verbal chest-beating medieval style. Not that Roland's the only epic hero to practice the ancient art of showing off. Reading the *Iliad* is like eavesdropping on a locker room for macho egomaniacs; and let's not forget Odysseus, bragging his name at the rock-hurling Cyclops. The feuding Icelanders of the sagas, or the knights of the *Nibelungen*, aren't much better. Smack talk has never lost its power – it still booms around gang culture, sporting rivalries, any scenario that's pumped with too much testosterone. Vincenzo and Sons made the most of the pre-swordplay banter, and they carried on hurling their taunts as the blades rattled and the bodies collapsed, blood simulated by flowing red silk.

An hour in this gaudy, gory world wasn't enough – I wanted more! But shuffling outside, back to his work cell, Vincenzo was phlegmatic.

'In my father's time, the crowds were very large – and they were local people,' he said. 'We knew the same audience would come back, so we didn't have to end it the same night.'

At its fullest extent, the Carolingian Cycle stretches to 270 episodes. In the past, the puppeteers could rely on a regular (traditionally male) audience, knowing they would return for each daily instalment, like the audience of a TV soap opera.

'The theatre of the pupi is the theatre of the poor,' said Vincenzo. Holding a cloven serpent that needed to be repaired, he shuffled back to his workshop and I walked alongside him. 'It wasn't for the children, it was for grown-ups. The rich went to the opera, and the poor came here.'

'Where has the audience gone now?' I asked.

'The young people today . . .' He shook his head over the battered serpent; furrows seared his brow like fresh carvings on a puppet's face. 'They just want to go to the bars, or watch television. They aren't interested in the pupi like their parents were. They aren't interested in our traditions.'

I thought of the guslars in the Balkans, who had been so hard to locate. Here is another long-standing folk culture, an offshoot of epic, narrowing to a niche activity. For now, the *opera dei pupi*'s popularity with tourists gives it a lifeline. But for how long, I wondered.

I spent a week in Palermo. After travelling at a hectic pace for the last few weeks, it was a relief to slow down. I hung out with my host Pietro, chatting about his girlfriend troubles and family pressures, the economic downturn, the bullying of the North: 'All the invest-ment, all the tax, goes back to the mainland,' he said. 'And then they tell us Sicily is dysfunctional!' I wandered around the Vucciria, got to know some of the vendors, browsed the surreal graffiti in the markets (Mafia dons snarling from pillars, European heads of state tagged across fences, Pinocchio's nose sprouting leaves across the block), which reminded me of Exarcheia in Athens. I visited a museum dedicated to the *opera dei pupi* (hundreds of knights with gleaming cuirasses, slung from hooks in a dimly lit hall, like captives in a gangster's abattoir) and best of all, I got to meet several pupari.

One of the most beloved was Gaetano Lo Monaco, who invited me into his sawdusty 'laboratory' near the courthouse. There, amongst prototypes and body parts, T-bevels and cans of oil, this master storyteller sat fiddling with a tin of tobacco. His eyes bulged under his leathery brow, as large and round as two-euro coins. Hanging over him was a chestnut-bearded Charlemagne he'd just finished and behind him was the new puppet theatre he was building, its frame locked to a sawhorse. He'd been involved with puppets since childhood, taught the craft by his uncle, and remembered watching his grandfather's shows when he was small.

'The tempo enthralled me! Rinaldo, why he's a cunning fellow. He's a rebel, I suppose that's why he's so popular. But Roland – well, he's the first knight, a man of strength, there is nobody you can trust more. I love them both!'

Of all the pupari I met, it was Gaetano who really communicated the love still so strongly felt in Sicily for these chivalric heroes. Grabbing my arm – tactile in the warmest, most Italian way – he threw himself out of his chair, plucked up a wooden sword and launched into a tale. It was a rhyming, chiming showdown between the two great heroes, Roland and Rinaldo. I was sucked into the rhythm of his performance, the deep bass thundering the verse, the clap of his feet, the beat of his sword: gesture, words and prop fusing with a centrifugal force that spun him to the scale of an orchestra. It was only when he stopped, with a casual flick of the wrist, that I realised: I'd forgotten we were still in his lab.

I'd been introduced to Gaetano by the novelist and poet Fabrizio Corselli, who I'd met, in the roundabout way that seems to be par for the course in Palermo, after sharing a table at a marketplace wine bar with an amateur acting company. One of the cast members insisted I should meet her son, Fabrizio, and set up a meeting for the next afternoon. So we sat among the brass poles and model *carretti* of the Spinnato Café, sipping a couple of frothy coffees.

Labelled by Italian critics as a 'Teller of Dragons', Fabrizio is steeped in the world of epic. He has co-written (with the philologist Gabriele Marchetti) a study of the epic tradition, *From Homer to Tolkien*, as well as a poetry collection called *Nibelung and the Black Swan* and an epic verse fantasy, *Drak'kast*, set in 'a realm of dragons'.

'You know what my greatest influence was?' His brown eyes glistened and his lips stretched a mischievous grin over his neat black beard. '*Beowulf*! That and Tolkien. You see, I really love dragons!'

As an oral storyteller, Fabrizio mingles prop-based physical performance with the traditions of rhyme and metre: *cuntastorie* and *cantastorie*. He presents his stories in public squares, and combines his performances with instruction, training up a new generation of professional storytellers, to be dispatched to tourist sites all over Sicily.

'We are not repeating the old ways,' he said. 'We are like Virgil. He was influenced by Homer, but when he wrote the *Aeneid*, he created something new. Each generation, the audience is different, but still they relate to the old stories, more perhaps than the new ones.'

Fabrizio's repertoire caught the breadth of Sicilian storytelling. He could rattle out tales about Roland, episodes from Homer, Virgil, the Arthurian Cycle (one of his most celebrated performances took place in the popular Square of Quattro Canti, where he told the story of King Arthur and Mordred). Sitting in the cafe with him – what a magical hour! – I lost count of all the stories and characters floating between us.

'Sicily is the land of myth,' he said, 'and our culture is deeply linked to the land. Look at Etna! Nowhere in Europe is like Sicily. Sicily had all these stories and myths around it, so of course it established a great tradition of storytellers.'

This fascinated me: Sicily as a storytelling storehouse. Its island location made it an incubator for these diverse tales; its central position in the Mediterranean pulled in stories from every direction. The same positional advantage enabled the Normans to run their lucrative empire. But the Mediterranean, the sea 'in the middle of lands', has fewer geopolitical advantages in the modern age. As Europe's political focus gravitated northwards, so Sicily's fortunes tanked. A German dynasty took up the reins from the Normans in the late twelfth century, and instead of sitting at the heart of a trans-Mediterranean trading network, the island dwindled to a southern outpost of the Holy Roman Empire.

In the evenings, the market of Ballarò is a dynamic place. Stallholders pull down their canopies and pile up their wares, sealing the sea bass in iceboxes, wheelbarrowing the swordfish and watermelons away. The smell of the fish lingers, mixing with the spicy tang of hash and the farting diesel of mopeds high-wheeling between the wooden benches, where dogs in spiked collars strain at their leads while their owners slump over their drinks. The lights of the mopeds mingle with the street lamps, tracking across the walls like search-lights, highlighting a graffitied slogan, a sticker for the Sicilian Communist Party or an oleograph of Jesus on Calvary.

Established more than a millennium ago, Ballarò was famous enough to be mentioned in the medieval diary of a merchant from Baghdad. Its name, derived from an ancient Arabic town, illustrates Sicily's pre-modern orientation: looking not towards Italy's more prosperous north, but south and east across the Mediterranean.

Amongst the crowd are many refugees and migrants. One of them, Khalil, is sitting in a bar called the Red Pig. More a social centre than a boozer, it's packed with new and recent arrivals, flicking through messages on WhatsApp or talking to the staff about work options. There are many people, all over Sicily, who are helping refugees – meeting them at the ports and giving them logistical support, offering rooms in their homes; or sailing out in fishing boats to rescue them from drowning. This is an island, after all, that's been welcoming refugees for centuries. But Sicily has problems of its own, and the refugees can't help getting absorbed into them.

'The boat cost 600 euros,' says Khalil. A Bedouin from western Egypt, he travelled to Libya in search of work. 'But everywhere in Libya is run by mafia,' he says. So, after a few months in pizza delivery, kicked around by aggressive bosses, he put his life in the hands of the smugglers. Only now is the irony dawning on him: setting off to Sicily to get away from the mafia.

'We didn't know about these criminal groups,' he says. 'We thought everything in Europe is better. But I don't want to stay in this place, I want to go to France. I have friends in Marseilles. Only, I have a problem with my papers. I wish the Italians hadn't stamped them.'

In the meantime, he's waiting for an opportunity – he's been in Palermo for five months – staying on a rooftop with around a hundred others.

'Is there space?' I ask, thinking of my poky *terrazza* at Pietro's.

'It is very tight.' Khalil clutches his shoulders, miming the night-time squeeze. 'And the problem is,' he adds, rolling up his sleeve, 'when a lot of people are close together, there are many arguments.' A few inches above his elbow is a russet scab the shape of a teardrop.

The worst brunt of Palermo's inequalities, according to a priest called Father Enzo Volpe, are borne by the African women. I have seen a few, lingering in the doorways of hair salons and other multi-tasking establishments. Many are victims of human trafficking, saddled with debt, enforced by traditional *juju*. Nigerian gangs like the Black Axe have muscled on to Mafia turf, striking a perverse alliance with the Sicilian crime-masters. The Mafia has no truck with prostitution, allegedly; but that doesn't stop it levying *pizzo* on the gangs that do.

'They are human beings,' says Father Enzo, 'but they are lost.'

Huge and bearlike, built like a bouncer, Father Enzo is a hard man to track down. He's parish priest of Santa Chiara, a Baroque church located in the heart of the district; but I struggle to find him at the church, because he's so busy roaming the parish. Eventually, I manage to get hold of his number and he invites me to his office, where we sit among scattered papers and ringing phones.

'There are many, many prostitutes from Africa, but only a few have the courage to flee,' he says. 'And if they do, they get far away from Palermo. Twice a week, I go out with blankets, fresh water and food, and try to talk to them. We tell them we are here if they want. It is to give them a human contact. But the number who respond is very low.'

The gangmasters might be new, but as far as Father Enzo is concerned, the thread in this particular labyrinth still winds back to the same place. Since the mid-1990s the Mafia has been weakened, with around 4,000 Sicilian Mafiosi arrested and an estimated

£25 billion of their assets invested back into Palermo's regeneration. But the Sicilian underworld has a way of enduring. In the latest sick twist, the criminal networks have been grabbing contracts on the construction of refugee camps, squirrelling away money earmarked for refugees.

'The Mafia are hidden,' says Father Enzo, 'but they manifest themselves in crime, in the drugs trade especially. And now the Mafia activities are co-ordinated with refugees. These people want work. There isn't a lot of work for Sicilians, let alone the refugees. And many of them are so desperate, they will accept anything.'

I think of Khalil. How much would it take to lure him? Promise of a doctored passport, perhaps? A route to his friends in Marseilles? The old criminal network is leaching off the refugee crisis, enlisting new arrivals as expendable street dogs. Eight centuries after the cultural zenith of Roger II (who welcomed scholars from every side of the Mediterranean in his court), here is a grotesque parody of the inter-faith fellowship that flourished under the Normans.

Back in the nineteenth century, critics of the puppet operas feared the violent tales were having a detrimental effect on the Sicilian youth (the criminologist Giuseppe Alongi asserted a direct link between the pupi and increased crime rates). 'Hence it is not rare,' wrote one critic, 'to see two rogues come across one another on the street and spin for themselves a genealogy of the Paladins; to wit, they gather themselves up as if they were two knights from the Middle Ages and they fly into one another . . .'

It's an old debate – you can track it back more than two millennia to Socrates' concerns over the impact of Homeric violence, and you can follow the line forwards to modern-day snuff movies. As long as people continue to tell violent tales, alarm bells are going to ring. Swap the 'young urchins' of nineteenth-century Palermo for disaffected youths on any modern sink estate, swap the tales of Roland and the Paladins for the latest gangster drama on Netflix: it's the same old problem, and it's epic storytelling that kicked it off. Which leaves the difficult question: if a few people get carried away, does that invalidate these dynamic stories for everybody else?

As for the connection between marionettes and the Mafia – surely this was taking things too far? And yet . . . the nickname given to the paladin Rinaldo – Roland's erstwhile love rival – suggests there may be something in it. For Rinaldo is known as the 'Mafioso'. Whereas Roland is slavishly obedient, following Charlemagne's commands to the letter, Rinaldo refuses to yield to authority. To quote the scholar Michael Buonnano: 'He was at once the rebellious baron of old French epic, the bandit of Sicilian popular narrative, and the Mafioso of the Palermitan streets.'

Sword-wielding paladins or pistol-packing hoodlums: with all the talk of honour and shame, the obsession with their outfits, threatening each other with violent deeds, is there much difference between them? Whether or not there's a causal link, there are certainly shared traits between epic heroes and gangsters, which is why crime movies often come closer to matching the grandeur of epic than the more anodyne fantasy and superhero movies that borrow so many epic motifs.

Now, in modern Palermo, the 'Mafioso' nickname is fading, as the city seeks to loosen the gangland grip. When I asked the pupari, most of them told me the moniker had fallen out of fashion. Wandering the Vittorio Emanuele on my last night in Palermo, I passed the red-chested 'Mafioso' on a playbill. Rinaldo was holding up his sword, staring defiantly back at anyone who caught his eye. I walked on by, wondering how long the Mafiosi will continue to glare down on this city they've been carving up for so long.

13

In Roncevaux this Roland I will kill,
The blood of Oliver I'll also spill,
The twelve peers cut apart upon those hills.
    Margaris of Seville, *Song of Roland*,
                                    Laisse 77

S ODIUM LIGHTS GLOWING on a shantytown of steel. A lemony
gleam across the high sea wall, where forklift trucks rolled across
the darkening docks of Barcelona. Seagulls swooped between cranes,
turning to white smudges on the lettering of Chinese and German
freighters.

I had been on the move for forty-eight hours: first a ferry from
Palermo, then a train across the rocky plains of Sardinia. Now I
was arriving in Spain, the setting for most of the action of the epic,
including the hero's death. A land, like Sicily, with grand epic
traditions (from the *Song of El Cid* to the post-epic burlesque of
Don Quixote) and a complicated history of Muslim–Christian interactions.

Against the giant steel cliffs of the ferries, the platforms and mobile
gantries, the workers were like tiny mechanical soldiers, as automated
as the machinery above them. Hundreds of shipping containers
bobbed on platforms, and I thought of the refugees in Chios, for
whom oversized toolboxes like these had been their homes.

There was no bus until morning, so I curled up on the floor of
Barcelona's bus station, bedding down amongst Africans with hessian
sacks and boxes wrapped in batik cloth. Climbing down at Saragossa,
I carried my pack into the swelling heat of the city. Ahead, round-
towered bastions gripped a high stone wall almost as formidable as

the citadel of Dubrovnik. Here was the Regional Parliament of the Autonomous Community of Aragon – which happens to be one of the finest surviving examples of medieval Moorish architecture.

In the *Song of Roland*, Saragossa is the Muslim capital, where King Marsile sits on his marble dais, winning over the treacherous Ganelon with an annual promise of 'Ten mules laden with the finest Arabian gold'. The poet's understanding of Islam may have been ropey (he turns monotheistic, iconoclastic Islam into an idol-worshipping polytheism), but he did have an eye for Islamic art. Men relax on seats of blue marble, on Alexandrian silk, in vaulted chambers 'inscribed and painted' in 'bright colours'. So appealing is King Marsile's court that Charlemagne's paladins adopt many of its features – even while they're plotting to kill the people who produced them: 'The knights on seats of silk brocade recline, / Amused by games of backgammon and chess.' Marsile baits Charlemagne with gifts of camels and moulted hawks, and when Roland dies his body is covered in oriental 'Galazine' cloth.

Amongst its many qualities, the *Song of Roland* is an early example of Orientalism, celebrating Moorish luxury even as it condemns the Moors. Beneath the military conflicts are more complicated cultural interactions, the same phenomena that were making Sicily and Spain the most intellectually fertile places in Europe at the time the poem was composed. But the narrative thrust militates against these subtleties: 'pagans [Saracens] are wrong', the poet declares, 'and Christians are right'. Just not, apparently, when it comes to interior decoration.

The Regional Parliament or Aljafería (named after an eleventh-century Moorish king) is contemporary with the composition of the *Song of Roland*; and it still sings the attractions that medieval Christian poets struggled to resist. Behind the imposing bastions and airport-style security check, you float among orange and lemon trees, marble and alabaster, soaking up the intricate designs of medieval Islam. Epigraphic bands roll over alabaster soffits and polyhedral archways, and latticework filigrees the surfaces as delicately as the carvings on ivory caskets. No wonder this palace was called the Qasr as-Surur – the 'Palace of Joy'. Wandering around, I could imagine myself as Ganelon, stepping into Marsile's orchard, mesmerised by the charm of ivory stools and the jewels of jacinth, amethyst and gold the Saracen queen Bramimonde presents to him.

Behind a row of orange trees in the Santa Isabella cloister, ivy hugs the columns. Vegetal arabesques dance between the blind pillars of a square oratory, where light honeycombs the latticework windows, spilling over carved verses from the Quran. Huge marble pillars tower like trunks in a forest, conjuring an illusion of depth as you approach the position of the throne. Embedded in the jungly tableau of a broad, blind archway, like a secret code buried in a manuscript, a plaster bird stretches its tail feathers. This isn't the only figurative decoration in the Aljafería: there's a winged plaster beast in the museum and two peacocks in the oratory. Moorish Spain was syncretic, in culture as well as the composition of its faith groups. The craftsmen who built this palace were not only Muslims but also Christians and Jews. Like Norman Sicily, this was a place where civilisations didn't collide so much as collude.

In Saragossa today, the Islamic influence is less public. The Reconquista wiped Islam out of Spain and it is only with the recent emergence of a migrant community from North Africa that a small mosque has opened. I was curious to know how Muslim life goes on, here in the old capital of the Bani Hud, so in the evening I wandered along a careworn alley, past a couple of young mothers puffing over prams.

Behind a plain metal door, a man with rolled-up trousers was washing his feet under a faucet. After prostrating himself before a simple niche, he came over and chatted about the weather: 'It's too hot in Spain! Of course, it is hot in Gambia too, but at least we have the rainy season!' Tattered adverts in Arabic hung from a sign-board, encouraging prospective hajjis to apply for the pilgrimage to Mecca. Standing in the grimy antechamber, I talked to one of the mosque regulars, an Algerian called Abdel-Kadir.

'I'm from Oran,' he said. 'There's a few other Algerians, but mostly they go to France. There's a lot of Moroccans here, and the blacks of course. It's not easy living here, but it's better than back there.'

Another Algerian, wearing a dishdasha, his head squeezed under a filigree cap, pinned a notice on the board behind us. Like Abdel-Kadir, Mohammed had dark memories of home, where 'we couldn't do anything'. But he wanted to go back one day. 'Everybody wants to die in his homeland, don't they? And we are Muslims.'

Above a wiry beard, his lips pushed forward, the groove soft over his shaven upper lip. 'I hear in England many have found Islam.'

I smiled weakly. 'I don't think . . .'

'But you are curious? This is why you are here?'

For a moment, he held my gaze, and I felt the pleasure of a stranger's approval. But it was an ephemeral goodwill. 'I'm afraid I'm not a very good Christian,' I said at last, 'and I'd make an even worse Muslim.'

North-west of Saragossa, beyond the wriggling Ebro and the roughly matted foothills of the Pyrenees, the road twisted between forests thick with pine and silver birch. Pitched roofs and Alpine-style balconies tilted over heaps of freshly chopped firewood. After the broad plains, the rise was precipitous. Pity the odd cyclist, pushing their aching thighs against the pedals. The road lifted us high up the mountains, nearly a thousand metres above the sea. When I stepped out of the bus, I could taste the iron on my tongue.

Roncesvalles is a towered, stone-clad refuge. A frieze battened to a rock marks the battle of 778 – at least, the fictionalised contest narrated in the epic. Cavaliers fight with spears and shields, while a chainmailed knight plunges his sword into the side of a mace-bearing Saracen.

The pilgrims' hospice here dates back to 1127, if not earlier (one theory for the composition of the *Song of Roland* in the eleventh century is that it was a cynical commercial strategy, designed to draw in the pilgrims on their way to Santiago). It's run by the Augustines, and Roncesvalles retains the atmosphere of a monastic commune, packed tight around the cloisters and chapter house. You can glimpse the bones of long-dead pilgrims in the ossuary known as Charlemagne's Silo (traditionally believed to contain the remains of Roland and his fellow paladins). You can pray before a medieval wooden Virgin under the delicate vaulting of the Church of Santa Maria. And you can visit the chapter house, with its tomb of Sancho VII, King of Navarre – a seven-foot, four-inch Moor-slayer who accompanied Richard the Lionheart on the Third Crusade.

In the epic, the traitor Ganelon tips off the Saracens to attack Roland at 'Sizer Gate', or the Col de Cize as it's known today: the old Roman road cut through the Pyrenees. It's on the saddle of the mountain pass that Roland's fall takes place. Now, I followed a path towards the site. Horse droppings and blackberries studded a dirt track between buckler ferns and bushes of pink gorse. Rock hauled the track into a beechwood, where my nose filled with the mossy, antiseptic smells of the forest, and that's where the dreamland began.

Cottony whiteness filling every pocket of air. Pasture stretched between the woods, but the mist coralled the cows, so I could only identify them by the tinkling of bells and their disembodied moos. It was a whiteout, mummifying the fields, until the arch of an old hermitage broke through like the hull of a storm-wracked ship.

The blanketing intensity emphasised how high up and isolated was the battle site. It showed why Roland and his fellow paladins have to fend for themselves and there is no hope of Charlemagne's army making it back in time to rescue them. On a double platform of stone, marking the spot where Roland is believed to have died, a grey flagstone stele punctured the mist. I sat on a rock to jot some notes, but the wind was so fierce it pulled my glasses off my face.

The cold was biting through my layers. But at least, under the hermitage porch, I was spared the lashings of the wind. I rolled out my sleeping bag and snuggled inside. A fieldmouse nibbled at the remains of my sandwich and gnawed a hole in the side of my backpack; a couple of bats loop-the-looped over the stone altar and a cluster of votive crosses, as if they needed to wind themselves up before they swooped across the sky. I watched them in a state of numbed appreciation. Up here, it felt like anything could happen.

Come the morning, the air was still clotted with mist, muffling any hope of a picturesque ramble to France. Mossy, grey-pink cliffs, starred with blue columbines, plunged to invisible streams. The Rio Luzaide (or Nive d'Arnéguy to the French) split the two countries, and the road followed the north–south axis of the valley.

By mid-morning I was breakfasting on gritty coffee in Carlosvalles – the Valley of Charlemagne – where tradition claims that Charlemagne turned his army around after hearing Roland's oliphant. Sitting around me, locals in berets rustled their newspapers and sipped sloe-flavoured patxaran liquor, cajoling each other in a mixture of Spanish and Basque. One of them stumbled by my table and leaned in to peer at my Kindle. He performed a theatrical bow, pulling off his beret and clicking his esparto sandals together, before skipping to the mini-market next door.

Before the days of the Schengen Agreement, the frontier was a thriving smugglers' passage, moving everything from livestock to lingerie, radios to resistance fighters on the run from the Nazis. Now, you barely know you've crossed. The give-away is the sign-posts, where the Spanish tilde over doubled Ns is swapped for French circumflexes, occasionally accompanied by the massed sibilants and hard Ks of Basque. The border is so indistinct there are residents who receive their electricity from the French grid and their security from the Spanish Guardia Civil. Firewood was heaped against stone granaries and solar stars carved over windows, and donkeys peered among apple trees and pines.

Downhill to Saint-Jean-Pied-de-Port, the path flowered into a riot of Frenchification. The houses lost their mountain squatness, their walls narrowed and roses crawled around iron balconies; the warm smell of lunchtime baguettes and sticky cheeses wafted under signs for *salle climatisée* and I passed enough crêperies to satisfy any Francophile. But there were also posters for Basque specialities like *Goyotik* singing and *pelota* (the popular Basque racket sport); and on the covered market over the fairground, a banner read: 'Regroupement des Prisonnieres Politiques Basques'.

In the *Song of Roland*, the hero is bombarded by the might of the Islamic army. But reality was both less and, in some ways, more dramatic. Because Charlemagne's paladins did fall, only to a far lower-profile assailant: the people who've inhabited these valleys since the Stone Age. Their excision from the poem is telling. After all, European powers have been trying to rub them out ever since.

A few weeks later, I'm back in Roncesvalles, climbing off another bus. It's 15 August, the anniversary of the battle recorded in the *Song of Roland*, and the square beside the Church of Santiago is awash with red flags, borne above a crowd of several hundred.

Across one banner is written *Independentzia*. Another is emblazoned with the number 778 in gold – the date of Roland's fall. Trumpets blare across the square, and the crowd thickens around a brass band; a man in Harlequin-like black and white performs a traditional dance, which involves a lot of leaping and kicking. There are speeches too: one by a bespectacled lady in a red cardigan; another by a bald, professorial man in a green polo shirt. I hear rolled Rs and lisped Zs, the agglutinative language of the Basques. But I can't understand a word of it, so I ask the people beside me.

'He's talking about Charlemagne,' says a man with curly brown hair, holding one side of a banner, 'and how we defeated him!'

'For us,' says the woman beside him, 'the Battle of Roncesvalles is the first war the Basque people won.'

'And,' her partner adds with a mischievous smile, 'the last!'

'It was revenge on Roland and Charlemagne,' the woman continues, 'for destroying Pamplona. For killing so many Basques. We say this is our Independence Day!'

When it comes to ancient land tenure, nobody in Europe can hold a candle to the Basques. Geneticists have traced them to Near Eastern farmers mixing with hunter-gatherers, occupying the valleys of the Pyrenees for the last 7,000 years; although new theories are always on the horizon. Less controversially, we can be sure there were Basques in these valleys when Charlemagne's army barged through.

'The battle here was a milestone,' says Dr Aitor Pescador, an archivist, historian and archaeologist of the Aranzadi Science Society, the man who's been addressing the crowd. While the singing carries on in the square, he leads me down the path to the collegiate buildings, so we can hear each other. 'It was the first time the Basques fought together. It's a reference point that remains in our collective imagination.' It was the Basques, he insists, who ambushed the Frankish rearguard and killed Roland. The epic may give a different account, but contemporary sources agree with him. Far from crusading against the Saracens, Charlemagne was lured to Spain by a joint embassy from the Muslim rulers of Barcelona and Saragossa, enlisting his support against the growing power of the Umayyads to the south; and it was the approach of the Umayyads that drove the Franks back across the Spanish pass. There, according to the contemporary chronicler Einhard,

> the Vascones [the medieval term for the inhabitants of these valleys, commonly identified today as Basques], who lay in ambush on the top of a very high mountain, attacked the rear of the baggage train and the rearguard in charge of it and hurled them down to the very bottom of the valley. In the struggle that ensued, they cut them off to a man; they then plundered the baggage and dispersed with all speed in every direction . . . Eggihard, the King's steward; Anselm, Count Palatine; and Roland, Governor of the March of Brittany, with very many others, fell in this engagement.

Although Pescador disputes some of Einhard's details (he points out, for example, that Charlemagne's troops were already 'in the bottom of the valley, because they were using the old Roman road, so the "Vascones" used this disadvantage to attack them from the heights'), he broadly agrees with Einhard's narration.

'The *Song of Roland* gets so many things wrong!' he says. Charlemagne's army was 'a foreign, imperialist, centralising power. He attacked Pamplona and turned the Basques into his enemy.' Here is another case in which history was written by the losing side – the more powerful side, this time – and reshaped for their greater glory. Call it Carolingian propaganda, or (to use the modern term) fake news.

'It was shameful for them to be defeated by the Basques – a small country without an army,' says Pescador. 'So when they told the story, they needed a more powerful enemy. The Muslims gave them the honour in their defeat.'

This matters today: 'People need to know their own history,'

Pescador insists. 'The problem here is that Spain was built over the defeat of the Basque Country, Navarre, Catalonia and other countries, so the Spanish mindset is still imperialist.'

Here is one of Europe's most enduring separatist movements, drawing off the memory enshrined in one of Europe's most enduring epics. Spain's wrestle with its secessionists has often turned bloody, with the recently disarmed Basque group ETA responsible for some particularly violent episodes. The growth of Europe's independence movements reflects declining confidence in the nation-state, but also expresses the organic flux in which European polities are bound – the never-ending shifting of ground between localisation and centralisation, encapsulated in the image of Basque ambushers seeing off the rearguard of Charlemagne's mighty, pan-European army in 778.

A farrago of historical inaccuracies the *Song of Roland* may be, but it follows the same principle as Hollywood historical movies: never let the facts get in the way of a rollicking story. This afternoon, I sit inside the small, Gothic church of Santiago and join a reading from the poem. A Spanish literature professor starts us off with a nineteenth-century verse epic by the Spanish author Bernardo del Carpio (who reimagined the battle as a contest between France and Spain). A priest called Padre Joachim tramps inside with a party of pilgrims and reads a couple of stanzas from the *Cantar del Roldan* (a Spanish translation of the *Song of Roland*). A little boy called Martin works through some verses (he gets a big round of applause). And I read out an English translation from a laminated printout. Loudest of all is a Basque activist, big-shouldered with a theatrical beard, who bursts into the church, followed by a companion with a camcorder, and barks some lines from a nineteenth century account of the battle. '*Independentzia!*' he declares, shaking a fist, and marches back out, his cameraman at his tail.

Reading the poem is a reminder that, for all its troubling politics, the *Song of Roland* is a work of astonishing literary craft. I'm swept up in the graceful, plainchant-like *laisses* (or stanzas), the formulaic repetitions, assonances and multiple rhymes winding around my ears like incantation. Zealotry doesn't usually make for good poetry, but the *Song of Roland* is an exception, and we need to understand this in order to appreciate its impact. Not only is this the earliest known masterpiece of the French language, it's a manifesto for that language's rippling, coursing genius:

> Ço sent Rollant que la mort le tresprent;
> *Now Roland feels death is pressing hard;*
> Devers la teste sur le quer li descent.
> *It's creeping from his head down to his heart.*
> Desuz un pin i est alét curant;
> *He hastens to a pine-tree set apart,*
> Sur l'erbe verte s'i est culchét adenz.
> *And there he stretches down upon the grass,*
> Desuz lui met s'espee e l'olifan'.
> *And lays beneath him sword and oliphant.*

The readings give me an urge to revisit Roland's monument. But this time, instead of mist, it's drenched in sunlight, thronging with more than a hundred demonstrators. Banners are raised and slogans shouted (many are the same banners I saw in the square), an accordion is squeezed and songs are chanted. Group photos are taken and a microphone is handed around for speeches about socialism, anti-imperialism and feminism. This demonstration, it occurs to me, represents a counterpoint to the Sicilian perspective. There, the story of Roland had been detached from its setting, mined for its story: an almost purely cultural legacy. Here, it's the setting that matters above all. The semi-fictionalised account told in the epic has been stripped back to its historical source, hinged to a battle over political identity.

One of the speech-makers, silver-haired in a Che Guevara T-shirt, breaks away from a group chant. 'We are having an assembly to discuss our objectives,' he explains. 'We have five. Firstly, the Pays Basque [French Basque Country] and Navarre [Spanish Basque Country] must be united, then socialist, feminist, ecologist and Basque speaking. All over Europe, things need to change. We need to change the way we structure our economies.'

'So you're choosing the anniversary of a battle from the Dark

Ages,' I ask, 'to campaign for a separatist progressive utopian future?'

He tugs my arm, a gentle smile crossing his face.

Listen – this is an important day for us. Back then, it was a period of German-Frankish imperialism. They had all the power, and Charlemagne was ruthless. Did you know, when he attacked the Saxons he slaughtered thousands of people! But we still managed to kill Roland, who was Charlemagne's most famous soldier. We showed you can still change history, even if you are small. It's important for us all to remember that.

14

With Durandal so many blows I'll send,
My goodly sword that from my side depends
I'll smear with foemen's blood from end to end.
                    Song of Roland, Laisse 85

U P TO NOW, my Roland journey had carried me to an island
where the tale is retold with marionettes and the frontier region
where the events of the epic took place. Now, I was crossing the *Song
of Roland*'s original homeland. So pan-European are the poem's references – with Danes, Bavarians and even Saxons listed in Charlemagne's
army – it's easy to forget: this is the national epic of France. Or, as
my French sister-in-law said: 'Oh yeah, the *Chanson de Roland*, we
had to read it at school when we were twelve. It was so boring!'

The local train from Saint-Jean-Pied-de-Port, the TGV from
Bayonne, then a switch to the scruffier local train, from Bourdeaux
to Brive La Galliarde. Sitting around me were lanky teens with long
hair and pale faces flattened to studied nonchalance, a Gallic *froideur*
that was strangely refreshing after the light bulb expressions of the
Mediterranean. A lone bastion of enthusiasm was barrelling up and
down the aisle: a little boy in a *Minions* T-shirt, ignored by all the
phone-glued waifs. When the train pulled into his stop, he clambered
down to the platform and leaped into the arms of an elderly lady
– presumably his grandmother. I felt a lump in my throat as I watched
them hug. I'd been away from home for too long.

The TGV offered the consolation of free Wi-Fi and plugs for
your phones. I could even use the WC to shave. But there were no
such extras on the local train. I disembarked, after the day's fourth
ride, at the station of Rocamadour. A pilgrimage town with some

unusual possessions, it claimed to have the famous Durandal – Roland's beloved sword, 'fair, hallowed, and devote', to quote the warrior himself. With the town a few miles from the station, I set off on another ramble, grinding my feet on the bitumen. The long walk out of Roncesvalles had delivered a fresh raft of blisters, so I was thankful when a car pulled over.

'It isn't safe in the dark!' A kindly pair of eyes gleamed under a blonde pelmet. 'We don't want you to get run over!'

Anna and her friends were from Lyon. Where I'd been drawn by steel, their intentions were spiritual. They had a full day of prayer ahead and had booked themselves into a hostel. I admitted that I hadn't prepared for my visit quite so thoroughly, and they offered some advice: 'If you want to do wild camping, go somewhere out of the way – so the police can't catch you!'

That night I was a vagrant, sitting in the shadow line of a poplar in a park beside a medieval hospice. Between the branches, the pilgrimage town was spilling light into the thickly wooded valley of the Alzou: a forested secret. Dawn shed a honeyed light on a warren of houses and shops, churches, chapels, stairways and gates, grafted on to a fifty-metre cliff pocked with grottoes and caverns. Rather than projecting out of the cliff-face, the buildings clung to it, hugging their environment like some imaginary collaboration between J. R. R. Tolkien and Frank Lloyd Wright.

Hobbling along the cobbled lower market street, I dragged my latest blisters past a crêperie, a *maroquinerie* and more foie gras specialists than I've ever seen on a single street. A stone stairway soared above them, like some celestial ladder dragging us away from those symbols of French provincial worldliness. Churches and chapels crowded around a dizzying forecourt – seven sanctuaries floating over the flagstones. They were angled so tightly they seemed to be spawned by the ribbed limestone cliff that sheltered them.

Rocamadour's most popular shrine is the twelfth-century Chapel of Nôtre Dame. Under webbed vaulting, candlelight flickered against the grotto wall; stone angels hovered over the nave and stained-glass windows showed scenes from the life of the Virgin. Irons and shackles were nailed to the cliff face, mementoes of freed prisoners and pardoned sinners; and there was a 'miraculous' bell, forged before the ninth century, which has been said to ring of its own accord. Standing over the tabernacle was the chapel's holiest possession, a 'Black Madonna', the walnut body draped in a cream mantle, long arms enfolding a baby Jesus.

I sat in a pew, relishing the cold stony air, the flickering shadow play of the candlelight, the gothic occultism of the Black Madonna (a homage to the dark beauty of the Song of Songs, as some have suggested, or maybe just the candle-stained result of centuries of pyro-worship). Filing into the chapel came a group of Girl Guides, assembling for Mass. They wore blue shirts and neckerchiefs, and their flag-bearer had kidskin gloves. They channelled their Psalms towards the Madonna, voices yoked in a single, adoring alto.

I stood behind them, biting my lip over the guest-book. It was nosy of me, but I couldn't help looking: a woman's request to 'guide my steps along the way', a young man hoping for his *oncle Louis* to be reconciled to his *grand-père*, a wish to *apporter la fertilité* (like many visitors to Rocamadour, the supplicant was hoping the Black Madonna would help her to conceive). Slowly, I was absorbed into their prayers, willing the Madonna to do something for all of them. I had been brought up in their faith, and had spent my life wrestling with Catholicism – the stifling rules, the violent history, the misdeeds of some of the priests and monks I'd known, but most of all Catholicism's failure – the failure of all religions – to satisfactorily explain death. But it was like a wrestle with a loved one, because there was so much that drew me in: the chiselled, often charming storytelling, the peaceful values of the Gospels, the humble kindness of so many of the people who devote their lives to the Church. Now, feeling a little weary, nursing my latest limp, I was yearning for the comforts of familiarity. It's the agnostics, I often feel, who get the most out of going to Mass.

No epic could be as Christian as the *Song of Roland*, with its Crusading ethic, its images of shriving monks clouded in incense, nuns in wimples praying in the convents of Aix. Charlemagne is presented as especially pious, celebrating holy feasts, performing solemn rituals and receiving visitations from the angel Gabriel. But Roland, with his hawkish appetite for battle, is as distant from the Sermon on the Mount as you can imagine.

'Spend all your life, if need be, in the siege,' he declares, when Charlemagne's court is debating whether to make peace with King Marsile, 'Revenge the men this villain made to bleed!' So much for 'turn the other cheek' and 'blessed are the peacemakers'. Roland makes vague references to Christianity, but he only prays at the very end of his life; and even then, he devotes fewer lines to God than he addresses to his beloved sword, Durandal. Like the heroes of Germanic and Greek mythology, from Achilles to Beowulf, his true idol is worldly status, measured by the blood you shed and the blood shed on your behalf. You read the vaunting and taunting of the battle, Roland's fiery pride and Charlemagne's wrath, and you wonder how much attention the poet had given to the Gospels, or if he took his values straight out of Homer.

And yet . . . As the critic Marianne J. Ailes has written, 'The Christian warrior, exemplified by Roland, does not make the poem less Christian, even though today we might find his military stance difficult to accept.' The *Song of Roland* is a plunge into the medieval headspace, the emotional pull that led men from sermons about mercy and forgiveness to acts of slaughter and pillage. In old French, *recreire* is the word for surrender. This is the one act that Roland will not countenance. The word is derived from the Latin *recredere* – 'to change your religion'. Wave the white flag and you're an apostate. Here is the ideology of the Christian soldier, which epic tales like the *Song of Roland* did so much to nurture.

With its odds and ends of ritual and relics, Rocamadour can feel like a theme park for pious Catholics. Cast your wishes to the Black Madonna, ascend the steps on your knees (reciting Ave Marias on the way), say a few prayers in a grotto slung with the shirts of leading French rugby players, sprinkle coins over the burial place of Saint Amadour and gaze at a gleaming sword impaled in the rock face. That's what I was here for: to feast my eyes on Durandal, the French Excalibur.

Such was the animistic power attributed to heroes' swords, they were given names and embedded with precious relics. According to the epic, Durandal contained Saint Peter's tooth, drops of Saint Basil's blood, some of Saint Denis's hair, a fragment of the Virgin Mary's gown. Each relic tightened the bindings between the hero and the Church Militant, amplifying the powers of his blade. Pledging to keep Durandal safe from 'pagan hands', the dying Roland lies down on top of it, after beating off a Saracen's attempt to steal it. Folk tales claim that he managed to hurl the sword until it struck the cliff of Rocamadour. A less fanciful version suggests it was presented to the monks after the battle by Charlemagne as a gift, having been blessed at Rocamadour before the battle (an event that is recorded in a bronze bas-relief under the Black Madonna, which shows Roland weighing out pieces of gold to match Durandal).

Originally, the sword was located at ground level, but it became the subject of 'unsavoury rites'. Now it's mounted higher up the rock face, warding off the more determined pilgrims. But the sword still receives plenty of attention, mostly from photo hunters showing off their impressive zooms. There, amongst the selfie sticks and iPads, I noticed more than one woman clasping her hands in prayer, quietly associating this talisman of death (or so I imagined) with the possibility of life.

What was palpable here in Rocamadour wasn't so much the invisible power of stories as the lure of physical objects. Catholicism has always juggled the tangible and the abstract, drawing much of its spiritual power from the tension between them. 'Ne'er shall base ballad be sung of them in hall!' says Roland to Oliver, when they are in the thick of the battle ('them' being their swords). For the sword is a hero with a name, a history, a reputation, addressed in song and prayer; a repository of all the skirmishes in which it's played a part.

15

From Spain does Charles the Emperor advance,
And comes to Aix, first citadel of France.
              Song of Roland, Laisse 268

I F YOU WERE living in Paris in the winter of 1870, you had little
hope for haute cuisine. 'Ragout of cat' was served in the hotels,
the *pot au feu* was made with crow, according to an eyewitness, and
'to go out decently dressed would now expose you to risk of arrest
as a Prussian spy, or that which is worse, to be recognised as an
Englishman'. The army of Prussia was besieging Paris and the residents were rapidly losing morale, sinking under news of defeats from
the Loire communicated by hot-air balloon.

For Gaston de Paris, the pre-eminent French medievalist, it was
time to give his compatriots a pep talk. So he delivered a lecture
at the Collège de France entitled 'La Chanson de Roland et la
nationalité française'. In the process, according to the scholar Fernanda
Moore, Gaston 'secured *Roland*'s spot at the head of the French literary
canon'.

'From within this iron circle the German army tightens around
us', he declared.

> Yes, eight centuries ago, when many European nations had no
> conscience of themselves as such, when many, like England, still
> awaited the formation of its essential elements, the French nation
> was formed. National feeling existed already in its most intimate,
> noble and tender character. In the *Song of Roland* the divine
> expression 'Sweet France' appeared for the first time, such a grateful
> and adoring formulation of the love which all its children feel for

their homeland. Sweet France! The Germans have envied us this notion, as they fruitlessly searched for a similar formulation in their own national literature.

The Germans weren't feeling much envy the following month, when they ended the siege with a bombardment of large-calibre Krupp siege guns. Within days, the armistice had been signed, and Wilhelm I was declared Emperor of the Germans at the Palace of Versailles. This was a mortifying sight to French pride – to witness German triumph at the glittering symbol of French civilisation. But if any literary text could provide solace, it was the *Song of Roland*.

'We have just seen defeat, once again,' wrote another scholar, Léon Gautier, introducing an 1872 edition of the poem, 'but we know how to repair the nation from the Roncevaux of the nineteenth century.' Its long history of civilisation, Gautier believed, would fix the nation: 'To you Germans . . . you who suffocate today my poor France, I will show very clearly how eight centuries ago we were a grand nation.'

Basque identity may feed off the historical Battle of Roncesvalles, but it was French national identity that was nourished by the epic poem. Gaston and Gautier weren't just kicking their words like pebbles into the Seine, they were dealing with a story and characters that held a profound emotional appeal. A year after composing 'La Marseillaise', in 1793, the French army officer Claude Joseph Ruget de Lisle produced a war song about Roland, entitled 'Roland at Roncevaux, or: Let us Die for the Fatherland'. The hero was adaptable to monarchist and revolutionary sympathies – a royalists' darling in the 1830s, fighting for his king; a patriotic martyr in the 1850s, dying for 'douce France'. The rediscovery of the *Song of Roland*, in 1835, led to a publishing phenomenon: Gautier's was one of twenty-six editions in the space of thirty-one years.

That was the *Song of Roland*'s prime – the excitement of its rediscovery coinciding with a period of national crisis. But its influence has continued to be felt. 'Douce France' became the title of a hit song during another period of crisis – Charles Trenet's nostalgic ballad from 1943, which fondly remembered the *vieilles chansons d'autrefois* ('old songs from yesteryear'). More recently, in the speeches of the Rassemblement National (formerly Front National) leader, Marine Le Pen, this malleable story continues to beat. Writing about Le Pen in *Le Monde*, the literary professor Cécile Alduy observes: 'one is always in a mythological register, that of the Crusades. The *Song of Roland*, the first national epic which sings this "sweet France" so much cited by Le Pen, poses the founding axiom of this xeno-phobic ideology: "Christians are right and Saracens are wrong."' And so it goes with the politicisation of epic. For Gaston de Paris, the *Song of Roland* was a consolation for a besieged nation. France may not be under siege today, but try telling that to Le Pen and her followers.

Stepping off the night train from Brive, I wandered the Left Bank, climbing past the mansard roofs and iron gates of Gaston de Paris's Collège de France. At the Musée de Cluny, I admired the gigantic ivory oliphants – those sawn-off bits of elephant with their echoes of Roland's fatal horn blowing – before crossing the Pont au Double to the Île de la Cité.

A huge crowd filled the square in front of Notre-Dame Cathedral: scooping up pigeons in their arms, waving selfie sticks and licking ice creams at the base of an equestrian statue. As a resident of Paris a few years before, I'd often schlepped past this statue, struck by its dramatic composition. Now, immersed in the *Song of Roland*, I saw it enlarged, almost animated, as if the warriors on that high pedestal were about to go crowd-surfing.

Charlemagne was a fork-bearded bronze giant, jabbing his sceptre at the pigeons. Leading his horse were his *leudes*, his two most steadfast warriors: Roland and Oliver. With their downturned moustaches and strapped breeches, they looked like early prototypes for Asterix. Roland carried a double-headed axe in one hand, Durandal in the other, his oliphant dangling from his waist like a Victorian's fob-watch. All three of them gazed across the river, towards Germany.

The timing of the statue is revealing. Sculpted by Louis Rochet, it was unveiled at the World Fair of 1867. Very much of its time, it represents the same themes channelled by Gaston de Paris and Léon Gautier: enshrining Charlemagne and Roland as emblems of an ancient nation. As the sculptor's brother Charles explained: 'The idea of this statue was conceived by my brother to take back from the Germans this historical figure they wanted to steal from us.'

Which pinpoints the problem with Charlemagne and why he's a risky symbol: he can be claimed by either side. He was German-speaking, holding court in German cities like Aachen, Worms and Paderborn. His people were the Franks, a Germanic tribe (with a mythical ancestry in ancient Troy) who had established themselves in Roman Gaul a few centuries earlier. Under the Merovingian dynasty from the fifth century, the Franks became a nation; it was a Frankish commander, Charles Martel, who held off the Arabs at Tours in 732, preventing the Islamic conquest of western Europe. Charlemagne was Martel's grandson.

But how does this make Charlemagne French? Because it was through the Carolingians that, over time, a French-speaking monarchy emerged, assuming the *oriflamme* symbolising Charlemagne's kingship. Because he ruled over the territory known today as France, and because he is the 'King of France' in the national epic of the French. The Franks may have started out Germanic, but the Gallo-Romance language got them in the end, turning Clovis into Louis, Hruoland into Roland and Karl der Grosse into Charlemagne.

But when national identity is at stake, do you really want to rally behind a symbol that's so ambiguous? This is a subtlety that doubt-less passes by Marine Le Pen. When she's bashing the Germans and rallying her cohorts with appeals to *douce France*, she is also praising a Germanic tribe under a German-speaking ruler who's been cred-ited for more than a millennium as the architect of European unification.

The battle over Charlemagne's legacy has been fought for centu-ries. 'I am Charlemagne,' declared Napoleon in 1806, regarding his relationship with the Pope; and when Jacques-Louis David painted him crossing the Alps, the name of Charlemagne was written in the rocks beneath Napoleon's horse. Equally, German rulers coveted association with Charlemagne – from Kaiser Wilhelm, who com-missioned a copy of Charlemagne's crown to show he was the true heir of the Holy Roman Empire, to Adolf Hitler, who brought the crown back to Nuremberg. Showing their cynical expertise in matters of identity, the Nazis even came up with a Carolingian compromise.

Massaging the sympathies of French fascists, they named a regiment of French *Wehrmacht* volunteers the 'Charlemagne Division'.

The truth is, Charlemagne doesn't belong to either nation. He ruled in an era of tribal networking and feudal allegiances rather than demarcated borders and the nation-state. Like so many heroes, he's been co-opted by those who could make use of him. But, by retaining a joint French and German following, he remains a figurehead for western and central Europe – as broad-reaching as the epic poem that celebrates him.

At the end of the *Song of Roland*, after Charlemagne has avenged Roland's death, slaughtered several thousand Saracens and conquered Saragossa, he returns to his royal capital at Aix, or Aachen (today a German city, a few miles east of Belgium). Ganelon is found guilty of treason, 'His every limb wrenched from the socket' by four stallions, and thirty of his kinsmen are hanged. As for the Saracen queen, Bramimonde, she is led to the city's famous baths to be baptised, a symbol of Charlemagne's spiritual victory. Which reminded me: it was quite a while since I'd had a decent wash.

In the riverside hangar where Flixbus operates like some low-budget Bond villain, passengers were scrolling phone apps to show their tickets, pouring inside a wobbling double-decker. Sprawled across the back seat behind me was a pair of Syrians. An Italian businesswoman was barking into her phone across the aisle; a Liberian family was arguing with the driver about the enormous wicker baskets they wanted to stow in the hold.

'So how can I fight for Assad?' asked one of the Syrians, talking over the headrest. His brother, he explained, was in the 'Free Army' fighting against the forces of President Assad. 'Maybe I would have to shoot my own brother!'

British arms trading, they pointed out, wasn't doing their homeland any favours. Many of the weapons sold to countries like Saudi Arabia and Qatar had ended up in the armouries of Islamic State, part of Britain's £6 billion-per-year arms industry. 'Why don't your people stop your government from doing these things?' one of the Syrians asked. Bashfully, I turned to greet the man beside me. He was blond and Teutonic-looking, but he introduced himself as

'Hassan'. He was half Palestinian – and he had a few things to say about Britain too.

'Maybe you heard,' he said, a little waspishly, 'about the Balfour Declaration?'

I was still apologising, eleven hours and at least as many Belgian canals later, as I climbed down from the bus – for the missiles, bombs and fighter jets the British arms trade was shipping to the Saudis, the Sykes–Picot Agreement, Mandate Palestine, the Suez Crisis . . . Being British amongst Middle Easterners is to be a sackcloth-wearing, self-flagellating sinner. Which was a fitting attitude to carry along the cobbled streets of Aachen.

Gargoyles leered and Gothic arches looped. Nothing cried out for makeshift sleeping arrangements, so I settled on a fountain beside the cathedral. Sitting down on the cool stone ledge, I drifted in and out of consciousness, reflecting that I had probably made the right decision not to tell my fellow passengers I was following the story of a Muslim-killing soldier of Christ. After all, you can trace a direct line from Charlemagne's battles against Islam through to the colonial era and the so-called 'War on Terror'. This historical interconnectedness was at the heart of one of the most intriguing interpretations of European epic currently doing the rounds: *The Song of Roland: the Arabic Version*, which was scheduled to debut in Germany a few weeks later. At some stage over the coming months, I hoped to catch it.

Now, slumping on my fountain ledge, I rubbed all those guilty feelings away, too tired to process them, and slumbered into dreams of the bed-sheets I'd promised myself as soon as I made it to the Rhine. When my eyes blinked open, a few hours later, I found a bag of Bounty Bars beside me on the ledge. I stared at it for several moments, as if it was an apparition. *Who . . . ? Why . . . ?* At last, I held it up, gazing in wonder; warmed by the gesture, faintly confused, and touched a little by shame.

Charlemagne remains a powerful symbol of European unity, distant enough from our own age to be more palatable than other, more recent conquerors. In 1950 a 'Charlemagne Prize' was established, presented annually in Aachen to an individual deemed to have made a significant contribution to European unification (recipients have included Henry Kissinger, Tony Blair and Pope Francis). The prize's inaugural winner, Richard Nikolaus Graf Coudenhove-Kalergi, used his acceptance speech to champion 'a renewal of the Empire of Charlemagne as a confederacy of free nations . . . to transform Europe from a battlefield of recurring world wars to a peaceful and blooming worldly empire of free people'. He was conflating ideas about a 'Union Charlemagne' with broader concepts of European interconnectedness which, a year later, would form the European Coal and Steel Community, paving the way for the European Union. What Charlemagne represents, above all else, is the power of the centralised state.

In the *Song of Roland*, the feudal heroism of the paladins exhausts itself. When they fall at Roncesvalles, the state machinery kicks in, pursuing a rigorous revenge against the Saracens. Far from neutralising the power of Charlemagne's army, the Saracen ambush has fuelled its motivation, jump-starting the engines of the super-state.

This isn't an anachronistic projection of modern concepts on to the medieval. The nation-state may have flowered in the nineteenth century, but it derives from organisational principles established in Charlemagne's time. So much of modern Europe tracks back to the medieval: our universities, military hierarchies, trading guilds and banking system (down to specific details like double-entry bookkeeping and bills of exchange), as well as the ideological divisions between eastern and western Europe and the development of fortified frontiers. It is also in this period that we find the post-classical rebranding of 'Europe'. The term was in sufficiently wide currency for the author of an epic ninth-century Latin poem about Charlemagne to describe the emperor as 'Europae . . . pharus' – 'the beacon of Europe'.*

---

* This poem, the 'Aachen Epic' or 'Charlemagne and Pope Leo', focuses on a particular episode in Charlemagne's career: the visit of Pope Leo, fleeing from knife-wielding conspirators in Rome, and his coronation of his protector, Charlemagne, as 'Emperor Governing the Roman Empire' (later known as the Holy Roman Empire), inaugurating a western European, German-led imperium that would last 1,006 years, until the rise of that self-styled new Charlemagne, Napoleon Bonaparte.

Charlemagne is ubiquitous in Aachen. He presides over a fountain opposite the city hall, his image adorns boxes of Printen nut sweets; his fork-bearded statue appears in cafes, over fasciaboards, even in the lobby of a spa. To many residents, Charlemagne is more than just a king, more even than a Holy Roman Emperor – he's a saint, to whom several miracles have been attributed. In the twelfth century, a Latin prayer was composed in his honour – the *Karlssequenz* – which is still sung in a Mass held on Charlemagne's feast day. His sanctity was officially acknowledged back in 1165, by Pope Paschal III. However, Paschal was an anti-Pope, following a disputed papal election, who was currying favour with the Germanic emperor (and Charlemagne devotee), Frederick Barbarossa. At the Third Lateran Council of 1179, Paschal's pronouncements were abrogated. The only concession to the emperor's acolytes has been a 'local cultus', which means he can officially be known as 'Blessed Charles'.

'Many people in Aachen consider him a saint,' said Stefanie, a willow-haired guide in the cathedral. 'They pray to him and they say miracles happened because of him. But the Vatican refuses to accept this because of all the Saxons he killed. As if all the other saints were so pure!'

In a city with ye olde bar names like At the Golden Unicorn, where knights' helmets project under timber-framed windows, the desire to swim in the past is strong. And Charlemagne certainly gives a lot to the visitor. Behind the carved eagle pulpit in the cathedral, you can see his shrine: a golden casket carved with scenes from his life, surrounded by the figures of sixteen successors. In a gallery upstairs is the emperor's marble throne: an unadorned chair fastened with bronze clamps, underneath which sinners used to crawl as a penance. But to feel the emperor's majesty, the place to visit is the treasury.

There, a lustrously bearded bust glows behind the Roman sarcophagus in which he was buried, with his so-called hunting knife and book covers from Charlemagne's art school (reflecting the development of illustrated manuscripts under the emperor's auspices, and their legacy in the Carolingian minuscule, which initiated the lower cases and spacings we use to write today). The emperor is wavy-haired, his shoulders and neck decorated with gems and ivory cameos:

a serene figure gazing back at the viewer, the cares of his kingdom lightly drawn by a pair of frown lines.

I was too dirty for such a mighty king. A mile out of the old city, behind a fork-bearded Charlemagne statue in the lobby of the Carolinus Thermen, I collected a yellow coin and a wristband. Aachen's association with healing waters reaches back before the emperor's time; and they still provide a balm to local residents after a tough day at the office, just as they close out the combat of the *Song of Roland*. Amongst all the bronzed, ripped, beautiful people, I must have looked a bit of a freak; but fortunately nobody seemed to notice when my toenail fell off. I picked it up, along with my towel, and made my way back towards the changing room.

My adventure in the *Song of Roland* was drawing to a close. But a few weeks later, I stopped in the northern German city of Bremen. Looming over the old medieval marketplace, near the cathedral and the elaborately sculptured city hall, is an eighteen-foot-tall statue of Roland. He's one of the largest civic statues in Europe, a formidable presence. Gold streaks his legs and the edges of his red cape, spans his shield and colours the claws of a double-headed eagle inside gold embossed lettering: the gaudiness of the Sicilian *pupi* on the scale of the Paris Charlemagne.

Most statues are commemorative, but the Bremen Roland has a more practical function. 'I manifest your freedom,' reads the inscription, 'as granted to this city by Charlemagne and many other rulers. For this, be thankful to God, that is my council.' The statue, mounted in 1404, embodies an imperial gift by the Holy Roman Empire. It stands as a symbol of the independence of the 'Free Hanseatic City of Bremen', with its own parliament and legislative powers, a city-state within the German federation.

Life whizzed around the statue all through that afternoon. Under the city hall, a band of Hare Krishnas in dayglo orange were playing guitars. Across the square, a stag group was pushing a guy dressed as a giant dummy-sucking baby in a shopping trolley. A crowd of demonstrators swept past the statue, handing out flyers for the Open Borders campaign, while anarchist tunes roared out of a boom-box. The most poignant moment was the arrival of a Syrian couple who had just exchanged their wedding vows. Dressed in black tails and a long creamy dress, they danced in the square, while friends recorded their sinuous arm moves on their phones.

'My parents see this right now,' said one of the group. 'They are in Syria and they see this. They are so happy!'

When the dancing was over and the phones discreetly lowered, the bride pushed back her veil to smoke a fag, before drumming the cobbles with her four-inch heels. Above her towered the giant Roland, reinvented as a figure transcending religious identity: a secular guarantor of civic rights, under whom the Syrian couple's marriage had been celebrated. The epic's audience may have grown from the conflict of Christianity against Islam, the clash on which so much European identity was built. But the hero had moved on, to champion legislative freedom – as European a value, surely, as his earlier iteration.

Walking away from the square, I was thinking about the multiple roles in which Roland had manifested: the chivalric deed-doer and cross-eyed lover of the Sicilian puppet operas; an inspiration for the Crusaders; a symbol of oppressive centralising powers for the Basques; a fertility god for visitors to Rocamadour; a monarchist or a revolutionary patriot, defender of *douce France* against the Germans; Charlemagne's obedient henchman.

This diversity of roles answers the question I had been asking since Dubrovnik: why did this haughty Frankish knight become a hero for such a vast span of the continent? Because, more than any of Europe's epic heroes, Roland is malleable, his character and identity sufficiently broad for different nations and ideologies to claim. Ironically, for a warrior so proud of his resolute inflexibility, as a cultural icon he's as loose as a feather.

But Roland doesn't hold the monopoly on role shifting, and many of his fellow epic heroes share his versatility. Which is what makes them so dangerous. Because, if there's no limit to how you can remould them, what's to stop the unscrupulous? The Balkan epic had already taught me that, but down in the depths of Germany I would learn about a tale with a history even more deadly.

PART FOUR

The Taste of *Götterdammerung*

The Nibelungenlied

The beauty of Princess Kriemhild is sung across the Rhine, so the dragon slayer Siegfried, holder of the lavish treasure of the Nibelungen, sets out to win her. He makes himself indispensable to her brother, King Gunther of Burgundy, by fighting off an army of Saxons, and does a further service for Gunther when he uses his cape of invisibility to trick the formidable warrior-princess, Brunhild of Iceland. Gunther is no match for Brunhild, but the invisible Siegfried engineers his victory in a contest of leaping, hurling and stone-throwing that compels her to accept Gunther as her husband.

Reluctant to submit to Gunther's caresses in the marriage bed, Brunhild binds him with her girdle and hangs him from a nail. So Siegfried is called upon once again: disguised as Gunther, he wrestles Brunhild into submission in the royal bedchamber, leaching her of her superhuman strength. But he also steals her girdle and ring, which he gives to Kriemhild, who is now his wife.

When a dispute erupts between Brunhild and Kriemhild, the latter shows these powerful tokens, shaming Brunhild and King Gunther. As far as the councillor Hagen is concerned, there is only one solution: Siegfried must die. However, the hero has been invulnerable ever since bathing in the blood of a dragon he slayed, with only a small patch of mortality on his back where a linden leaf fell. After learning this detail from Kriemhild, Hagen launches his spear against the hero.

Kriemhild is distraught at her husband's murder and determined to avenge him. But she has to wait many years for the opportunity. It comes, at last, after she accepts a marriage proposal from the warlord Attila the Hun. Inviting her kinsmen to a feast, she stokes a conflict that hurtles beyond the point of no return when Hagen beheads her young son. After tens of thousands of knights have fallen, Gunther and Hagen are finally subdued. Kriemhild executes her brother and beheads Hagen herself, with Siegfried's old sword. This is too much for one old knight, Hildebrand, who cuts her to pieces, bringing a bloody end to the carnage.

16

In Worms they held their sway beside the river Rhine,
Supported in their day by many daring, fine
And honourable knights until one day there brewed
The very worst of fights – two noble ladies' feud.
                         Nibelungenlied, First Adventure

I S THERE SUCH a thing as the uber-epic, jam-packed with more
'epic' strands than any other? A nearly immortal, monster-slaying
hero. A beautiful but inaccessible princess as strong as any man. An
extravagant treasure guarded by dwarves. A dramatic betrayal. A
journey across a perilous wasteland. Female water creatures with the
gift of prophecy. A final battle of fire and blood, infanticide, a smat-
tering of cannibalism, and bombastic speeches about honour . . .

Only one epic's got it all, and if not the very greatest, it certainly
holds off allcomers in terms of dramatic intensity. It also happens to
be the one that's suffered the most unconscionable misuse. Because
this is the one the Nazis got their paws on. Whereas the *Song of
Roland* branched out from Roncesvalles to encompass western Europe,
the transmission of the *Nibelungenlied* (or 'Song of the Nibelungen')
has worked the other way: a story that swings from Iceland to Hungary,
narrowed down to an anthem for German nationalism. Over the
coming weeks, travelling towards the old Hungarian capital of
Esztergom, I wanted to learn how this had happened.

Like the *Song of Roland*, the *Nibelungenlied* was lost for many
centuries. It was a Swiss doctor, Jacob Hermann Obereit, who found
the poem, in 1755, browsing in the ducal library of Hohenems in
the Austrian Alps. He suspected he had discovered something of
real worth and contacted Johann Jakob Bodmer, a noted medievalist,

who began the task of disseminating the poem to the wider public. The story, as with the *Song of Roland*, was well known through other versions. Still, its rediscovery was a major moment in German literary history because of the superior poetic craft of the *Nibelungenlied*.

In story terms, there are also correspondences with *Roland*. Both epics depict an ill-fated stand, in which a few brave knights fight off an enemy army (the Nibelungen against the Hun, Frankish paladins against the Saracens), and in both cases the knights take great pride in their loyalty to their king. But the storyline of the *Nibelungenlied* is more complex, its characters more ambiguous. Amongst them – a telling contrast with the French epic – are two of the most dynamic female characters in the European epic tradition.

Whereas women in the *Song of Roland* are reduced to war trophies and mourners (Roland's intended, Aude, is so superfluous to the poet that on hearing of Roland's death she immediately drops dead), in the *Nibelungenlied* the queens Kriemhild and Brunhild are drivers of the plot, refusing to be silenced by the male status quo. Brought to the foreground, they rail against each other and the men around them, while Kriemhild uses every available resource during the story's blood-drenched final battle scenes, even wielding her late husband's sword to decapitate her enemy. But let's not mistake the *Nibelungenlied* for some medieval version of *Kill Bill*. The poet makes it clear where he stands from the beginning. Kriemhild 'came to be a beautiful woman, causing many knights to lose their lives'. This is a story for a patriarchal society, in which female combativeness is something to wince and marvel at, like scaly, fire-breathing dragons.

The *Nibelungenlied* is still inspiring new stories, and I hoped to meet some of the artists creating them. Which is why I had come to the ancient Rhineland city of Worms during the *Nibelungen*fest. For a fortnight every summer, Worms goes *Nibelungen* crazy. There are posters in shop windows, brochures in cafes, articles in the latest edition of the local paper, the *Nibelungen Kurier*. You can debate the epic's themes in 'discussion groups' in the back rooms of museums; listen to reciters from the Nibelungen Society reading in Middle High German; watch it on the big screen – a showing of Fritz Lang's monumental 1924 silent movie *Die Nibelungen*; bid for artworks inspired by its episodes. And most excitingly of all, you can sit in the raked auditorium behind Worms cathedral, watching characters from the *Nibelungenlied*: forging alliances, betraying each other and falling to the tune of a Wagnerian dirge sung by a *Valkyrie*, or shield-maiden, in a triple-horned cap.

'It's the weather that makes it such a challenge,' says Florian, assistant director of this year's festival centrepiece – *Siegfried of Arabia*, by the Bavarian playwright, Albert Ostermaier. 'Last week there was so much rain, we had to shuffle the scenes around. But,' he adds, allowing a cautious smile as we pass a couple of tech crew pulling rainproof covers off a russet train carriage, 'those are the most satisfying ones to get through!'

Behind him, the *Valkyrie* is unstrapping her baby-carrier, handing over parenting duties to her partner. Out of the caravan behind her steps the hero Siegfried, buttoned into his greatcoat. There's a Turkish actor smoking a fag beside the canteen; and an Ethiopian actress, who's playing the avenging Kriemhild, passes by.

'This isn't just a story about Germans,' says Florian. 'It's about the whole world.' Although its source, he admits, is 'Germany's most famous legend': 'Some locals did ask me, "What does this play have to do with the *Nibelungenlied*?" But at the end of the play, the question is: is war really the final answer? Which is the same question that's asked in the legend.'

This revisioning of the tale is set in the First World War, in the Middle East. *Siegfried of Arabia*: the title evokes T. E. Lawrence and the geopolitical wrangling of that time, when German double agents were nearly as active in the Middle East as their British counterparts. 'The trick is not minding,' says Siegfried in an early scene, cunningly quoting the movie version of *Lawrence*. On a screen mounted over the actors, jackboots stomp under barbed wire and battle smoke. Hagen – a warrior and a murderer in the original tale, here presented as a stodgy army lieutenant – is told, 'you can prove your Nibelungen loyalty in the carnage'. This is the deadly idea at the heart of the epic – *Nibelungentreue*, loyalty defined by the shedding of blood. So resonant an idea that in the lead up to the First World War it was cited by the German chancellor as the glue binding Germany to its ally, Austria-Hungary, and later as a slogan for mobilisation. Even now, a century on, it remains a powerful concept in German political discourse. To give an example: when the invasion of Iraq broke out in 2003, the newspaper *Die Zeit* characterised the alliance between the UK and the US as a *'Nibelungentreue'*.

Siegfried of Arabia took the *Nibelungenlied* out of Worms and dragged it through the Middle East. But I had come here to track the story to its source. Worms . . . it can be a misleading name for English speakers, conjuring underground crawlers and the diet of Roald Dahl's Twits, rather than the formidable city described in the *Nibelungenlied*. It began life as a Celtic camp, co-opted by the Roman army, evolving into one of Charlemagne's favourite bivouacs. Seven centuries later, it resurfaced in the history books as the setting for Martin Luther's interrogation: that favoured historical event of tittering English schoolkids, the Diet of Worms. 'Here I stand,' he famously said, standing here, on the east bank of the Rhine.

'There is no place in the world that was so important in former times – and now so unimportant!' said local artist Thomas Eichfelder. But it's the much mythologised era of the Burgundians that sealed Worms's place in the national memory: a fragment from the 'Age of Migration'. Wandering out of Scandinavia and eastern Europe, the Burgundian tribe settled on the Rhine, the traditional border between the Roman Empire and the 'barbarians'. If you were born in the first year of King Gunther's reign (roughly AD 413), you'd still only be in your mid twenties by the time of his death, ripe to get yourself trampled by the Hunnish mercenaries who smashed up Worms for the Romans, or join the trail of refugees wandering over the Rhine. Keeping their tribal name, along with their penchant for good vineyard country, the survivors established themselves in the Savoy, in the region of France still known as Burgundy.

Although the *Nibelungenlied* braids together several moments from history, they are fused through centuries of oral retelling and a medieval poet's relish for dynamic fight scenes. Modern-day Worms struggles to evoke King Gunther's Dark Age capital, but of all the buildings that survived the Rhineland bombing campaign of the Second World War, it's the cathedral that offers the most insight into the epic. Not only does it play a key role in the narrative; its twelfth-century core is contemporary with the poem itself.

Inside its sinewy musculature of fanning vaults and buttresses lurk several archetypal creatures: a gryphon, a monkey on a mason's back, a bug-eyed lion tearing into a man's head. There's a metre-high boulder in the courtyard known as 'Siegfried's Rock' (according to tradition, he impaled his lance inside and hurled it), although it's probably an old winepress from the seventeenth century. Strangest of all is the tetramorph over the main gateway, an eerie creature bearing a plump queen on its back, with four different heads, beaked, snouted and horned.

These carvings are echoed by the many wild and strange creatures in the *Nibelungenlied*: from treasure-guarding dwarves and prophetic river-maidens to the woodland bear that Siegfried wrestles on a hunt. But none of the epic's supernatural episodes is as famous as the dragon slaying, the source of Siegfried's oh-so-near invulnerability.

Downhill from the cathedral, a caped Siegfried poses in front of the city library, barefoot and bare-chested, his brawny physique slightly undermined by his smooth mullet. The statue was carved in 1904, and this was apparently considered a suitable heroic hair-do at the time. But the sculptor hasn't done Siegfried justice – he looks too stately, a far cry from the charismatic jock who bounces through the early chapters of the epic: He-man with a goofy grin.

In the sculpture, he's trampling his defeated foe: a scaly, snakelike 'Lindwurm'. From which comes 'Worms'. So enthusiastically has the city embraced its mythical identity that dragons are visible all over the place – spurting from a 'fortune wheel', lime-green in a knitwear display, bristling off the corner of a brewery, covered in newsprint outside a local newspaper office, grappling over the city's keys and glaring back at the cathedral gargoyles. The dragons are so ubiquitous, I lost any sense of awe. I found myself leaning against them and using them as picnic tables. They were particularly useful when I needed somewhere to rest my notebook and scribble up a diary entry.

I had booked myself into an Airbnb, but I arrived in Worms a day ahead of schedule, so on my first evening I set myself down at a late-night drinking hole – the Siegfried Fountain Sports Bar (the *Nibelungen* fan has plenty of choice – there's also a Kriemhild restaurant behind the cathedral and the Zum Hagen bar, named after Siegfried's killer). A drunk Bulgarian brickie was stumbling around the fruit machine, and a retired policeman called Moritz was sitting at the bar, grazing on a Bitburger. On a mirrorwork wall mural behind them, Siegfried was depicted, relishing his victory over the dragon.

In the time-honoured way of strangers in a bar, Moritz and I ran through a raft of topics, while sipping our way through a couple of pints: from his reminiscences about Beatles-era Hamburg to the current problems he saw in Worms.

'This city,' he fumed, 'has a lot of problems! Our crime rate is too high – and do you know why? Because of the Turks! The problem is they have no respect. We are open in Germany, we are democratic, we can't throw all these migrants out. But they come from Romania, Syria, Africa . . . *ack!*' He waved a hand in the air. 'The good ones stay in their country, but the bad ones come here and do so much crime!'

Moritz wasn't alone. Germany's national election was looming, and in the last weeks of campaigning, the far-right Alternativ für Deutschland was on the offensive, sniffing electoral gains. Angry middle-aged men were out in force: I saw them a couple of days later, handing out flyers beside a blue-painted van, holding a jar of sweets for the children. I was tempted by a dolly mixture; instead I got a diatribe.

'If these immigrants have four or five children and we only have one, then in two generations they will be as many as us. It will be a big problem,' said a balding man in a gingham shirt. 'And these Africans, they have very low skills, so what can we do with them? They are not qualified to do our jobs. We are working for them to stay in our country!'

This was conservatism with a capital C, nurturing a honeyed vision of the past, desperate to keep things 'the way they were'. When I told him I was here for the *Nibelungen*fest, he admitted he hadn't been to this year's show:

They've changed it so much. They're trying to appease this liberal agenda. Now, if they were going to tell the original story, I would be the first in line! But I heard they set it in the desert this year. In Arabia! Why do they need to do that? Isn't the story interesting enough?

Over the coming weeks I would hear many similar views. I would be told that Germany was losing its discipline, that foreigners were taking advantage, that refugees were sex pests and thieves. But I would also hear the opposite, from activists holding banners for 'Open Borders' or collecting funds for refugee soup kitchens, and from refugees themselves – guys like Okba and Mahmud, who I met over a bowl of hummus at the recently opened Damaskus Restaurant.

'The AfD are Nazis,' said Okba.

'But they are not popular here,' added Mahmud. 'They have a following in East Germany and the south. *Not here.*'

Okba and Mahmud had both travelled from Syria, paying 1,500 euros to the smugglers in Turkey.

'Assad destroyed my village,' said Okba. 'The smugglers brought us here by walking – one and a half months. We slept by the roadside, in the woods. We had to hide from the wild animals and the bandits. When we got to Germany, I thought, "Now I can begin my life again." I'm studying German and I've reached B2 level. I want to get a job and start working.'

My Airbnb was a two-bed walk-up near the cathedral, owned by a young couple who spent their evenings watching horror movies. Occasionally, I was woken by a blood-curdling scream or the screech of slashing knives. But I had been reading the *Nibelungen* tale over the last few days, so nothing in the modern world was likely to trouble me. Besides, I relished the creature comforts after several nights outdoors: the crisp sheets, access to a fridge and a kettle, the easy Wi-Fi to skype home.

Lying on my bed that night, I thought about the ordeals described by Okba and Mahmud: the long hours of walking, the aggression of border guards, tense glimpses of wild boars when they were hiding in the woods. Ingredients, I couldn't help thinking, for an epic tale. Sure, Siegfried's a glory-hunting prince blessed with near invulnerability. But the value of plays like *Siegfried of Arabia*, as with other adaptations of epic literature, is in drawing connections across time and culture.

And here's another striking parallel. 'Siegfried follows the chaotic model of knight-errantry,' writes the scholar Edward Haymes. 'From the standpoint of traditional values, Siegfried represents chaos.' Anarchy, disorder: the terror of all conservatives, from right-wingers in modern Germany to the councillor Hagen, fretting over the stability of the Burgundian Kingdom. Siegfried is something new, a socially mobile soldier of fortune, bending the hereditary structures of feudal society. But in disposing of this dangerous champion, the Burgundians are unable to recover their lost order. Because you never can roll back to 'the way things were'. Here is the profound lesson of the *Nibelungenlied*: in striking at the root of the chaos, the Burgundian elite unleashes a chain of events that leads to the greatest carnage in all of European epic.

17

Now Brunhild, you have brought dishonour on your head.
No woman who's been bought could to a king be wed.
Kriemhild, *Nibelungenlied*, Fourteenth Adventure

'WE WERE LUCKY,' said the old woman, 'all these wine cellars. They are good places to hide.'

A couple of blocks from the apartment where I was staying, the alleyway of Maugasse was painted with *Nibelungen* scenes, lush and shiny as new silk curtains. A green dragon glided over the trees of the Odenwald, the Worms coat of arms tucked inside its tail. Around the corner, lines from the *Nibelungenlied* were printed in gold lettering over a doorway, recalling the *Nibelungen* loyalty of Prince Giselher ('I never broke my faith with any friend') in the epic's final battle.

A similar fondness for tradition dominated the decor in the neighbourhood bar. Behind doily-like curtains, paintings of old Worms were mounted among beer steins and decorative plates. Smoke blossomed over the heads of card-playing old-timers (no bothering with EU regulations in this little pocket of the past) as they slapped down aces and queens under photographs of buildings lost in the war.

'Well,' said a man with horn-rimmed glasses, 'it brought everything to an end, that is the important thing.'

'I remember messing around in the rubble.' Another player blinked his rheumy eyes, puffing on a cigarillo. 'When you're small, you think it's exciting. It's only later you realise the danger you were in.'

Worms was one of twenty-three Rhineland cities heavily bombed in the Allied air strikes. On 21 February 1945, British bombers flew out of East Anglia and dropped 900 tons of explosives over the city, wiping out two-thirds of the houses and immolating the medieval city centre. A month later, on 18 and 20 March, American bombers dropped a further 1,100 incendiary bombs. In his bestselling study of the air raids, *The Fire*, historian Jörg Friedrich quoted from the *Nibelungenlied*, linking those apocalyptic events to the 'national epic of self-destruction'. For Friedrich, the epic's influence on wartime Germany was palpable, a will-to-death fuelling the slaughter. He wrote:

> Four weeks earlier, the defenders could have entrenched themselves behind the Rhine. They could have lost just as easily, but at least saved Worms. But this did not correspond to the requirement of the battle of the Nibelungs as depicted in the epic. The Burgundians took their world with them to their ruin; there was no after.

Wandering around Worms, the devastation is still visible in the jarring disjunction between the surviving monuments and the predominantly modern city centre; the vast open space in front of the cathedral. A sandstone relief of Siegfried's entry to Worms and a bust of the fiddler warrior, Volker of Alzey, flank the city library, all that's left of the much admired Cornelianum. Standing before this old bomb-site is the Siegfried fountain – remarkably untouched, proving itself even more invulnerable than its subject. In the State Archive there is a devastating photograph, showing Siegfried upright in front of jagged ruins and heaped rubble: an invincible warrior surrounded by carnage.

Another war survivor stands, at the edge of the city, on the east bank of the Rhine. Hammered out of Galvano plastic in 1903, Hagen von Tronje (the surname, in medieval fashion, hints at Trojan ancestry) is the quintessential medieval hard man. He looms over the Rhine, raising the treasure of the Nibelungen on to his shield, ready to sink it in the river, to keep Kriemhild from weaponising the wealth of the man Hagen has slain. Ruthlessly pragmatic, he bullies the rest of the court into following his policies, making them all complicit in his murder of Siegfried. But he's more than a Macchiavellian schemer, for it is Hagen who inspires the *Nibelungentreue* – the 'Nibelungen loyalty' quoted by so many German and Austrian politicians. Less obviously heroic than heroes like Siegfried or Roland, he proves to be just as heroic in the long run, 'the boldest warrior that ever bore sword'.

Beside an anchored pleasure boat, a cormorant was perching on the wharf. A riffle in the air and its wings fanned the breeze; long black neck flattening, legs back. It hurled itself downstream, flying towards the turreted Nibelungen Bridge like a spearhead. Leaning over a railing, I peered into the grey, oily water. A ferry was floating a cargo of lumber upstream, a crewman dangling his feet over the gunwale. This could be any European waterway; it happens to be the most famously mythologised of all the continent's rivers. Brewed in the Alps, the Rhine spends itself in the North Sea, drawing a frontier that's been one of Europe's great dividing lines, from the days of the Roman Empire (when it distinguished the imperium from the barbarians) to the Rhineland battles of the Second World War.

I peered into the murky water, imagining the legendary stash, which metal detectorists are still searching for (as local artist Thomas Eichfelder put it, 'The first question everybody asks when they come to Worms is: "Where can we find the *Nibelungen* treasure?"'), a treasure described in drooling terms in the epic, with its nuggets of gold, precious gems and a golden wand, which 'if any had found its secret, he could have been lord of all mankind!' It remains one of the world's great undiscovered hoards, like the treasure of the Knights Templar or the gold of Eldorado.

'I dreamed I reared a falcon,' declares Kriemhild, 'a strong, beautiful, wild one, which two eagles clawed to death. No greater sorrow could have happened to me!'

The tragedy of the epic – and particularly Hagen's murder of Siegfried – is foreshadowed at the beginning of the story when Kriemhild recounts her macabre dream. The same dream narration opens Irene Diwiak's *The Icelander*, inspired by the *Nibelungenlied*, which was playing at the Lincoln Theatre by the old market.

I'd heard this play would focus on the epic's females, and having spent most of my time among macho warrior types, I was keen for a change of perspective. Foregrounding two dynamic women, the

Nibelungenlied poses significant questions about gender relations that still resonate. So I went along to watch the show and talk to the playwright about her adaptation of one of the epic's most iconic episodes – the 'Quarrel of the Queens'.

Kriemhild and Brunhild have been married to their husbands, Siegfried and Gunther, for several years when they meet on the steps of the cathedral. Kriemhild, distressed by Brunhild's jibes about her husband's status, approaches the cathedral ahead of her sister-in-law. But Brunhild is furious: 'A liegewoman may not enter before a Queen.' Defiantly, and ruthlessly, Kriemhild clinches the argument by producing the girdle and ring that Siegfried took from Brunhild when he subdued her for King Gunther. 'My dear husband Siegfried was the first to enjoy your lovely body,' she crows, 'since it was not my brother who took your maidenhead.' The humiliation is absolute – not only for Brunhild, but also for the king. 'Are we to rear cuckoos?' asks Hagen. 'His boast that he enjoyed my dear lady shall cost him his life.'

I had already seen this dramatic episode depicted in several paintings. Now, at the Lincoln Theatre, I was watching it in action. 'Who should take seriously a king who marries an Icelander?' demands the matriarch, Ute, rasping over her feathery black coat. 'One would think he'd ordered her from a catalogue. One would think he couldn't have anyone else!' Kriemhild, blonde plaits dangling over her shoulders, welcomes Brunhild's arrival. 'She will bring new wind to our sails.' Their argument echoed the debates about immigration taking place on the streets of Worms. The Icelanders, insists Ute, are too different. Not only do 'they have other gods than us', but 'a girl isn't worth much . . . The politics are corrupt, the provisions bad'. This isn't the medieval poet's Iceland – a land of ordeals to test knightly valour – but an imagined dystopia against which to map an older generation's resistance to change.

With the arrival of Brunhild, a different tension emerges. Hands swoop the air in failed high-fives and a mobile phone is lifted for a double princess selfie. But these sitcomesque touches only defer the inevitable fallout. 'Do you know what it means to be fucked?' asks Kriemhild, spinning from modern directness to medieval pomp: 'Your honour is my souvenir!' she declares, presenting her rival's stolen girdle. Only by dragging the characters away from the narrative constraints of the epic was the playwright able to suggest a finale built on female solidarity. Kriemhild, pregnant with a girl, declares 'Burgundy is no place for girls' and determines to follow Brunhild back to Iceland, where 'the men are all extinct'.

The play intrigued me. It was the most direct example I had come across of epic narrative material poured into a modern mould. I had been in touch with Irene Diwiak by email, and after the applause died down, we sat at a table in the theatre bar for a chat.

'I found the *Nibelungenlied* boring when we did it at school,' admitted Irene, sipping a glass of Sekt, 'but when I was fifteen, I started to become interested in Kriemhild, when I played her in a school play. She was presented as something like Princess Diana.'

It was easy to imagine Irene as Kriemhild. She cast watchful eyes over her glass, under sweeping lengths of rich blonde hair. There was calm steel in her eyes, camouflaged by her floral dress. Although only in her mid-twenties, she had already published a novel and authored several plays, garnering a spate of prizes. For *The Icelander*, she had been influenced by the news events around the time of her writing, 'the high point of the migration crisis' and political turbulence in Austria. 'But I was also thinking a lot about eastern European women, when they come to the West to marry rich men. Everyone says they are whores, they judge them very quickly, but they don't judge the men who marry them.'

Of all the women depicted in European epic, Kriemhild's character development is the most striking. At the beginning of the tale, she is King Gunther's dutiful sister, who promises she 'shall always be as you wish, and do whatever you command'. By the end of the story, she is the 'she-witch' who has her brothers killed and carries Gunther's head to taunt her enemy Hagen. Just as significant – though less noted by critics – is the psychological shift. She transforms from an ingénue, naively giving away the secret of Siegfried's mortality, into a champion schemer who waits thirteen years to dish out her revenge, using postcoital persuasion to get her kinsmen invited to a fatal feast; manipulating the oaths and ambitions of the men whose brawn is fit for purpose. In terms of political craft, this is some serious upskilling.

'I deliberately kept the men off the stage,' said Irene. 'I wanted to show that power isn't always where we think. We have a saying in Austria: "Wars should be conducted by others, but you, happy Austria, marry!" I wanted to look at this. To show that politics is also about these situations.'

After Siegfried's death, Brunhild barely figures in the story. But Kriemhild continues to play a leading role. So central is she to the narrative that the first published edition, in 1756, was entitled *Chriemhilden Rache* – 'The Revenge of Kriemhild'. Playing on the weak spots of the knights around her, Kriemhild spreads carnage like a frenzied puppeteer, dooming all the men whose strings she pulls. Her character trajectory reinforces an uncomfortable truth, particularly resonant in a country with Germany's complicated history: under the wrong circumstances, even the most innocuous person can turn into a monster.

18

The conflict could not reach a happy resolution,
And so out of this breach there flowed blood-drenched pollution.
Nibelungenlied, Thirty-Sixth Adventure

ALL ALONG THE road you find them, from Worms to Ezstergom: carved or painted, beaten out of bronze, twisted out of iron; protruding from church walls, inscribed on medieval houses, installed in the chambers of castles. They are knights from the *Nibelungen* tale, the occasional lady, the odd dragon, dwarf or river-maiden. Breastplates are buckled, helmets horned or winged, hair braided down the backs of pleated gowns. This is their territory, for this is the *Nibelungenweg*, the path followed by Kriemhild and later the ill-fated knights of Burgundy to the court of Attila the Hun.

I was running against the flow of the Rhine, catching trains south to Heidelberg and Bad Schönborn, then an afternoon's hike in search of German literature's most notorious murder site. Wasps danced over puddles of leaking blackberries and insects hummed in the linden trees, boasting of midsummer excess; oak leaves pulsated in tunnels of submarine light.

At the foot of a wooded mountain slope, I washed my feet (Damn! More blisters!) and unrolled my sleeping bag on the sapless grass. Dragonflies the size of toy helicopters were droning over the arrow-shaped channels of the stream. The spring poured itself under a small stone arch and an inscription recording Siegfried's death, where 'still the fountain flows'. The earliest known manuscript of the *Nibelungenlied* – the thirteenth-century copy found by Dr Obereit in the Austrian library – records Odenheim as the setting of the murder; although such is the prestige of the story, several other villages have launched their own bids, like nations competing to host the Olympics.

How do you mark a mythical murder site? Odenheim signposts the event with a bas-relief, carved in 1932 by a Jewish sculptor called Sigmund Odenheimer, which shows Hagen gripping his spear and pointing towards the cross on Siegfried's cloak (sewn there by Kriemhild in the expectation that Hagen would protect him). The hero kneels over the spring, oblivious to the danger, quenching his thirst from a drinking horn. Frozen in the last moment before the mortal wound is inflicted. 'Then,' the poet narrates, 'as Siegfried bent over the brook and drank, Hagen hurled the spear at the cross, so that the hero's heart's blood leapt from the wound and splashed against Hagen's clothes. No warrior will ever do a darker deed.'

This is the iconic moment of the epic – so iconic that Sigmund Freud used it to explain his analytical method. Asking patients to repeat their dreams, he would look for the 'weak spot' in their account: 'they serve me as the embroidered mark on Siegfried's cloak served Hagen'. But so malleable is the death of Siegfried, it has been used in other, more political ways.

'Just as Siegfried fell to the treacherous spear of the terrible Hagen,' declared General Paul von Hindenburg in 1919, 'so did our exhausted front line collapse.' Here was the *Dolchstosslegende* or 'back-stabbing legend', cited by the two most senior officers of the First World War, von Hindenburg and Erich Ludendorff, repeated by Adolf Hitler in *Mein Kampf*: the belief the German army wasn't defeated fair and square, but leached of its strength by insidious forces. And like Kriemhild, unable to forgive her husband's murder, many Germans were unable to see past the perceived betrayal of 1918. German culture has no more striking image for the stab in the back.

Travelling across Europe is a journey amongst rivers. I had already straddled many, from the Balkan bridges to the Ebro in Spain, but it was on the *Nibelungen* leg that storytelling formed most actively around them. The Rhine may be Europe's most mythologised river, but now I was moving towards the quintessential European waterway. It splits more great cities than any other and plays a significant role in the *Nibelungenlied*: the Danube.

This was the route pulling me into Bavaria. The previous year, I had wandered around Bavarian castles with my family, and the painting of Siegfried slaying the dragon at Neuschwanstein had been a key moment in kick-starting my journey. Now, I was keen to learn more about Bavarian connections to the epic. Climbing 300 feet over the Danube at Regensburg, I saw a plaque to 'the poet of the *Nibelungenlied*' inside a neo-Hellenic folly bristling with Doric columns: the pantheon of Germanic heroes known as 'Walhalla'. But I was seeking people more than monuments. Two in particular: one, I hoped, would give me a perspective on the *Nibelungen* resonances that had informed his recent plays; the other had uncovered some disturbing evidence about the worst period of *Nibelungen* exploitation.

Climbing off a muggy Flixbus in Munich, I walked under monumental statues of King Ludwig I and tried to make my way to the Literaturhaus without getting mown down by the ubiquitous cyclists. Albert Ostermaier arrived at the same time, and we sat down with a couple of coffees.

In Worms, it had excited me to see Albert's play, *Siegfried of Arabia*: epic retold as a political thriller, with echoes of Alfred Hitchcock movies and *Lawrence of Arabia*. All the more so, given this was one of three plays he had written about the *Nibelungen* story. The epic has an extraordinarily rich theatrical history – from Friedrich Hebbel's renowned nineteenth-century trilogy to Fritz Lang's iconic 1920s movies (and not forgetting Wagner's *Ring Cycle,* which encompassed the great composer's fascination for the many different versions of the *Nibelungen* tale). The productions I'd seen on this journey showed the tradition is in good health.

'It is such a rich subject,' said Albert, letting out a barrel-chested laugh. 'I could have written five more!'

Given the breadth of references in his plays, quoting from Shakespeare to the Persian poet Hafez, I was expecting an old-school Teutonic egghead. Instead, the playwright languidly stretching across the cafe bench looked as though he could be the goalkeeper for Bayern Munich (not surprisingly, he's goalkeeper for the German authors' team).

His trilogy began, in 2015, with *Gemetzel* ('Carnage'). 'It's set in a mystical, medieval time,' explained Albert, 'from the eyes of Kriemhild's son Ortwin.' Using role-play and storytelling, he played around with the narrative of the *Nibelungenlied*, asking 'if they talk to each other, would it be different, could there be a different way to solve the conflict?'

The second play, *Gold*, followed in 2016, set in modern times, telling the story of a famous film producer. 'He dreams of doing a really artistic *Nibelungen* movie,' explained Albert, 'so he engages a director, who's a Tarantino/Lars von Trier type, breaking all the rules, provoking the cast to break their hearts.'

This was meta-theatre amped to the max: stories within stories, filling the stage with neo-Nazis, politicians, refugees, confronting the audience with the troubling legacy of the *Nibelungen* story.

'They're modern characters,' said Albert, 'but in the end they *become* Hagen and Kriemhild and all these characters, because the original characters are inside them. It's about how the *Nibelungen* story is still very lively and contemporary and it's always stronger than any interpretation.'

Above all, it was the final play, *Siegfried of Arabia*, that dramatised the epic's history of political exploitation.

'That period of the First World War,' said Albert, 'was when the whole *Nibelungen* story was raised as a national anthem. They were using it to militarise Germany and prepare the war. They didn't understand a thing about it, but they used it. They violated it.' Reading around the history of the period, he found a true story about a 'mission impossible in the Middle East. This troupe of actors on their way to the slaughter.' It was a way to tell the *Nibelungen* story in a fresh light, exploring the history of its exploitation as an engine of the drama. 'It's all about stories,' said Albert, 'because that's what politics is – it's about who has the better storyline.'

The epic had been a military tool since the early years after its rediscovery. In 1814 a field edition was handed out to German officers to inspire them 'with pride and trust in the fatherland and the people', as the epic's first translator, Friedrich von der Hagen, wrote, 'with hope for the future return of German glory and world-rule'. Still, Germany was an idea rather than a unified state, a late starter among the nation-states of Europe, and it took the best part of the nineteenth century to glue all those principalities, kingdoms and duchies together. Several decades after Greece and Serbia had secured their independence, contemporary with the Italian Risorgimento, Germany slowly stitched itself together, with Otto von Bismarck (the 'Iron Siegfried', as one poet labelled him in a panegyric) wielding the needle.

'Germany had never really existed the way France had,' said Albert. 'It was struggling for this common idea, so it needed myths like the *Nibelungen*.'

When war broke out in 1914, the Western Front was labelled the 'Siegfried Line', another flank was known as the 'Alberich Line' (after the dwarf who holds the Nibelungen treasure) and there was a 1918 attack against the French known as the 'Hagen Offensive'. The Great War began with the *Nibelungentreue*, the 'Nibelungen loyalty' binding Germany and Austria; and it ended with the *Dolchstosslegende*, the 'backstabbing legend' associated with the murder of Siegfried. The national epic had become the lens through which Germany explained its swings of fortune. And like Kriemhild, unable to come to terms with the death of Siegfried, Germany was determined to reverse the narrative its enemies had imposed.

'This is why the *Nibelungenlied* is so popular,' said Albert.

> Because it's open. For me it's reflecting the madness of war. It's an anti-war piece at its best, and I really don't know how anyone can say this is a national epic, with the story that's inside it! It's one of the most fantastic pieces of literature in the world. But a lot of people misunderstood it and they used it for their own purposes.

We sat in the cafe for over an hour, throwing ideas around, jokes about Kriemhild as a medieval Margaret Thatcher (with Attila the Hun as her Denis), bemoaning the neo-Nazi movements widely supported in East Germany. I had enjoyed talking to Albert: his erudition and laughter, the arty pragmatism of a working playwright. Now I would be focusing on the period after the First World War. For, rather than snuffing out the epic's power, defeat in 1918 paved the way for a new era of *Nibelungen* abuse. It was time to turn my attention to the most troubling of all the manipulations of European epic. And that meant visiting one of the loveliest places in Bavaria.

'The news that a great number of foreigners were fast approaching,' records the anonymous poet, 'reached the Bishop's town of Passau . . . and emptied the houses and the Prince-Bishop's palace, too; for everyone was hurrying up through Bavaria in the direction of the strangers, where Bishop Pilgrim soon met lovely Kriemhild.' In one of literature's unlikeliest matches, Siegfried's widow has agreed to give her hand to that celebrated Romeo – Attila the Hun. She hasn't suddenly caught a taste for 'life in a strange land'. Instead, she's eyeing up the advantages of a union with the most powerful warlord of her day. 'Since Etzel [Attila] has so many fighting-men,' she muses, 'if I am to have command of them I shall achieve whatever I wish.'

Sunshine balmy over ripe wheatfields, signs for thermal spas and village *Biergartens* with antlers mounted under the gables, rivers running so fast you could hear them playing over the stones, like fingers on piano keys. Horn-shaped Passau snuffles into the rivers that surround it, so widely hemmed it feels like an island. The domes of the cathedral swell like prize onions over houses splashed in peach, peppermint, custardy yellow and the pale pink of strawberry mixed with cream. The Ilz oozes underneath, black and sombre, meeting the green of the inn in a confrontation that shapes the city between them, while the Danube discreetly joins them, awaiting its opportunity to engulf them.

Passau plays a minuscule part in the *Nibelungenlied*, but it's mentioned in glowing terms. 'The strangers were comfortably quartered,' we are told, 'and when the merchants of the city learned that their prince's niece had arrived they gave her a warm welcome.' Given its lack of narrative significance, its inclusion in the story has led many scholars to locate the poem's composition here, under the influence of a later bishop-prince, Wolfgar von Erla.

A wheeler-dealer of the late twelfth century, Wolfgar had the political clout to press for the release of Richard the Lionheart from the castle of Durnstein, petition the Pope to approve the Teutonic Knights and build a castle at Obernburg. He was also a noted patron of the arts, with a flourishing court (among his acquaintances was the great *minnesinger* Walther von der Vogelweide, who wrote the famous song 'Under the Linden-Tree'). But he wasn't against using the sword to shore up his power. One grisly siege he orchestrated, at Graben am Main in 1199, resulted in mass burnings, drownings, maimings and, according to a contemporary chronicle, choppings of noses and lips. This is the world of the *Nibelungenlied*: juggling courtly graces with the savagery of battle.

I was staying in the Oberhaus, the old bishop-princes' palace, which towers over the Old City, gripping its cliff like an eagle on its eyrie. I had a bunk in a youth hostel installed near the drawbridge. On the other side of the 'Bear Moat', a reconstructed treadmill crane leaned towards a well, and coats of arms of bishop-princes stamped the surrounding walls. There were suits of armour, lances and swords, a thirteenth-century *Streitaxe* and torture implements with atmospheric names like the *Schandemask* or 'mask of shame', testifying to the sadistic ingenuity of Bishop Wolfgar's epoch.

Back down the hill, in the double-towered convent of Niedernburg, a skull grinned in a cage of cusped stone. It belonged to Princess Gisela, a German princess whose marriage to the Hungarian saint-king Stephen, in AD 995, may have influenced the *Nibelungen* poet's descriptions of Kriemhild's marriage to an earlier 'King of the Hun'. Wreaths had been laid, in the red, white and green colours of the Hungarian flag, amongst ribbons inscribed with the donors' origins from Hungary and Austria. A guest-book was chatty with prayers and good wishes. Here were reminders of the connections between identity and faith that join the modern world with the medieval, even today. But Gisela was a prototype, at best. It was Kriemhild herself I wanted to see.

And here she is – braided plaits flowing over her golden cap, ermine hugging her shoulders. She gazes out, proud and calm, sitting on horseback, looking like she could ride out from the gilt frame containing her and come to a stop between the marble pillars of the Old City Hall. Half-dressed peasant children hold out flowers towards her, while her uncle, Bishop Pilgrim, leans across from the horse beside her. Gripping the bridle, leading Kriemhild under the bannered balconies of Passau, is the artist, Ferdinand Wagner, who used his skill with oils to indulge in a classic nineteenth-century fantasy, magicking himself into the world of the *Nibelungenlied*.

The Old City Hall is hushed and church-like, with light oozing through stained-glass windows, shining off the tiles of a *Kachelofen* stove. Although the painting on the other side of the main door isn't the kind they hang in cathedrals. It shows Hagen on a riverbank, facing three very naked, very curvy women: the 'water fairies endowed with second sight who were bathing there to cool themselves'. Hagen steals their clothes, forcing them to give him their forecast. 'If you ever get to Hungary,' they warn him, 'you will be sadly disappointed . . . All who ride to that land have linked their hands with Death!' Judging from the painting, Wagner's taste was for the sort of buxomness fetishised in traditional Bavarian beer-halls. His water fairies are all fleshy hips and breasts, lustrous gold and red hair, mermaid scales tattooing their thighs. A classic of Romantic eroticism.

Forget the Middle Ages, the European epics come to us through the curation of the Romantics. Digging for roots, rose-tinting the past, idolising anything that smelt of nature, the Romantics built a podium under the ancient tales of Europe. Ferdinand Wagner, like his namesake Richard, was part of a romantic chain that stretched from the likes of Walter Scott and William Morris, retelling chivalric tales in the north, all the way to the romantic poets wandering around Troy and fighting for Greek independence in the south. The *Song of Roland*, *Beowulf* and the *Nibelungenlied* all share this period of rediscovery, while the Serbian epics and the Icelandic sagas captured cross-European attention and there was a spike of Homerphilia. Eighteenth- and nineteenth-century preoccupations still define these stories, just as much as the mistier periods in which they were conceived.

This was the era of the 'New Mythology', which provided 'the orcs and trolls, the elves and dwarves and dragons and werewolves which now crowd the shelves of every bookstore', as the scholar Tom Shippey has written. And what's the harm in this? Can't we enjoy these paintings, poems, plays and stories as good-natured representations of a rediscovered folk identity? Not when we recognise the issues these stories were intersecting with. The playwright Friedrich Hebbel, for example, was assembling a trilogy of *Nibelungen* plays at the same time as he was reading the 'Communist Manifesto'. The *Nibelungenlied*'s definitive nineteenth-century translator, Karl Simrock, was also engaging in the nationalist debate over the ownership of Jutland, in common with his fellow story collector Jacob Grimm, who did much to spread the concept of a greater 'Germanic' culture. Meanwhile, Richard Wagner was dabbling in the new Darwinian theories on natural selection, and at the same time nurturing his own rabid anti-Semitism, pouring these ideas into his *Ring of the Nibelungen*. These storytellers were part of a politically active web, spooling ancient tales around the preoccupations of their tumultuous century.

This matters. The *Nibelungen* material cannot be detached from the political issues with which it became so intimately entangled. And certainly not in Passau. Across the city's chivalric, medieval imagery – archangels spearing dragons, the totemic Wolf of Passau filling medallions and shields – falls a darker shadow. For it was here that Adolf Hitler lived (not for long and only when he was very small, between the ages of three and six). Now it's Passau's dirty secret, but there was a time when the city wanted everyone to know.

Hitler's boyhood home at number twenty-three Theresienstrasse bears no number, and of course there is no plaque. Other local celebrities have been recognised – such as the poet Hans Carossa, next door. But the only reference I found to Hitler on his old street was a sticker on a downpipe: a cartoon Führer slashed by the slogan 'Nazis Stoppen' – the work of 'young socialists' of the Social Democratic Party. Along with other street postings, stickers and stencillings printed on walls and pavement slabs ('Space Invaders Against Racism', 'Zona Anti Fascista', 'Refugees Welcome'), this evoked the *Kulturkampf* colouring the forthcoming election: a struggle over history and how you respond to it. *Vergangenheitsbewältigung*, to use one of those characteristically polysyllabic German words: 'coming to terms with the past'.

Passau's remembrance of the Nazi era has been especially ambiguous. A lid was shut over the period until the 1980s, when a determined local student decided to find out what had really happened, here at the forgotten edge of Germany. For her pains, Anna Rosmus received death threats in the mail, a shut-out by the city archives and the label Hexe von Passau – the 'Witch of Passau'. She published her findings in a series of controversial books, and became the subject of an Oscar-nominated movie, *The Nasty Girl*, released in 1990.

'It was the bishop who got me going,' she said, sitting under gilt-framed paintings in a kitschy, pseudo-traditional cafe near the cathedral. 'He lied to my face, he told me there were no Jews in Passau – which is funny, because his best friend when he was a schoolboy happened to be Jewish. And I proved it by reintroducing them!'

Lively and warm, with a wide-eyed, owlish expression, Anna is nothing like the grim subject matter she has exhaustively researched. Whether shouting down neo-Nazis at demonstrations or rigorously exploring obscure archives, she has been on a heroic, decades-long hunt for the truth. During the 1980s, while Passauers stayed in denial, she uncovered the murder of 1,700 Russian prisoners-of-war in a nearby forest, several concentration camps nearby, the compromises of local church leaders, the forced abortions and child murders at Hutthurm and the 'baby farm' of Sallach where infants were murdered with spoiled milk; and she published her research in spite of considerable local resistance. But what does this have to do with the *Nibelungen*? For Anna, whose most recent book is entitled *Hitler's Nibelungen*, quite a lot, as it happens.

'When I was ten years old,' she recalled, 'they took us to the Old City Hall to see the Ferdinand Wagner paintings. It was a deliberate strategy, to tie us into Passau's identity. To see Kriemhild, this noble queen who is not too proud to visit our city. And for most of us, it worked.'

Refusing to submit to the culture of compliance, nor the 'Passau tradition of "let the past be the past"', Anna dug out old newspapers and files in the state archives, interviewed old residents and uncovered the multiple associations between Passauers' pride in the *Nibelungenlied* and their pride in the Führer. 'When Hitler came to power,' she said, 'the local paper bragged that he was a son of Passau, how he had lived here and given his first public speech here, in 1920. A vast number of locals got swept up in this feeling of greatness.'

Talk of a 'Greater Germany' was beguiling for Passau's businessmen, whose incomes were vulnerable to political tremors, with the Austrian and Czech frontiers so close. Instead of being out in the boondocks, how much better to sit at the heart of a Greater Germany, a city with close personal ties to the Führer himself.

In a characteristic speech, delivered in March 1938, Mayor Max Moosbauer declared: 'A thousand years long shall you murmur, in every day and time, how the new Siegfried besieged the dragon of disunity.' No prizes for guessing who had been identified as the dragon slayer: 'Adolf Hitler, you have made us the greatest people in the world.' Such comparisons delighted the Führer, who 'had been intoxicated by tales of the ancient German heroes' since childhood.

Newspapers were full of references to the 'Nibelungen Loyalty'; and in the months leading up to the war, a play about 'Rudiger of Bechelarn', who brings Kriemhild to Hungary in the epic, was performed in Passau by the Bavarian poet Hans Baumann (the so-called 'troubadour of the Hitler youth').

'The papers reported about it for weeks,' said Anna, 'and all the local children had to take part – my mother was one of them. The *Nibelungen* mythology had a massive impact at this time, in mass media, in schools. If you look at the school yearbooks from this time, they are full of essays on the *Nibelungen*. It was part of a strategy.'

From schoolchildren to professional writers, from theatre to movies, throughout the 1930s the *Nibelungen* theme was all the rage. Hitler had written about Siegfried in his polemical autobiography, *Mein Kampf*, back in the 1920s, and his admiration for Wagner's *Ring of the Nibelungen* was well known. Although Wagner's version was based on other sources, the Nazi elite's fondness for the themes of the *Nibelungen* tale – especially the will to death that drives the final act – encouraged a cottage industry of *Nibelungen* material, nourishing a revival of interest in the epic.

Fritz Lang's *Die Nibelungen* movies were rereleased with a new Wagnerian score, praised by Joseph Goebbels as 'so modern, so contemporary, so topical', and their monumental aesthetic was absorbed into the designs of the Nuremberg rallies. So enamoured was Goebbels of the *Nibelungen* tale that he named a publishing company after it, conceived to disseminate anti-Bolshevik and anti-Semitic tracts. His colleagues in the Nazi elite, such as Heinrich Himmler and Hermann Goering, used the *Nibelungen* in major speeches, dipping into the powerful wellspring they were poisoning.★

'These things didn't end with the war,' said Anna. She should know: during the 1990s she took part in protests against conventions of the far-right Deutsche Volksunion, who gathered in their thousands at Passau's 'Hall of the Nibelungen', which had been built during the Nazi period. 'They picked that place because of its association with the Nazis,' said Anna. 'They believed World War Two wasn't the end of the story. In their minds, that was just the first attempt.'

And so the Nazi legacy continues: cherished by neo-Nazis, on one side of the debate, challenged on the other by the likes of Anna Rosmus, members of what she sees as a generation of historians who 'confronted the past'. The positive effect of their work, she believes, has been felt in the refugee crisis.

'Young people know what happened, and they see the connection. You could hear teenagers saying, "There were people fleeing then and now it's happening again, so this time we have to help them."'

History unburied, creating the circumstances for positive action in the present. As for the *Nibelungenlied*, it's still volatile, even if its claws have been pared. AfD leaders have cited the legend in recent speeches, alongside their founder's slogan, 'we have the right not only to take back our country, but also our past'.

'These things have deep roots,' said Anna, 'and people can use those roots. This can be very dangerous.'

But surely, I asked, there isn't any chance of *that* kind of exploitation resurfacing? *Is there?* But Anna had lived through personal attacks and death threats, sinister late-night phone calls and vilification at public demonstrations. Looking at the world today, she confessed

---

★ Goering, for example, used this 'tremendously heroic song' to egg on Germany's 6th Army at Stalingrad, while Himmler, after the notorious 'Night of the Long Knives', compared his SS crack troops' slaughter of the SA to Siegfried bathing in the dragon's blood (overlooking, with a telling and probably deliberate myopia, the detail of the linden leaf), claiming the slaughter had made them invulnerable.

she wasn't so sure. 'The border between reality and parallel realities is shrinking,' she said, stirring her coffee. Later, I thought of something the artist Thomas Eichfelder had told me in Worms: 'After the war, nobody wanted to talk about the *Nibelungen* any more. It was almost forbidden, too negative. And there is still a lot of that. It tastes of something.'

That 'taste' is hard to define, but if there's one word for it, I'd call it *danger*. It's there in the story, with all its bloody slayings, and it's certainly there in the way it's been used. Danger always attaches to the forbidden, gleaming like the *Nibelungen* treasure, shining in the depths, waiting for somebody to dive down and dredge it up.

19

I tell you I am loath to turn on you my sword.
But I have pledged an oath, so blood must now be poured.
Rudiger of Bechelarn, *Nibelungenlied*,
Thirty-Seventh Adventure

A LL ALONG THE Danube you could see the rain: stabbing the
river, bouncing off the muddy sward, forcing the swifts to
tack across the wind. Although I was in a new country, the landscape and architecture had barely shifted, the language was still
German, the dialect very close to Bavarian, and it didn't matter
which side of the border you were on – you still had a good
chance of bumping into guys in lederhosen or meeting a girl in
a *Dirndl*. The only discernible shift on those first days in Austria
was the weather. After a few balmy days in Bavaria, now the
clouds were gathering in darkly: predatory birds spreading their
wings. Gobbling up the sun, they revelled in greyness, chewing
the blue.

In Passau, the Danube had been a dwarfish trickle. Stepping down
from the train line at Pöchlarn, I was confronted by a giant, breasting
through the valley of the Wachau, carving out a spectacular region
where vineyards and orchards cascade towards tangled waterweeds
and castles sail in and out between the clouds.

Epic and geography can be unreliable companions, but here's a
region where they lock together, landscape and place names meshing
with the storyline. So accurately rendered are the journeys to the
court of Attila that many scholars have pinned the poet round here.
As the travel writer Helmut Berndt has written, 'The *Nibelungenlied*
is the earliest German travel guide, about six hundred years older

than Baedeker's handbook.' I was planning to hike along the tract known as the Nibelungengau, or 'Nibelungen Province', as far as Traismauer, where I could catch a train to Vienna.

The gateway is Pöchlarn, a fishing village associated with the 'March-Lord', Rudiger of Bechelarn. It is Rudiger who woos Kriemhild for Attila the Hun – an embassy for which he ultimately pays with his life. Escorting Kriemhild towards Attila's court, he breaks up their journey at his 'broad palace, a very handsome building past whose base the Danube flowed' and entertains his guest with a lively jousting tournament. Later, Kriemhild's brothers rest here too, and so magnificent is the hospitality that her youngest brother, Giselher, marries Rudiger's 'enchanting' daughter.

The happy couple were depicted in a pair of stand-up metal cut-outs, installed near the river, serenaded by the music from a waterproof speaker. The rain was drowning the romantic atmosphere; a patch-eyed Hagen, brooding upstream with his hands tight around a spear, was more in tune with its mood.

Behind Hagen, flags and oak trees flanked Pöchlarn's chief memorial to the poem: an arc of painted shields, representing sixteen cities, from Metz to Verona, from which knights gathered in the *Nibelungenlied*. Panning across this heraldic hemisphere – the dragon of Worms, the wolf of Passau, the white cross of Vienna – was to be reminded of the poem's continental reach. The flags could have stretched even further: the poem incorporates Danish knights and Brunhild's court in Iceland, and Kriemhild's marriage to Attila draws 'men from Greece and Russia . . . Poles and Wallachians . . . from the land of Kiev, too', framing the story's Germanic fulcrum in the wider trans-European network.

Recalling such a breadth of alliances has a political resonance. In an explanatory plaque, the monument's patrons expressed their aim to make 'a contribution to European peace-thinking'. The *Nibelungenlied* dramatises a matrix of allegiances, asylum granted, oaths and favours exchanged that spans the continent. This is a united Europe, yoked not by a common currency but by a common code of conduct; a feudal ethic that sucks everyone down the same destructive spiral.

Everybody understands the code – which means they all get squashed by it. And nobody's death is more ridiculous, more maddeningly unnecessary, than Rudiger's. When battle erupts at the court of Attila, Rudiger finds himself pincered between his duties of hospitality to the Burgundian knights and feudal fidelity to Kriemhild. 'Whichever course I leave in order to follow the other,' he protests, 'I shall have acted basely and infamously – and if I refrain from both, they will all upbraid me!' Regretfully arming himself, he hands over his own shield to Hagen (to replace the damaged one the latter was given by Rudiger's wife), then throws himself against Hagen and his fellow Burgundians, 'giving ample demonstration how very strong, brave, and well-armed he was by the great numbers of stalwarts he was slaying'.

Imagine boxers at a prize fight, handing out apologies between their punches! Praises and regret are volleyed between blows and 'they all wept because none could compose this heart-rending agony'. The sequence verges on farce, but it's composed with such passion and excitement, there's little appetite to laugh. So great is the 'wild lamentation' after Rudiger's death (slain, predictably, by a sword he gave as a present), it's tempting to wonder if the poet is calling into question the ethical code that forces this deeply honourable man to throw away his life.

Planning the journey, I had been really looking forward to that week of Danube walking: a gentle ramble with easy camping and provisions. But I'd sure picked my moment! Rain-clouds scudded overhead, filling my boots with their offerings. Scampering under the fusillades, I stopped for shelter under oak trees and willows and hurriedly wrapped my gadgets in plastic.

In the town of Melk, I slept on a bench outside the train station and passed a wall inscription quoting the *Nibelungenlied* (when Kriemhild passes Melk, 'magnificent gold goblets filled with wine' are handed to her party). Further up the Wachau, rain dribbled through the canopies of black pine and hornbeam, slushing the path to Aggstein Castle, where an exhibition of *Nibelungen* dioramas filled a dank cellar. Crow-haunted bastions and brambly buttresses were wreathed in mist, or 'Nebel', from the same root as 'Nibelungen', the 'mist-land' where strange things happen.

They were sodden days, and they were making me prickly. I'd

been trying hard to keep my budget down, eating out of supermarkets, sleeping outdoors, spending a lot of time inside my own head, chafing at the misappropriation of this extraordinary epic. Because I loved the *Nibelungenlied*, as I loved so much of medieval German culture. Fifteen years earlier, I had read the chivalric romance of *Parsival* while researching the legendary priest-king Prester John, and I had dipped into this fascinating culture many times over the subsequent years. I hated how Germany's medieval literature, which did so much for the development of European humanism, had been violated by the crude tastes of those bludgeoning thugs. Thinking about this, or bumping into AfD activists, gave me *Weltschmerz*, to put it in the German way – 'world-grief'.

Sometimes it can be hard to know what's getting you down. Is it the political issues you've been thinking about, or something more personal? Is it homesickness, or too much rain, or are these issues drilling into your own, deeper frailties? With all its slaughter, the *Nibelungenlied* deals out a lot of grief, and that often got me thinking.

When Rudiger arrives in Worms on Attila's embassy, Kriemhild is a 'doleful lady', given over to frequent lamentations. 'Through one man,' she says, 'death has inflicted such suffering on me that I can never be happy again.' Her grief is so all-consuming that even after she has married Attila and borne a child by him, it still eats away at her. When the Burgundian knights arrive for the feast at Attila's court, Attila's vassal, Dietrich of Verona, warns them that 'every morning I hear Attila's queen piteously weeping and lamenting'; so damaged is she by her grief that, when her beloved brother Giselher appeals for mercy, she admits 'my heart has none to show!'

This is grief on the scale of epic storytelling, formalised and amplified. But Kriemhild's nihilistic passion is consistently drawn, an aggressive egoism that bears a ring of truth. 'My grief is my castle,' wrote the Danish philosopher Søren Kierkegaard; 'nothing can storm it. From it I fly down into reality to seize my prey'. Grief, that cancerous emotion: God knows we all have to go through it. Reading about Kriemhild's lamentations, I couldn't help feeling for her, in spite of all the deaths her grief unleashes. Isn't this the power of epic, after all – to dramatise our deepest emotions on a scale that matches the terrible feelings inside us?

When my father died, I was afraid to talk about it, anxious to put across the impression I was coping. And I felt guilty, because I had been in the wrong place. I didn't feel I had the right to make a lot of noise. So I held my breath and held it in. It was only later, much later, that I started to recognise the damage it had done. Now, reading about Kriemhild's emotional incontinence, I felt a strange, soothing catharsis. She lets grief take over, submits her entire being to it, allows it to fission into something powerful enough to tear down the world. That's the power of grief, right here in this extraordinary story.

Black-hearted clouds prowled overhead, occasionally pouring down their wrath. They looked like they were impersonating dragons, dark and spiky, hurling down drizzle instead of fire. I was already a sodden mop when a party of apricot pickers scooped me into their minivan and swooped me along the river to the town of Krems. The rain fell back at last, sun glowing over a park; I harvested some bread and biscuits from the local branch of Netto and sat down to dine.

I was sitting on the ledge of a monument to Helmut Schmidt, a nineteenth-century field marshal, laying out my drenched socks on the plinth. There were voices on the other side, and a smell of tobacco smoke. I recognised the glottal stops and rapid guttural speech of Arabic. Eventually, after a wobble of hesitation, I poked my head around the corner and introduced myself.

'Our papers are not in order.' One of them, Moussa, banged a fist against a palm, miming a border stamp. 'In Vienna, they are asking too many questions!'

They came from Morocco. A boat had carried them from Libya, close enough to Lampedusa for the coastguard to pick them up. But their passports had been stamped by the Italian authorities, which meant they were forbidden from crossing any further borders. According to the Dublin Treaty, they were obliged to seek asylum in the first country they reached. If the Austrian authorities found them, they were likely to be deported.

'I guess it's a struggle to get work?' I asked.

Moussa clicked his teeth. 'That's why we left Morocco. If you don't know the right people, you haven't got a chance. We thought Europe would be the answer.'

'Do you know how many diplomas I have?' asked his friend. 'Four! I have a diploma from the University of al-Azhar in Cairo. But what can I do with it? I am trained as an engineer. I can work as a hairdresser too.'

He flicked his cigarette on to the path. A few moments later, he lit another. We shared my biscuits and their jar of olives, spread on slabs of pitta bread. By sun-fall, most of my clothes were dry, so I packed them up, restoring Field Marshal Schmidt to his customary dignity. The plinth wasn't the comfiest place to sleep, but we were spared further rain. Judging from the glow of cigarettes between the fir trees, we weren't alone.

Reading the *Nibelungenlied* immerses you in a world where bold knights can travel wherever they please – as long as they have a keen sword, ready cash or decent contacts. But it's barred by frontiers, much like our world. When Hagen tries to cross the Danube, he faces resistance from a ferryman, charged with guarding the frontier. The ferryman smacks him with his punt, provoking Hagen to lop off his head. Not that Hagen is opposed to borders on principle. Meeting a knight near Pöchlarn, he gives him six bracelets of red gold and commends him as 'a fearless warrior, lying all alone at the frontier though you do'. Siegfried, similarly, is delighted to find one of his castles well guarded by a giant. He keeps his identity hidden, like an undercover boss checking on his staff. 'Siegfried was in no small fear of being killed by the mighty blows of this gatekeeper,' we are told, 'a fact that much endeared the man to his liege lord Siegfried.'

These are violent lands and the men who guard them are little better than thugs. Many of us like to think of modern Europe as the continent that's moved beyond borders. The Schengen Zone, at least: unfrontiered, unfortressed. But the refugee crisis has dismantled our cosy self-image. Some of the most unsettling ordeals I heard about from refugees were their experiences around borders: cuffed by aggressive guards, chased by sniffer dogs, pepper-sprayed around fences. I was alarmed by the erection of border fences in Hungary and Austria, and by the isolationist rhetoric of populist politicians.

Is 'Fortress Europe' really the answer? Surely there was a more sophisticated way to handle this? Surely this was the moment for Europe's union to kick in? But all I could see was the raising of drawbridges – razor wire, referendums, the rise of populists. As if the problems next door can be ignored if your walls are high enough.

'Europe is changing too fast' was a sentiment I heard many times on this journey. But isn't Europe always changing? Aren't the epics themselves – the evolution of the super-state in *the Song of Roland*, the growth of cities tracked in the *Odyssey*, the self-destruction of sclerotic feudalism in the *Nibelungenlied* – records of change?

I thought of my travels around the Sahara a few years before, of the heartbreaking stories I heard amongst nomads who'd lost all their livestock and city dwellers fed up with the grinding poverty. And as usual, I circled back around the same old question: what would I do if I was in their shoes? Wouldn't I want to make my way towards the land of so-called plenty?

The roar of traffic on a bridge over the Danube; the beautiful sight of Gottweg Abbey on a hilltop, a cupola at each corner; orchards and vineyards shading the road snaking east. For most of the day, the clouds held back. But rain gave chase on the outskirts of Traismauer. I hurried into the village, drenched all over again, seeking shelter under a garage roof. I stood there like a mop, dripping between a pair of BMWs so lovingly tended that my bedraggled face was mirror-clear in their bonnets. Why all this rain? It was late July! Diving through a last rainy onslaught, I leaped behind the glass door of a *Stüberl*. Peace from the rain, a chance to change out of my wet clothes, and a brace of delicious Weissbiers. The rain was still falling, and I watched it through the window, where the medieval walls appeared like the backdrop in a spectacular aquarium.

'*Grüss Gott!*' A member of a bowling team chatted about the rain and bought me an apricot schnapps, before joining the team song and clomping into the dark with his mates. I watched them go a little sadly, wishing they had stayed longer; but it was past midnight, chucking-out time was imminent. Trudging out in search of a nightspot, I could find nothing cosier than a porched alcove behind a block of flats, where there was enough dry space beside the wheelie bins to roll out my sleeping bag. I lay myself down and keyed the alarm on my phone, so I could pack up my gear before anyone came out with the morning trash.

The streets of Traismauer follow the outline of the old Roman fort, which survives in the form of a Roman tower, a mud bastion 1,700 years old. It was only a few yards from my night spot. Grafted on top was a medieval turret, painted with a scene from the *Nibelungenlied*. Mounted in 1933, the fresco shows Rudiger, with golden horns on his helmet and a stately beard, turning to Kriemhild as they ride side by side, her golden cape matching her long braided hair. Traismauer plays the tiniest role in the epic – a 'splendid fortress' belonging to Attila – one of many places where Kriemhild dispenses largesse on her way to her new home. But that's enough for a small town to celebrate its place in the grander story.

Fifty miles separate Traismauer from Vienna, and the grand head-quarters of Mitteleuropa was my next destination. Passing under the tower, I gave Kriemhild and Rudiger a wave, and carried on towards the station. Through the windows of the empty train carriage, the fields looked as drenched as paddy fields, uninhabited except for the odd rain-battered scarecrow: a flattening flood plain after the vege-tative riot of the Wachau. Slowly, suburbia clawed back the orchards; towers and domes scaled the sidings and flyovers. I climbed out and boarded the Metro to Karlsplatz, passing a musical toilet where Mozart's operas muffled the tinkle of emptying bladders and a busker playing 'Blue Danube' on a taped-up viola. No doubt about it: I had reached Vienna!

20

To mercy's kindness I will not be reconciled
When slain my men lie, as does my butchered child!
Attila the Hun, *Nibelungenlied,*
Thirty-sixth Adventure

FOR ANY MEDIEVAL Mitteleuropean, there was no more prestigious wedding venue. Which is why the poet of the *Nibelungenlied* sets Kriemhild and Attila the Hun's nuptials in Vienna. Not that the city cares to broadcast the link: it's hosted enough history to turn its nose up at legend (although that hasn't stopped it from having a Nibelungengasse, which gets you from the Opera House to the Museum Quarter).

Where Vienna offers insight into the *Nibelungenlied* is in its enduring Mitteleuropeanness. In the block where I was staying, and others that I visited, brass plates were engraved with *Doktor, Magister, Dip. Ing.* and even *Hofrat* (a high-ranking magistrate). Sabine, my Airbnb host, mischievously pointed them out and moaned about the local obsession with rank and regulations: 'Everybody knows this is a city with a stick up its butt.' The kind of place where you can imagine the obsessions of the *Nibelungenlied*: Kriemhild and Brunhild falling out over who should take precedence; knights like Rudiger sacrificing themselves on spurious points of honour. Norse versions of the *Nibelungen* legend don't dwell on these matters so obsessively, because they were composed in more egalitarian climes; but here in the heart of Europe, the concern for position prevails.

For me, this was all part of Vienna's charm. It's plugged into the twenty-first century – from refugee soup kitchens to silent head-phoned dancers at a nightclub by the Danube Canal. But it's also a city ratcheted to its past, where the much romanticised Empress Sisi dangles bejewelled ringlets down cafe facades and Litfass columns. Launching out from Sabine's low-ceilinged apartment, whoozy from Aperol spritzes and chain-smoking political confabs, I wandered around the city, revelling in all the things I'd loved about Vienna before: reading the *Donau Zeitung* while sipping an espresso topped with whipped cream in a padded cafe booth; listening to jazz in an underground cafe on Franz-Josefs Kai; joining an Iranian family for a 'grill party' on the banks of the Danube.

Now I have an appointment with a performer of medieval tales. A few years earlier, I met traditional storytellers in Iran, who knew hundreds of verses by heart; and I came across similar traditions among the griots of Mali. One of the most pleasing discoveries of my journey through Europe has been to learn that, while this tradition is limited, it isn't extinct.

My Austrian bard is Eberhard Kummer. Eyes lucid in a nest of wrinkles, he beams over his lap-harp, his voice thrumming from a stout barrel chest. In his parlour, a cuckoo clock hangs over a pine-cone handle and glazed pots adorn the cupboards, amongst framed photographs and an old-fashioned coffee grinder. Eberhard has recited the *Nibelungenlied* at various festivals and recorded a series of discs, notching up more than 100,000 views on YouTube.

'It is wonderful,' he says. 'There is still such a big audience for this!'

Fascinated by singing traditions in other cultures, he enthuses about many of them – a 'duelling' verse form still practised in Corsica, the stories recited by griots in Niger, 'where each hero has his own melody'. Like many reciters I've met, Eberhard sees his own performances within the context of a larger tapestry, and he relishes the others because he knows how great a challenge is his own.

'People respond to the *Nibelungenlied* in a very deep way,' he says. 'The story takes over them, just as it takes over me. When children are in the audience, they are always hooked.'

Talking to Eberhard in my erratic German is a struggle. I'm glad of my Dictaphone, which enables me to play back the interview later, but the greatest pleasure is to hear him performing some verses. He caresses the strings of his lap-harp, his chest expanding to a spicy *fortissimo*, spiked by rolled Rs, softening in lighter moments with the gentleness of falling feathers:

Uns ist in alten mæren wunders vil geseit
There are in ancient stories such wonders we can read,
von heleden lobebæren, von grôzer arebeit,
Of famous heroes' glories and all their mighty deeds,
von freude un(d) hôchgecîten, von weinen un(d) (von) klagen,
Of joy and feasting-days, of grief as well as tears,
von kuner recken strîten muget ir nu wunder horen sagen.
Of bold knights in the fray, such wonders now you'll hear.

Performing the *Nibelungenlied* is a more solitary pursuit than the songs of the Bosnian guslars. You don't sit around in a bar, passing the lap-harp between glasses of schnapps. But Eberhard is keeping up the oral heartbeat of these stories. The *Nibelungenlied* was composed to be recited, not to be read from a book, so listening to this mercurial performer is to edge a little closer to the old epic spirit. This isn't a continuing tradition, like the guslars. The tune and tempo are speculative, not handed down over the generations. Still, it's exciting to listen to the *Nibelungenlied* in this way, and to be reminded of the German language's instinctive musicality.

Rolling towards the final setting of the *Nibelungenlied*, I was leaving behind pastel facades and stucco, spa signs and wind turbines for overgrown brush, broken-down tractors and slaloms of construction stores, like the highways of Kosovo. On one side, the Danube slid its silver thread between the willows. On the other, hills flattened to the Hungarian steppe, the horizon broken occasionally by the gleaming jagged blade of a town and the lush overspill of frantic graffiti. With the signs in Magyar – nailed to posts, slanting over the highway – you could feel the continent turn. Stooped backs and shuffling feet aligned with the frequency of liquor stores and billboards advertising job opportunities in Austria.

At Budapest, I swapped the bus for a minivan to Esztergom.

Cyclists in lycra zipped alongside us, racing down the Danube cycle path. Families piled inside, carrying buggies and kayaking equipment. Between willows and waterweeds, I watched games of badminton and Frisbee, picnickers laying rugs over their cars to stop them overheating; a wedding party sipping champagne outside a marquee. The bride's hair had been trained into ringlets, which reminded me of paintings in Viennese galleries from the Biedermeier era.

Around a bend in the Danube, the fields shrank under the weight of willows and osier-beds. Bitterns skimmed the shallows under swamp-like thickets, stripy feathers twitching between the reeds. At last, like a temple in a jungle, Esztergom raised its cupolas and belfries, and a huge lead dome swelled above a ring of Palladian pillars, capping the cathedral like the lid on a treasure casket.

I stayed at a riverside sports hall, sleeping in a dormitory with half a dozen Slovenians from the other side of the river. Actually, I wasn't sleeping *with* them – they were sleeping with each other, and they didn't need the dormitory to do it. They were out on the patio for most of the evening, limbs entwining tighter with every slammed-down shot of palinka. Gradually, they moved inside, shedding extraneous clothing and camping out on the sofas. 'Happy night!' they called, when I minced past around midnight. It sounded like a report.

Esztergom was a fitting end to my *Nibelungen* search; for this was 'Gran', the city identified in the poem with Attila the Hun's capital. Here, according to the poem, Kriemhild hosts her kinsmen at Attila's midsummer festival. Thousands of knights cross the Danube to join the festivities, oblivious to her murderous designs. Here they gather in the hall of Attila the Hun, tipping over the wine and board, hacking wounds through chainmail, battering the Hunnish helmets with footrests; and here the story boils into a giant pan of blood.

As with the *Odyssey*, the final battle revolves around a hall. A place of shelter, food and warmth, transformed into an abattoir. It's a common occurrence in Europe's great stories – the Icelandic *Njal's Saga* pitches towards a farmhouse burning; Beowulf protects the mead hall from predatory monsters. In European epics, this happens more commonly than elsewhere (the dust-caked battlefield duels of the Persian *Shahnameh*, for example). As the epics move ever northwards, that role strengthens, reminding us how much climax is designed by climate.

The Arpad Palace is where the old kings of Hungary held their court – a stone-walled keep sprawling over the hill beside the cathedral. Although Attila the Hun never lived here, it was the Hungarian capital during the time the *Nibelungenlied* was composed, and this is the palace the poet was imagining when he put his story together. After Frederick Barbarossa stayed here on his ill-fated journey towards the Third Crusade, reports would have filtered back to the poet in Passau (or whichever court he frequented), supplying background details for the epic's ferocious final act.

In a Gothic chapel deep in the palace compound, two knights peer from a pillar, under a gold-starred vault. One of them carries a bow, the other a dagger and shield. Less reverent than the surrounding assemblage of august saints, this sculpture is a glimpse into the warrior culture of the epics, reinforcing how the pacific message of Christianity struggled to match the thrill of martial deeds.

Esztergom's grandeur drips through the *Nibelungenlied* – the sophistication of the court of King Stephen, husband of the German princess Gisela. Their marriage united Germans and Hungarians; and something comparable happens in the *Nibelungenlied*. For Kriemhild and Attila preside over a realm where 'the Christian life and the heathen existed side by side. But whichever rite a man followed, the king's magnanimity saw to it that all were amply rewarded.' Considering the epic was composed during the era of the Crusades, this is remarkably open-minded, starkly contrasting with the binary prejudices of the *Song of Roland*. But religious tolerance doesn't prevent bloodshed: you don't need ideological enmity when you're nursing a more personal vendetta.

Wandering between the terrace cafe and the cathedral, you could easily imagine Hun warriors scurrying along the heavy stone walls, bearing Kriemhild's murderous commands. In the palace, I visualised King Gunther and the dauntless Hagen, blood streaming around their ankles, fire glowing in the beams above them. On the surface, the epic's final battle is a conflict between settled Germans and nomadic Huns from the steppe, tying into that quintessential theme of southern European epic: Europeans against the people on Europe's fringe (the opposition of the *Iliad*, the *Song of Roland*, the *Kosovo Cycle*). But the *Nibelungenlied* straddles northern and southern Europe – this is the epic of Mitteleuropa, after all. Not only in its treasure and dwarves and dragon (those staple elements of fantasy fiction that thrilled the romantics) but also in its brutal carnage, its obsession with loyalty and courage, the German epic directs us northwards, towards stories like *Beowulf* and the Icelandic sagas.

'What terrible vengeance she took on her nearest kinsmen,' the poet announces in the opening chapter, 'for slaying him [Siegfried] in days to come!'

Here is a theme that binds Europe's epics, on both sides of the Alps. Roland and Miloš Obilić are betrayed by men on their own side; the *Odyssey* ends with the hero slaughtering his own subjects. Repeatedly and powerfully, the epics show that 'outsiders' or 'strangers' are not the ones who pose the greatest threat. This felt like a telling point to consider as I prepared to return to my own fractured homeland. Politics was ever thus: internal disputes sending out polluted ripples across the world.

Nazis and ultra-nationalists have been inspired by the *Nibelungenlied*. For all its fantastical charms, this is a brutal story of will to death. The mythological furnishings only deepened the story's attraction to Hitler and his ilk, mingling with their *völkisch* appetites, their fetishisation of 'manly' sports and relish for the retrograde. As I had learned during the course of this journey, the *Nibelungenlied* is deeply rooted in German popular consciousness. Those charming story elements – the dragon slaying, the Rhine treasure, the prophetic river-fairies beloved of romantic painters – conceal the more troubling will to death that can be extracted from the tale's core. All the great epics are disturbing stories, and none more so than the *Nibelungenlied*. Just as Siegfried's colossal strength proved his undoing, turning Hagen and the Burgundians against him, so the epic's greatness is also its weakness, rendering it susceptible to all our projections.

'The *Nibelungenlied* is reflecting the madness of all wars', Albert Ostermaier had told me; a couple of days later, Anna Rosmus insisted 'it is certainly glorifying war'. Could it be doing both? The poem cunningly rises beyond a single interpretation. The anti-war argument doesn't explain the relish for martial deeds, the verbal glitter of clashing swords and severed body parts, the lavish praise heaped on the most violent characters. But nor does the counter-argument resolve the melancholy pall that descends over the vast shedding of blood. 'It's not perfect,' Albert said, 'and that is its power. It's like Shakespeare.'

That power, those thrilling battle scenes, the histrionic speeches – it's all there for the taking. You only need a few to tarnish the tale for everyone. But what colours the fascists are missing: the tragedy of Rudiger, the complexity of Hagen, the naivety of Siegfried. Reading the *Nibelungenlied* in Worms, I remember putting down the Kindle when I reached the end, exhaling across the *Stüberl*. I felt shaken, chemically altered, like I'd taken a drug. What a powerful thing for a poet to do – and how reckless!

Take the epic's devastating finale. Hagen declares a toast 'to the dead' just before he strikes his hosts' son 'so that the blood washed along the sword to his hands and the boy's head fell into the Queen's lap'. Courtly music is transformed into a dance of death by the fiddler Volker, another in the line of epic soldier-storytellers: 'His tunes are sinister, his strokes are red: / His melodies strike many a hero dead.' And with no wine to hand, the thirsty knights cannibalise their fallen comrades. 'If any of you are plagued with thirst,' suggests Hagen, 'let them drink the blood here – in such heat it will be better than wine!' There is no final victory. Hagen's greatest fear is realised and he is slain by a woman; and Kriemhild has no time to savour her enemy's demise before she is hacked to pieces by an indignant elderly minion of her husband's vassal.

Is this how the Greeks felt as they sailed away from the burning pyres of Troy? Is this how the Visigoths looked on the ruins of fifth-century Rome? Is this what the Allied soldiers experienced on trawling through Berlin in the summer of 1945? Reading the last, horrific stanzas of the *Nibelungenlied* is to be confronted by the bitter taste of *Götterdammerung*: the end of everything, the twilight of the gods. There is no hope in the ruins, nor does the poet offer any consolation to cushion the approximately forty thousand deaths that have occurred. 'There lay the bodies of all that were doomed to die,' he tells us grimly; 'The King's high festival had ended in sorrow, as joy must ever turn to sorrow in the end.'

PART FIVE

How to Kill a Monster

Beowulf

Heorot is a mighty mead hall, planked with wood and plated with gold. But its owner, King Hrothgar of the Danes, is suffering the predations of the monster Grendel. After twelve years of terror, help arrives from across the sea: Beowulf, a lord among the Geats,* promises to rid Hrothgar of his grisly gatecrasher. When Grendel breaks into the hall, Beowulf engages him in a deadly wrestle and wrenches off his claw. The monster flees across the fen, fatally wounded.

But the trouble isn't over: Grendel's grief-stricken mother assails the hall, thirsty for revenge, and Beowulf follows her to the underwater hall where she lurks. There, unable to slay her with his sword, he grabs a giant's blade and runs it through her neck. Back in Heorot, celebrations resound across the mead hall and Beowulf listens to tales of old before sailing back across the sea.

But there is one more battle to face. After a reign of fifty years, Beowulf sets out to slay a dragon that has burned his hall and the dwellings of his folk. Twelve thanes accompany him, but only one of them stays the course, his loyal kinsman Wiglaf, and together they bring down the fifty-foot beast. Victory has come at a mortal cost to Beowulf. Mourning his death, his thanes burn him on a pyre and fill a magnificent mound with treasure, singing heroic chants to their fallen king.

---

* Inhabiting an area of southern Sweden remembered today by the name 'Gotaland', the Geats were subsumed by their rivals, the Swedes, although they remained an enduring presence in Swedish history. As late as 1973, the King of Sweden's official title was 'King of the Swedes, the Geats and the Wends'.

21

I shall grapple with the fiend and fight for life,
foe against foe.

Beowulf, Sixth Fit

S OMEWHERE DEEP IN the so-called 'Dark Ages', so deeply obscured
we're not even sure which century he lived in, nor which region,
there was a genius so gifted that he conjured out of the language of
the Anglo-Saxons the earliest English literary masterpiece. *Beowulf* is,
simply, one of the most beautiful things that England has ever made.
It was written down on a manuscript round about AD 1000, but
two-thirds of a century later the country succumbed to the Normans
and the language underwent a rapid transformation. Falling into
obscurity, the Anglo-Saxon epic lay neglected for more than seven
centuries. Forgotten, perhaps, but its *wyrd* (to use the Anglo-Saxon
term for fate) was strong. It fell into the possession of a distinguished
collector, Sir Robert Cotton, who opened his library to seventeenth-
century scholars like Sir Francis Bacon and Sir Walter Raleigh. Later,
when the Cotton Collection was gifted to the nation by his grandson,
it would become the foundation of the British Library.

Ignored by native researchers, *Beowulf* would depend on visiting
scholars to wriggle its way out of the darkness. Grímur Jónsson
Thorkelín, an Icelandic bibliophile, tracked it down in the late eighteenth century and carried his transcripts to Denmark. There, it was
feted as a great Danish story, and continental scholars wrestled over
its provenance; in Britain, meanwhile, recognition slowly began to
flare. The characters and narrative were less tightly wound into popular
consciousness than those of the *Nibelungenlied* or the *Song of Roland*,
so its political impact was less direct. Not to mention that Britain

already had plenty of cultural archetypes for its propagandists to marshall, from the Arthurian legends to Shakespeare's history plays.

Although many literary titans turned their attention to *Beowulf* through the course of the nineteenth century (amongst them Sharon Turner, Alfred Lord Tennyson and William Morris – now most famous for his flowery wallpaper designs), it wasn't until the twentieth century that the epic really took off, following its robust interpretation by, and influence on, J. R. R. Tolkien. Now it is one of Europe's liveliest epics, inspiring stories by blockbuster authors like Michael Crichton and Neil Gaiman, an existentialist masterpiece by John Gardner focusing on the monster Grendel, an episode of *Star Trek: Voyager*, the name for a computer cluster and a pioneering motion-capture movie featuring Angelina Jolie as a decidedly ungrisly version of Grendel's mother. More broadly, the imagery of *Beowulf* – monsters emerging from dark, murky fens, mead halls glistening with soon-to-be-shattered joy, dragons jealously guarding their treasure – have become staples of Western storytelling consciousness, lifting *Beowulf* alongside the *Odyssey* as the most accessible of European epics.

But where was it composed, and why? What inspired the Anglo-Saxon bard to fashion this tale about macabre monsters and the pleasures of the mead hall, laced with the sweet sadness when 'the riders sleep, heroes in their graves'? I was thinking about these questions as I relaxed at home in Dorset, catching up with my family, spinning from *Beowulf*'s dragon to the somewhat friendlier dragon in Julia Donaldson's *Zog and the Flying Doctors*. Epic has cast a huge influence over children's literature, from monsters to mythical quests to specific plot lines. Reading *The Wind in the Willows* with my eldest, I was struck by the parallels with *Beowulf*: the sinister threat of the deep, dark wood contrasting with the homely comforts of the hall. When Toad declares, 'You are in the hands of the famous, the skilful, the entirely fearless Toad!', Kenneth Grahame could be parodying any epic hero.

Epic was in my head, and there was still more travelling to do. It was lovely to be surrounded by the familiar, pressed to recognisable faces and voices. But the journey was incomplete and I was itching to keep moving. So, a couple of weeks after my return, I extracted bits of Lego from between my toes and bowled myself along a five-hour motorway slalom, towards a monastery in the Midlands. This would be the first of many Beowulfian visits over the coming weeks. Others included a remote East Anglian church, the famous barrows of Sutton Hoo and a pagan burial ground in Denmark. Trailing *Beowulf*, it's fair to say, sends you off to some spooky places.

What sounds might those creatures make? Would they growl or roar or hiss? Standing in the church of Breedon-on-the-Hill, perched on a 122-metre turret of Leicestershire limestone, I could hear a low rumble, but at least that was external. Wind blustered at the stained-glass windows, a fierce westerly bowling against the Norman tower; and the twin jets of an aeroplane shrieked on a lowly flight path, broadcasting the proximity of East Midlands Airport.

The creatures were encased in lead, embedded in the eastern aisle of the church. Predating the structure around them, they had been lifted from the monastery that stood on this site until the Viking incursions in the ninth century. Their lionlike faces scowled, twisting backwards over bulbous bodies that plunged towards goatlike hooves. They looked like the hybrid mutants of a Last Judgment, or decorative fiends in the margins of an illuminated manuscript. One of them was sinking its teeth into another's back. Its spade-shaped tail curled over the rump of another beast, which appeared to be mounting its fellow, whose legs were tangled in another's.

Looking at them, I was reminded of the carved beasts in Worms Cathedral, and they reflected a similar instinct: the medieval fondness for the fantastical. For the scholar Richard North, these 'Anglian Beasts' are symptomatic of 'a house filled with biblical, apocryphal, fabulous, classical, and homiletic books, just as it was with Middle Eastern, Classical and Insular styles of stone sculpture'. Such a minster, North speculates, 'could be the community where *Beowulf* was composed'. There is a possible dynastic connection too: a ninth-century king of Mercia, Beornwulf, who was succeeded by Wiglaf – the name, in the poem, of the hero's most loyal follower.

Tucked behind the box pews, in the western aisle at Breedon, is a fragment of a cross. The lower panel shows Adam and Eve beside the Tree of Knowledge; the upper panel shows a warrior with a drinking horn beside a hooded man, possibly at the gates of Valhalla, the hall where fallen warriors are greeted by the gods in Norse mythology. 'I guess whoever made it was hedging his bets,' one of the parishioners suggested, when he found me stooping there. Here is a characteristic of so much Anglo-Saxon art: the creative fusion of the Christian and the pagan. It's a striking feature of *Beowulf*, which is echoed by another cross fragment showing a series of beasts. One of these is a serpentine creature with a split tongue. In *Beowulf*, this is the *wrætlicne wyrm* ('wondrous serpent'), the dragon that lures the hero to his final battle.

Later that evening, wizard beards of cloud drifted across the sky, moving briskly, as if in search of the bodies from which they'd become detached. The wind was scooping up the leaves on the tombstones, hurling them like some macabre confetti thrower. It was no night for camping, so I climbed into the car and laid out my sleeping bag on the back seat. No wonder the wind was so fierce: this is the highest point all the way east as far as the Urals. This wind-buffeted bluff would be a fitting gathering point for 'grim spirits' like the monsters of *Beowulf*. Like the monsters grimacing inside the church.

If you like monsters, then *Beowulf*'s for you. With its misty marshes, its dragon caves and underwater lairs, it carries us across a landscape of chills and thrills, where the natural and the supernatural overlap, like interlaced patterns in Anglo-Saxon sculpture. Not even the *Odyssey*, with its one-eyed giant and flesh-chewing sea beasts, and certainly not the *Nibelungenlied*, which dismisses its dragon in a handful of lines, can match it for supernatural intensity. *Beowulf* shares many narrative qualities with the *Nibelungenlied*: a monster-slaying hero, let down by those whose loyalty he should have been able to count on; a king's demise betokening the end of a civilisation. Melancholy might be a Greek word, but as a storytelling motif it's the keynote of the north. Where *Beowulf* and the *Nibelungenlied* differ is in personnel: the latter hinges on the slaying and betraying of men, whereas *Beowulf* is structured around its remarkable monsters. For J. R. R. Tolkien, who confessed to a 'profound desire' for dragons, how could this epic not exert a powerful spell?

According to Tolkien, it is the monster-intensity that makes the poem so important. Above all other Anglo-Saxon scholars, it was Tolkien who recognised these merits, redirecting scholarship away from the historical and philological, towards the imaginative. In his hugely influential lecture, 'Beowulf: The Monsters and the Critics', delivered in 1936 (around the same time as he was completing *The Hobbit* and a year before he started writing *The Lord of the Rings*), Tolkien argued: 'It has been said of *Beowulf* itself that its weakness lies in placing the unimportant things at the centre and the important on the outer edges . . . I think it profoundly untrue of the poem, but strikingly true of the literature about it.' Too often misunderstood as 'the confused product of a committee of muddle-headed and probably beer-bemused Anglo-Saxons', *Beowulf*, Tolkien argued, was the zenith of northern literature, 'a poem by a learned man writing of old times' who 'put the monsters in the centre, gave them victory but no honour, and found a potent but terrible solution in naked will and courage'.

At the same time Nazi ideologues were plundering medieval literature for propaganda, Tolkien showed that epic could be recycled for more creative purposes. Take the Orcs (derived from '*orcneas*', fen-haunting demons mentioned in *Beowulf*), the name Frodo (from 'Froda', a warrior-king mentioned in one of the poem's many digressions), the golden hall of Meduseld (literally 'mead hall') in *The Two Towers*, which draws on the scenes of mead drinking, song and diplomacy in Hrothgar's hall. Or consider the plotting of the dragon's wrath in either *The Hobbit* or *Beowulf*: a solitary outlaw steals a single cup from the dragon's hoard, and in its fury the dragon destroys the nearest settlement and an aged king sets out, fatally, to tackle the threat. 'Tolkien felt more than continuity with the *Beowulf*-poet,' writes the scholar Tom Shippey, 'he felt a virtual identity of motive and technique.' Any reader who has responded to the cultural underpinnings of Middle Earth, to the raw world behind Tolkien's battles, will be rewarded by a visit to this astonishing tale. Its poetic rhythms, doom-laden atmosphere, and vivid, tactile monsters are welded together in 3,182 lines of hallucinogenic craftsmanship.

★

Ða com of more under misthleoþum
Then from the moor came, under the mists,
Grendel gongan, Godes yrre bær;
Grendel grasping — God's wrath he bore;
mynte se manscaða manna cynnes
meant the marauder from mankind
sumne besyrwan in sele þam hean.
to snare some of those in the high hall.

The voice is commanding, snarling with the monsters, drooping with the tender melancholy of the Blues, deepening in thunderous bass rolls that summon the spirit of the *scops* — the Anglo-Saxon bards. Benjamin Bagby — professional *Beowulf* reciter — is performing to an audience of nearly three hundred at the British Library. While the story is relaid in subtitles on the screen behind him, his fingers dance over the strings of his harp, his face scrunches to show the drunkenness of Unferth or the grimacing of Grendel when his claw is ripped from its socket, and stiffens to a stoical mask for the hero's boasts. Anglo-Saxon may have no native speakers, but this is a captive audience, responding to the tremors of the narrative with horrified gasps, laughter and warm applause.

Silvery tints glisten in Ben's hair, eyes deeply hooded, a studious cast that broadens to a warrior's burnish during the course of his recital. Now, sitting down at his dining table, he tells me how he became the go-to modern reciter of the Anglo-Saxon epic.

Hailing from Illinois, tracing his ancestry back to the Anglo-Saxons, Ben is steeped in the rhythms of medieval music. Unlatching the bespoke six-string harp that accompanies his recitals, he plucks the strings. I think of Nikos Xanthoulis playing his lyre in Athens, and of Eberhard Kummer with his lap-harp in Vienna. Ben could be a Greek rhapsode or a Balkan guslar; but the harp was made to precise specifications, enabling him to play the role of an Anglo-Saxon scop.

'I had this realisation,' he explains, 'that this poem was performed. There was a musical instrument involved and some kind of tones must have been sung.'

Already established as a significant interpreter of medieval European song, performing with his ensemble, Sequentia, he became obsessed with *Beowulf*. He contacted a harp builder, who made a copy of a seventh-century harp found in a nobleman's grave near Stuttgart, which had correspondences with a harp discovered at Sutton Hoo in East Anglia. He explains:

> I developed a series of hypothetical tunings based on a systematic idea that physics dictates the harmonic. If you tune according to basic principles of physics, you get an instrument with an octave, with a series of perfect fifths and fourths, you can't get around it. And once you have that, you've established a matrix where you have the tones of the instrument and the metrics of the poetry, quantifying time and pitch.

This is technical stuff and I'm no musicologist. At times, Ben might as well be talking in Anglo-Saxon. But the craft-specific language intrigues me. Forget clichés of bards inspired by the Muses. This is poetry-telling as a science: a practical how-to guide on how you put an epic performance together. I think of the scops in *Beowulf*, thrilling the mead hall with their tales, reciting 'with skill', their words 'truly bound together'. This isn't divine inspiration but an earthier, more human craft.

'Anglo-Saxon is an extremely rich palette of sounds,' Ben points out, 'and with the metrical structure, there's a huge amount of detail in there. It's about finding a performance with structure and a soul.'

Performing across a range of venues, all over the world, has introduced Ben to many different responses. Audiences vary from medieval experts to Tolkien enthusiasts, early music aficionados, and festival-goers snapping up tickets on a whim.

'Some of the most passionate audiences were in Australia,' he recalls. 'They get the funny bits, they get caught up in the drama, gasping and laughing and reacting.' In contrast, Scandinavian audiences could be hard work. 'I've done it in Denmark. It's a Danish story, after all! But they don't react to anything. They don't make a sound!' He reminisces fondly about the audience at a medievalists' conference in America:

They were way too excited, and by the time they got to my performance, many of them were a little tipsy. There were about three
hundred people at this performance and half of them had written a
book or a major article about *Beowulf*. They knew it so well, to the
point where they were laughing . . . in anticipation!

Not that all the experts approve of what he's doing: 'Let me tell
you about the metrists!' A rueful smile plays across his lips. 'I've
been verbally abused after performances: "How dare you break all
the rules!"' But a few heckles aren't going to snap his connection
to *Beowulf*: 'When I'm performing, I feel at home, I don't feel I'm
in a strange territory, I'm in a well-known zone, among friends.'

As Ben points out, there are 'thousands of epics' that will never
be recovered, and the hoard of Anglo-Saxon literature remains piti-
fully small.

But the fact that one little thing, the only epic poem in English, is
this text, makes it very precious. It's incredibly valuable for our sense
of who we are and where we come from. Many people tell me this
after a performance, they say, 'that really connected me with my
sense that I'm from somewhere'. It touches something archaic, it
touches something deep within everyone.

22

Take this cup, my noble courteous lord,
giver of treasure!

Wealhtheow, *Beowulf,*
Seventeenth Fit

KILL THE MONSTERS and you get a fabulous prize. For slaying Grendel, Beowulf is rewarded with 'two armlets, garments and rings, and the greatest neck-collar ever heard of anywhere on earth'. The poet dwells on the jewellery as gleefully as on the monsters; and for readers today, that glamour still shines. No wonder – the Anglo-Saxon was an age of treasure, when goldsmiths were expected to work miracles at the forge and kings were judged by their ability to hand out 'gifts of treasures . . . helmets and byrnies to the hall-sitters'.

One of the most successful of the Anglo-Saxon kingdoms was Mercia, which spread out from the valleys of the Trent. Staving off the Danes and building a dyke against the Celts, the Mercians traded with Wessex and the courts of the continent. Under rulers like Offa (famous for his diplomatic relations with Charlemagne, as well as his dyke) and the 'Lady of the Mercians', Ætheflæd, who drove the Vikings out of the Midlands, they developed a manufacturing economy that boasted some of the finest metalworkers and manuscript makers in the British Isles. This may not be recent history, but the past has a strange way of bubbling into the present.

In 2009, twenty-five miles south-west of Breedon-on-the-Hill, an amateur metal detectorist wandered around a field that had been used for growing turnips and Brussels sprouts, and happened upon the greatest of all Anglo-Saxon finds – the Staffordshire Hoard.

'Well,' explained Terry Herbert when I caught up with him, 'I was using a nineteen-year-old detector, I'd attached a new coil and I was using a customised programme that's sensitive to gold and silver.' His equipment could hardly be described as state-of-the-art. But, like treasure hunters since ancient times, he was convinced more ethereal agents were at work. 'I believe there was a spirit in that field, waiting for me to find the hoard. I had a saying, "Spirits of yesteryear, take me where the coins appear." But on that day, I changed the word from "coins" to "gold".'

When he wrestled the first treasures out of the floury soil, Terry suspected it was nothing more than 'costume jewellery, as the pieces looked like brass rather than gold'. Slowly, overwhelmed by the sheer volume of material, he realised he was on to a discovery far greater than he could ever have anticipated. He remembered a folded cross and 'a gold pommel with ornate decoration'. The first day yielded fifty pieces of jewellery; after four more days of digging, interrupted by raging thunderstorms, he realised he might never reach the end. He contacted the Finds Liaison Office, who brought in professional archaeologists and twenty-four-hour security. 'The workmanship was out of this world,' recalled Terry. 'The Dark Ages are more like the Golden Ages!'

Experts have identified the Staffordshire Hoard as primarily military in purpose, and there have been speculations that it represents a ransom for a king captured in battle. Valued at a whopping £3.3 million (which made Terry and the landowner immensely rich), the Hoard has been divided between several museums, including the Potteries in Stoke-on-Trent.

Imagine if we could pluck Beowulf out of the poem and show him those treasures. He would 'eagerly gaze on the bright gems of artful work', just as he does when he feasts his eyes on the 'old riches, the golden treasure' near the end of the tale. Sure, he might be bemused by all the information screens and downlights, but this is a guy who could dive into a monster-haunted lake, so he'd probably be able to handle it. He'd smile at the sword buttons of gold and garnet, gilt cheek-pieces and the ring of millefiori glass, wreathed in zigzagging gold lines. The latter's function might be beyond him (it's been speculated it was an early priest's headdress), but he wouldn't find the combination of pagan and Christian motifs confusing. The poet conceived his pagan hero in a Christian context, voicing praise to 'the King of Glory, the eternal Lord', and when his soul passes he seeks 'the splendour of the saints'. Addressing a Christian audience still familiar with their pagan heritage, able to pick up references to the necklace of the goddess Freyja and Thor's battle with the 'world-serpent', the poet mingles the faiths, much like the Staffordshire Hoard. It is this ambiguity that gives so much Anglo-Saxon art its distinctive tension: the push and pull of conflicting belief systems, intimately entwined.

It isn't the monsters that kill Beowulf, but treasure. 'Now have I sold my old life,' he admits, as the dragon's poison burns his ageing flesh, 'for the hoard of treasures.' He bequeaths it to his people, but the inheritance is bittersweet. His loyal thane Wiglaf predicts 'a time of strife for the people' and the treasure is sealed with a taboo, 'a curse laid upon it'.

Cursed treasure is a common theme among the epics – from the catastrophic homecomings of Odysseus and his Troy-plundering comrades, to the curse that haunts the *Nibelungen* hoard. In *Beowulf*, a gloomy thane, fallen on hard times, steals a single cup. 'Then the monster began to belch forth flames,' the poet records, 'to burn the bright dwellings . . . The loathy air-flier wished not to leave aught living there'. In a poem built around the deeds of the high-born, here is a faint acknowledgement that the worst suffering usually falls on those with the least access to the treasure.

The Staffordshire Hoard may have brought some glamour to the Potteries Museum, but the streets around the museum are no less dog-eared for its arrival. Who'd blame people around here for saying 'no'? Seventy per cent of Stoke-on-Trent's voters had turned against the EU, despite their dependence on EU handouts. The costs of austerity and social inequality, along with a combative media campaign, had exposed the fracture lines in British identity, where appeals to 'Anglo-Saxon' culture had been powerful weapons. For myths and legend have the ability to turn heads all over Europe, and Britain is no exception. 'The Anglo-Saxons had a view of life,' wrote Nigel Farage, while he was leader of the UK Independence

Party, 'that it is a bird that flies from the darkness into the warmth and community of the mead hall then back into the darkness.' He was paraphrasing the Venerable Bede, but also channelling *Beowulf*, in celebrating UKIP's 2014 by-election victory in the 'proud Anglo-Saxon town' of Clacton.

None of the politicians manipulating these terms were able to quote from the gems of Anglo-Saxon culture, nor to recognise the continental trading networks that helped Anglo-Saxon culture to thrive (as illustrated by the Staffordshire Hoard and the Breedon reliefs). Nor were they aware of the telling irony that the most iconic work of Anglo-Saxon literature is set in two nations still in the EU, with a narrative that dramatises the importance of diplomatic alliances. But what does that matter? Politicians have been mining art and history for millennia, grabbing whatever they can, like the hoard thief in *Beowulf*.

The masterminds behind the campaign to drag Britain out of the European Union were some of the most self-conscious politicians in recent history: MPs and strategists who read Sun Tzu's *Art of War* and, to quote the Conservative Eurosceptics' commanding officer, Steve Baker, 'applied the book as bloody hard as I could'; or, like the Svengali of the Vote Leave campaign, Dominic Cummings (whose Twitter handle, evoking the most famous of epics, is 'Odyssean Project'), followed the tactics of Otto von Bismarck and the Duke of Wellington's 'Waterloo Strategy' against Napoleon. For the elite players sitting around their war councils, this was their moment in history. Just as epic focuses on the elites and their war games, so does political reporting. But it is cities like Stoke that witness its effects; and in a democratic system, it is cities like Stoke that determine the outcome.

I had booked myself into a cheap room above a pub in the central area of Hanley. Wandering around the streets near the Potteries, I was never far from a Poundland, and every second shop front advertised a closing-down sale. In the old potteries centre of Longton, red-brick Victorian and Georgian foundries were blindfolded with boarding, chimneys and corbelling roosted by pigeons. Burslem was even more depressing, as you'd expect of the district with the most boarded-up shops in Britain (a 31.5 per cent vacancy rate according to a 2017 survey). There were cardboard fillers behind shop windows, nailed plyboard, shutters rolled down, taped-up windows, painted-over shop fronts.

Waving a placard near the Potteries Museum, a seventy-nine-year-old called Annie beckoned me over. 'I remember when it was all industry round here,' she said. 'Now you have to pay a tariff on everything. We need to bring back our industry, and we need to drain the swamp!' Her placard was emblazoned with the logo of the UK Independence Party and the slogan 'Holding the Government to Account!' Judging by the number of Stokies who gathered around her, she wasn't offering a minority view. 'They're coming in their hordes,' she said, throwing a defiant look, daring me to follow her drift. 'There's too many to cope.'

'Drain the swamp.' No doubt the fen dwellers of the age of *Beowulf* had thoughts of that kind. The association of natural excess and political turmoil explains why the imagery of *Beowulf* continues to resonate. Grendel, that troublesome swamp dweller, is a 'hateful monster', 'savage and raging'. Beowulf labels him 'a secret pursuer', who 'works on the dark nights evil hatred, injury and slaughter, spreading terror'.

After chatting to a policeman who had taken part in a surveillance operation focused on a far-right group called the Stoke-on-Trent Infidels (their motivations, he pointed out, were 'complicated and diverse'), I made contact with one of their spokespeople and asked what they were campaigning against. 'The Islamic takeover of Stoke,' he declared (through a series of messages – he was wary of meeting in person, after discovering I had written a couple of articles for the *Guardian*). 'The mass dominated areas of our city that have become no-go areas, the huge influx of mostly Muslim faith taxi drivers . . .' Here is the old pan-European theme – the fear of the Muslims, which I'd heard in Greece, Italy, Germany and elsewhere. This stance is particularly rife in the West Midlands, which has become the heartland of far-right groups like the English Defence League.

Those angry voices aren't growling out of a vacuum. Immigration in the UK has been conflated with industry, the decline in the latter fuelling anger against the former. Factory jobs have dwindled from 7 million in 1979 to 2.5 million by 2010; manufacturing, which represented 40 per cent of the UK economy after the Second World War, has shrunk to 10 per cent. The Midlands has paid a heavy price for Britain's economic evolution, especially since the financial crash of 2008. As local historian Fred Hughes told me, 'Stoke is in a good geographical position, in the centre of England. But it's not attracted the inventiveness and investment that comes with it.' I might disagree with the Infidels' diagnosis, but they do reflect a lived reality: something had gone wrong, and the potential of the English heartlands was being squandered.

Looking back into the past for a more prosperous future – never really works, does it? But there's a movement in the Midlands that suggests we should be looking all the way back to the age in which *Beowulf* was created. As far as the campaign for 'Independent Mercia' is concerned, the middle counties of England – twenty historic shires, from Cheshire in the north-west to Hertfordshire in the south-east – were illegally annexed in 1066, and it's about time they started claiming their rights.

'We've been living with this disease for a thousand years – well, that's a thousand-year-old disease the essence of which has never been dealt with.'

Sitting in his living room a few miles south of Stoke-on-Trent, Jeff Kent (aka the Convenor of the Acting Witan of Mercia) sets out his stall. Long silver hair spins off his chin and skull, weaving a Druidic glamour around his head; although his chequered shirt and slacks are more in keeping with his neatly kept house and the pretty garden through the window, where a stone Buddha squats beside the rose bed.

'Imagine,' says Jeff, 'if the Germans had won World War Two and we were looking back after a thousand years of their rule. Well, that's what happened! Look in the Domesday Book, so many villages were reduced to waste. The Harrying of the North – so many died of starvation, fleeing from the Normans. It was a holocaust!'*

---

* Across a range of more than a hundred miles, villages were razed, livestock and inhabitants slaughtered and food supplies burned. One hundred thousand (according to the historian Orderic Vitalis) died as a result of the ensuing famine, in which people were reduced to eating not only dogs and cats but also each other.

Not only is 1066 Britain's most iconic date, it also signifies the most controversial event in its history. Claiming kinship to the late English King Edward the Confessor, William of Normandy crossed the Channel and defeated Edward's much harried brother-in-law, Harold Godwinson, near the Sussex coast. What happened next has been debated for centuries. Was the nation enriched, shaken by a more rigorous organisation, its language expanded? Or was the Anglo-Saxon culture – the culture of which *Beowulf* is the greatest surviving example – mercilessly suppressed? The answer probably includes elements of both, and it has stoked passions ever since.

Blaming the Normans has a rich history. When the Peasants' Revolt broke out in 1381, its leader Wat Tyler demanded rights 'which the men of English race had lost at the Conquest'. During the seventeenth century, the growth in parliamentary opposition to the Crown was frequently expressed in terms of Normans versus Anglo-Saxons, by prominent politicians such as Sir Robert Cotton, who believed that William the Conqueror had left the Saxons 'in no better condition than villeinage'. As the nation's most significant book collector, whose library included the only copy of *Beowulf*, Cotton was an influential, controversial character. So dangerous was his collection considered, it was searched in 1630, placed under permanent surveillance, and officially closed during the run up to the civil war.

The image of an Anglo-Saxon golden age has gleamed throughout English history, a rose-tinted utopia like pre-Ottoman Serbia before the Battle of Kosovo. It inspired the Levellers to rage against the 'Norman bondage' and the Diggers to warn against falling back under the 'Norman Yoake'. More recently, the Eurosceptic MEP Daniel Hannan lambasted the Norman Conquest as the moment when 'England was wrenched out of the Nordic world and subjected to European feudalism', while Nigel Farage frequently sported ties decorated with the Bayeux Tapestry to remind voters of 'the last time we were invaded and taken over'.

Perceiving the Norman Conquest as 'the moment when it all went wrong', Jeff and his colleagues are keen to recover the best of the Anglo-Saxon age. 'There was a balance,' he says, 'because people lived on the land, and their survival was based on subsistence farming, this affinity with preserving the land.' The Acting Witan of Mercia's constitution is packed with Anglo-Saxon terms: 'regular folk, leet, hundred and shire meetings and a witan to co-ordinate the region's activities'; respect for 'historical precedents' for leet, hundred and shire boundaries; a plan to reassemble the *fyrd* – enlistment of the able-bodied. It draws on the sophisticated political structures and legal systems developed by Anglo-Saxon jurists, which ensured that, for all the turmoil of the era, dictatorship never flourished. As the medievalist James Campbell has observed, 'it does indeed look as if the history of constitutional liberty has important beginnings in Anglo-Saxon England.' These early political experiments, with their legal attention to practical examples rather than abstract principles, have survived in the division between 'Anglo-Saxon' (or 'Nordic') and 'Continental' models, which can be tracked to the non-feudal structures dramatised in *Beowulf* and the Icelandic sagas.

For Jeff and his fellow council members, Mercia has no place under the continuing 'Norman' rule. For all their fondness for the Anglo-Saxon, they are applying their interpretation of its history to the modern world: opposing nuclear technology and 'anti-ecological industrial activities', championing co-ordinated relief efforts. It's a campaign they've been waging for many years, having conducted a 'reaffirmation of Mercian independence' back in 2003.

Jeff recalls:

> It took place in Birmingham. We weren't sure if the UK police would try to stop us, but what right do they have? We are the legitimate acting government of the region and they are a foreign police force. We had banners and flags, stalls, books for sale. And we were interviewed on the BBC.

But the real breakthrough came six years later.

> With the Staffordshire Hoard – that really made people notice about Mercia! We went to the Potteries Museum and made a declaration in front of it, we put the hoard in the hands of the people of Mercia. After that, along with the financial crash, the interest in our campaign has gone up by 90 per cent.

There are currently 2,000 registered 'citizens of Mercia' (not, Jeff insists, an unfavourable number 'in comparison with the UK, which has no citizens but only subjects of the Crown'). But, as far as he's concerned, you can't measure success merely in statistical terms. Whether or not he will see an 'independent Mercia' in his lifetime, he is convinced this is 'the right thing to do'. 'Not everybody we've talked to is in favour of Mercia,' he admits, 'but we've found the degree of alienation with the UK to be near 100 per cent.' In such circumstances, he believes, and with the 'monumental ecological cataclysm that is coming', radical alternatives are needed. He quotes the ending of the tenth-century Anglo-Saxon poem, *The Battle of Maldon*: 'Courage shall grow greater, will the firmer, heart the keener, as our strength fails'.

'It's about standing together,' he says, 'even when the chips are down.' An attitude that Beowulf or Hagen, or any of the heroes of northern European epic could share.

23

. . . the great ravager relentlessly stalked,
a dark death-shadow, lurked and struck
old and young alike, in perpetual night
held the misty moors.

Beowulf, Second Fit

THE MIDLANDS MAY have the gold, but East Anglia is where the monsters hang out. Gloopy with fens and boggy marshes, quick sands and black muds, veiled in eerie North Sea mists, haunted by headless coachmen and the ghosts of hanged smugglers, England's spooky rump claims more supernatural creatures than anywhere else in the country. The churches of East Anglia are a freak show in stone – from the skiapod at Dennington to the tree spirit at Saxmundham, the spandrel imps at Mildenhall, the winged beasts on the southern aisle at Bungay, with its infernal black dog. And when it comes to the monsters of *Beowulf*, there are some very specific associations. Because *Beowulf* is far too rich and layered to confine itself to a single region. Sure, the poem has deep roots in Mercia, but it's just as deeply entrenched in the soil of East Anglia.

I had my East Anglian itinerary lined up – a couple of churches with infernal associations and a famous burial ground. Then I'd be setting off for Scandinavia, via the ferry from Harwich, to visit the land in which most of *Beowulf* is set. I'd packed my warmest clothes, including some thick woollen socks, as well as my sleeping bag and a one-man tent. After all the gear I'd lost back in Greece, I was now fully stocked, ready for the final Nordic lap.

Clacking points and chugging pistons, cheery announcements from the guard and whiny mobile phone chatter: the soundtrack to any English train journey. We were trundling towards the land of the 'south folk', where most of the town and village names have barely changed since they were listed in the Domesday Book: a dictionary of Anglo-Saxon mapped across the land. Swans floated on the Stour (the 'strong' river), and flaking dinghies bobbed at the boatyard of Woodbridge (which takes its name not from the local forestry but from the Norse god, Woden). We rattled through Saxmundham ('Saxmund's homestead') and Yoxford ('oxen's crossing') and I climbed down at Halesworth ('Hale's enclosure'), to make my way to the 'Stronghold on the pleasant stream', otherwise known as Blythburgh, a medieval church associated with one of East Anglia's most notorious monsters.

They call it the 'cathedral on the marshes'. Which explains why my shoes were mud-caked and soggy by the time I reached it. Suffolk roads aren't particularly walker-friendly, footpaths few and far between, so I had to keep assaulting the briar hedges to avoid the long-haul trucks. With all the road kill on offer, the walk was like conveyor belt sushi for birds of prey – a blackbird with its beak disarticulated, sinews spilling behind a clench of scaly legs; a pancaked hedgehog, spines jammy with blood. Rubber gloves, fast-food drinks lids, the plastic rings around beer cases. As for the signage, this was classic Little England, mixing old-school trustfulness with beady-eyed vigilance: sticker decals for Neighbourhood Watch stamped the windows behind honesty stalls with slots to pay for punnets of fresh eggs.

The church soars out of the marshes, gothic buttresses and elaborate stonework in stately contrast to the bedraggled grey estuary. Wooden angels float under the ridge of a tie-beam ceiling, golden hair coiling between carved bosses. Poppyhead figures perch on the pews, evangelists lurk behind a rood screen, and a Jack O'Clock, in knightly cuirass and codpiece, wields a hammer to strike the hour. All this figuration – it's like being inside a toy shop! But there's nothing twee about the visitation that happened here in 1577.

On the night of a mighty thunderstorm, the door of the church smashed open and a snarling beast, according to local folklore, darted through the church, leaving a couple of fatalities and paw marks on the northern door – black slashes have been gouged into the wood, either side of a broad metal hinge (although the more literal-minded might put this down to blacksmithery). Here was an appearance of the wild beast of the fens, the East Anglian monster that's been sighted from Colchester to King's Lynn, known as Galleyrot, Barguest, Old Snarleycrow, Scarp and most commonly the 'Black Shuck'.

'The Shuck is one of those totemic animals,' says Martin Newell, East Anglian cult figure and one of Britain's most prolific poets. 'It goes right back to ancient times. There's something in the human psyche that needs these bogeymen. I remember, growing up in Essex, I'd hear about someone who thought they'd seen the Shuck, incidents in the local papers.'

So fascinated was Martin by the Shuck that he wrote a poem about it, a rhyming ballad that he performs at folk festivals. Linking the Shuck to the invasions of Norsemen (many of its appearances are associated with Viking battle sites), he conceived the beast as a 'Hound of Odin' with 'burning-ember eyes' who 'sees the wounded wolfcoats / Arisen from the dead / The norsemen put to sleep on Saxon swords'.

The word *shuck* is linked to the Old English *scucca*, a word for 'devil' or 'demon', which King Hrothgar uses in *Beowulf* to describe Grendel. The link may be more than coincidental. Both monsters share vulpine characteristics and the 'fire-like, baleful light' emanating from Grendel's eyes is matched by the bright, hellish vision of the Shuck. A further linguistic connection with Grendel is raised by the East Anglian dialect: *grindle*, a 'ditch', suggesting the marshlands where many sightings of the Shuck have occurred, as well as 'the moors, the fen and the fastness' where Grendel roams. If the *Beowulf* poet lived around East Anglia, if he was inspired by the fens that lurked around his minster or monastery, it's likely that Grendel and the Shuck were spawned from the same source, the same folk horror tale that chilled the bones of Anglo-Saxon audiences.

The walk to Blythburgh had scooped out the heart of the day, but there was another haunted house in my sights – a church at Iken, on the estuary of the Alde River, associated with marsh demons back in Anglo-Saxon times. I'd never hitch-hiked in England before, but a few lifts on the continent had stirred the habit; and I was still in a travelling mindset. It didn't feel like I was at home: I was on the road, still moving around Europe, with the added bonus of a familiar language. So I strode down to the old trunk road and stuck out my thumb.

'Don't see many hitch-hikers these days,' said Mike, a gambling store manager from Lowestoft, who was only the second driver to pass by. Down the 'rat run' we went: the B-road to Leiston. Black pigs were rootling around hooped corrugated-iron sties embedded in the earth like giant tin cans. Above the grazing Red Poll cattle, distant spokes of wind turbines scythed at the sky, dicing the powerful westerlies off the North Sea. Mike dropped me at Leiston, and I carried on towards Iken. I was full of zip now there were only a few miles to go.

Walking with the traffic can be fraught – not only the danger of getting pancaked, but also the blast of engine noise and wind. So I sidled down fields of boulder clay and followed the meandering Alde. Hawthorn picked at my sleeves, bindweed tangled with my laces, and yellow roots of nettles softened underfoot. No wonder there were so many weeds: it was the dying days of *Weodmonath*, or 'Weed-Month', in the pagan calendar – otherwise known as August.

Worried about the fading light, I cut across the most direct route, clambering over fences, deep among pig farms. Black and dappled, pointing their snouts skywards, like meteorological equipment, they peered through tiny eyes hooded by floppy fin-shaped ears. They looked more studious than snarly: geeky counterparts to the tusked porcines depicted on the cheekpieces of the Geatish helmets in *Beowulf*.

At Snape Maltings, red-brick malt-houses towered over the Alde and a footpath ferried me to a duck-board platform. The river gleamed through the rind of marsh sedge, bright as tinplate under the lowering sun. I could hear a low creaking sound, like a rusty hinge. A rustle behind me, and a pair of ring-necked pheasants clattered out of the reeds, fanning the air with tightly sheafed tail feathers. Their flight path curved over combs of sedge and muddy runnels, where you could see the trails of feather presses and runes of birdfoot engraved in the flats. Midges swilled around me, and I windmilled my arms to beat them off. Across the bay bristled a tower of flint, half sunk in the tree line. It looked like the Grail castle in an Arthurian romance, obscured by thickening cloud, which backcombed over the pine trees. This was the church of Iken.

In the sixth century Saint Botulf established a monastery here. Timber has been found under the present church, as well as an Anglo-Saxon cross shaft. Reeds from the local marshes thatched the main body of the church, under the flint tower. Wood pigeons throbbed urgently in the trees, amongst a parliament of cawings, and a blackbird scooted under a beech hedge. It was nearly dusk and there was no lighting inside. Late shafts of sunlight skimmed off the benches, conjuring loopholes of light in the arch-braced nave, but the church was already cowled in darkness.

From the stone panels of a baptismal font, beasts were glowering, including a gryphon and a lion. I knelt behind them to study the cross shaft, holding my iPhone for light. Curling patterns gouged the stone, serpents coiling an ouroboros ring, a match for the winding shape of the Alde. This was the *Mithgarthsurmr*, the 'Middle Earth Serpent', winding itself around the world by biting its tail, an inspiration for the 'loathsome air-flier' that sends Beowulf to his doom.

Saint Botulf was known for his skills as an exorcist. He was drawn to this area to rescue the population from an infestation of marsh demons, the diseases associated with bogs and marshland, which is suggested today by the abundance of midges. It's a curious half-glimpse into the origins of Grendel and his mother, a reminder of the physical reality that underpins so many ancient tales. Grendel, like the spirits haunting Iken, is a disease spirit, suffering *cear wylmas* ('whelms of sorrow') which need a *bot*, or cure. Embedded here, deep in the Anglo-Saxon, is the image of monster as victim; the passion of Kriemhild pushed to its imaginative limit, which resonates all the more in the figure of Grendel's grief-stricken mother.

Only sorcerers or warriors could battle such deadly manifestations, which makes Botulf (or 'Bot-wulf', the 'cure-wolf') a monastic counterpart to Beowulf (the 'bee-wolf' or bear – a name that evokes the 'berserkers' or bear-shirts who worked themselves into battle frenzy before tearing into their enemies). One tackles the fiends with prayer and incantations, the other uses animal-like brawn. But in both cases, victory must be won through faith. When it comes to the challenge of Grendel's 'greedy, grim-minded' mother, strength isn't enough: 'holy God brought about war-victory', and the pagan hero is saved by the Christian 'Lord' he only dimly recognises.

All day I had been thinking about monsters, so walking demon-haunted byways in the twilight wasn't exactly plan A. It was like stepping out for a nocturnal wander after watching *The Exorcist*.

But it was magical! Wind howled over the frantic rustlings of pheasants and the broody chanting of the wood pigeons. Stream and shore mingled in the draining light, a brown-grey soup bitty with islets and the chirping nests of river fowl. Fluid and solid interfused, boggling the mind with the mirage of mingled mud and water, braided textures repeating themselves in the sky. If anywhere could conjure illusions and morbid phantasms, Iken was the place.

Still, it wasn't having a happy effect on my heart rate. Hurling myself down the by-lanes, I physically gritted my teeth to block out the marsh demons. Adrenaline became a whisk for the imagination, turning sporadic headlights into the Shuck's baleful eyes, conjuring fiends out of fence posts and stiles. 'And Shuck, / The black dog of the fens,' writes Martin Newell,

> *Will spring out on the traveller*
> *With burning ember eyes*
> *To haunt the ancient roads where he appears.*

What a relief to dive into warmth and light – the glow of racked glasses and the brass shields over the taps. The cheery familiarity of an English pub: my own 'mighty mead-dwelling' for an hour or two.

The next morning, after a night in a youth hostel in Blaxhall, I hitch-hiked a couple of miles towards Sutton Hoo. Apart from a shepherd moving his flock behind Tranmer House, the site was unpeopled. Crop spray pipes as big as water wheels loomed over the long, flat fields, framed by an ale-coloured skyline. Squeezing inside a gateway, I had to be careful not to let any of the black-faced ewes escape. On the other side of the burial mounds, dozens of pigs were roaming in front of their corrugated sties, like a muddy army on the morning after battle.

'Bid the men famed in battle raise at the sea-headland a gleaming mound', says a dying Beowulf. He falls in the land of the Geats, but it is at Sutton Hoo that archaeologists have found the closest parallel to the epic poem's barrow. Built on high ground, overlooking the upper estuary of the Deben, the Sutton Hoo mounds are uncanny echoes of the poem's funerary details. 'They laid on the barrow rings and ornaments,' the poet narrates, 'all such adornments as men, eager for combat, had erstwhile taken from the hoard; they let the earth keep the treasure of earls, the gold in the ground, where it yet lies, as useless to men as it was before.'

But it wasn't useless to grave robbers – the 'nighthawks' of earlier times. The wealth deposited in pagan burial mounds made them underground piggy banks, as tempting to gold-diggers as they were to the dragon who 'must needs seek the hoard in the earth'. Digging around at Sutton Hoo, the robbers siphoned off what they could find. It was their leavings, in the form of rusty ship rivets, that prompted the archaeologist Basil Brown to start digging in 1939, revealing the impression of an eighty-eight-foot-long ship.

What Brown uncovered was astonishing – only the Staffordshire Hoard can bear comparison. The trove at Sutton Hoo included silver-gilt mounts from drinking horns, fragments of a sword, a cauldron and a shield decorated with gold ornaments, as well as the ghostly impression of a ship (although the wood itself had rotted away). Among the most remarkable items were the remains of a six-stringed wooden lyre, stored in a beaver-skin bag and decorated with two gilt-bronze plaques, echoing the harp played by King Hrothgar in *Beowulf.* Brown also uncovered a whetstone engraved with a bronze stag (recalling the deer or 'hart' from which Hrothgar's palace of Heorot took its name) and a helmet with gilt-bronze boars' heads over the eyebrow pieces, matching the description of the Geatish helmets.

But are these parallels any more than coincidence? Does Sutton Hoo have a more specific connection to *Beowulf?* Archaeologically, it's hard to tell, since no body has been discovered. The barrow's occupant probably dissolved in the acidic soil, but its presence is suggested by phosphates found among the soil samples. A year after the excavation, the historian H. M. Chadwick wrote, 'All probability is in favour of the great and wealthy high king Rædwald, who seems to have died about 624–5.' Rædwald was the most powerful ruler south of the Humber, a convert from paganism who combined the new faith of Christianity with remembrance of the old, provoking scorn from the Venerable Bede ('in the same temple,' sniped the grouchy monk, 'he had an altar to sacrifice to Christ, and another small one to offer victims to devils'). This religious ambiguity may not have pleased everyone, but it was a common stance in an era of transition and it echoes the pagan–Christian intertwining of *Beowulf.*

The discoveries at Sutton Hoo don't constitute treasure, since they were buried without the intention of recovery. They belonged to Mrs Edith Pretty, owner of Tranmer House, who kept them under her bed when they were first discovered. In an act of remarkable generosity, she gifted the treasures to the nation, rejecting the CBE she was offered in recompense (for which her sister Elizabeth called her a goose!). At Tranmer House, you can pick out the etchings of land girls in the fireplace and sift through Basil Brown's workshop – a horse's hip bone, a box full of saws, pieces of Samianware. Around you, the clipped, cautious words of Neville Chamberlain play from a radio recording – 'Up to the very last, it would have been quite possible to have arranged a peaceful and honourable settlement . . .' – recalling the nightmare spreading across Europe in those very weeks when the Sutton Hoo mounds were opened up.

Standing outside, looking up at the cloud caul, I imagined all those warplanes launching from nearby airfields, some of them only a few miles away, thundering overhead on their way to bomb cities like Worms, where I had wandered a few weeks earlier. Chamberlain hadn't heeded the lesson of *Beowulf,* but his successor did: you can't just shake the monster's claw and trust his word, you need to grab hold of it and rip it out of the socket. Winston Churchill, who suffered from attacks of what he called 'the Black Dog' (not so much emanations of the Shuck, in his case, as perturbations from within), who filled his speeches with Anglo-Saxonisms and relished the pre-Norman history of these islands, certainly swallowed the Beowulfian principle: in order to battle the monsters, you need to be one.

Although most of the Sutton Hoo treasures are on display in the British Museum, there's an exhibition room beside the ticket office, containing replicas as well as a few originals. Iron shield bosses catch the light through the glass casing, while bronze and garnet and ivory glimmer on a *cloisonné* sword-belt buckle. Varied origins suggest the interconnectedness of seventh-century Europe – a Greek inscription gouged into a bronze basin, two silver Byzantine spoons, a hanging bowl of Celtic pattern. Artefacts for which the Anglo-Saxon metal-work is easily a match. Peer at the golden belt buckle, with its hinged backplate and locking mechanism, dragons writhing around the plate, and you're looking at metalcraft to set beside the word-craft of *Beowulf.* Like the sculptures at Breedon, the Sutton Hoo hoard articulates the continental network in which Anglo-Saxon culture was enmeshed – a network evoked by *Beowulf* itself, with its Danish setting, its references to Franks, Merovingians, Frisians and Swedes, and its mead-hall tales that include an early version of Siegfried's dragon slaying (which even has its own East Anglian association – the Suffolk village of Walsingham, derived from the Volsungs, the dragon slayer's clan). This may be a tale of the north, but it is also a European Epic, sending out and responding to signals across the continent. But in the text itself, there is one nation that is bafflingly ignored.

'It's a curious thing,' as the scholar Dr Sam Newton put it, '*Beowulf* is the primal English epic, our best surviving example of a great old English story, but it doesn't actually mention England!'

We tend to think of the Vikings as marauders, seeing them through the eyes of the monks who wrote about them, forgetting that Danish interactions with England were complex. For Sam Newton, the 'primal English epic' may not take place in England, but it grafts its Scandinavian setting on to the physical landscape of East Anglia, fusing the mythical Beowulf with the historical figure of King Rædwald.

I met Sam in the Prettys' old squash court. Casually dressed, jaw open in gleeful curiosity under a pelmet of dark hair, he sat behind a desk covered in papers, laughing readily as we discussed the poem. In his book *The Origins of Beowulf and the Pre-Viking Kingdom of East Anglia*, Sam identifies a dynastic connection between the Danish court of the Scyldings and the royal line of King Rædwald through Wealhtheow, King Hrothgar's wife. She appears twice in the poem, 'gold-adorned', presenting the goblet in the mead hall, like some Dark Age geisha: 'Then the woman of the Helmings went about everywhere among old and young warriors, proffered the precious cup, till the time came that she, the ring-decked queen, excellent in mind, bore the mead-flagon to Beowulf.'

This 'woman of the Helmings' belongs to a clan that gave its name to the Suffolk village of Helmingham. More broadly, Wealhtheow is a Wulfing, from the same ancestry as King Rædwald. 'I sent old treasures,' recalls King Hrothgar, rationalising Beowulf's journey to help him against Grendel, 'to the Wulfings over the back of the water.' The triangular alliance between Geats, Wulfings and Hrothgar's Danes is the diplomatic foundation on which the narrative rests. For an East Anglian, seventh- or eighth-century audience, these references would have been hard to ignore.

'So I think it does mention England implicitly,' said Sam. 'Wealhtheow is an illustrious ancestor, and the original audience would have got that. It was written by an Englishman for an English audience, looking back on a common English–Germanic ancestry.' If Rædwald's burial is echoed in the poem, so is the blending of Christianity and paganism that coloured his court, which Sam believes could give us the clue to *Beowulf*'s composition:

> Rædwald was a very great king, and that historically comes closer to making sense of the incredible quality and quantity of the stuff buried here. It was clearly a great centre of cultural activity, not just of the arts, but of verse as well. A king that brings good seasons so that the harvests flourish and people are happy and prosper and there's plenty of feasting – that's the ideal. And you could argue not much has changed today.

This is one theory amongst many. Others include Professor North's Mercian hypothesis – associating *Beowulf* with the monastery at

Breedon-on-the-Hill as a requiem for the Mercian King Beornwulf; and some scholars speculatively link the poem's patronage with King Cnut, who united Denmark and England in the early eleventh century, marrying the widow of Æthelred the Unready. *Beowulf* is too slippery to allow a single theory to pin it down. But of the many theories, I found Sam's the most compelling, because it's rooted in the landscape.

'Certainly,' he said, 'when it comes to fens, wetlands, the home of Grendel, it's the East Anglian landscape to me.'

> I think the Black Shuck and Grendel's kind, these monsters are more at home in an eastern English, wetland landscape, not just the folk-lore but the language. Remember, 'Shuck' comes from the East Anglian dialect. But then we have to remember that it's a poem. Yes, there's a historical strata, but this is also a psychic landscape. The boundary between the natural and supernatural isn't there. Just as when we go to the marshes around Iken and it's getting dark and cold, the mist is coming up and you can't tell the difference between the land and the sea, the sea and the sky, it's all disorientating and those normal elemental references are all wrong.

Walking towards the train station, I remembered the strange inter-fusion of the elements at Iken: as Beowulfian as any place I had visited. No, I thought, this is one quarry the scholars are never going to wrestle down. *Beowulf* eludes definitive categorisation. It spins around in an eternal circle, like the Middle Earth serpent biting its own tail.

24

TIME TO BOARD 'the foamy-necked floater' and cross 'the bath of gannets'. More prosaically: the Stena Line Ferry from Harwich was due to depart.

When Beowulf and his retinue launch themselves at sea, they 'plough the deep water'. Not that there's much chance of farming analogies now, unless you're harvesting the fruit machines. But out at sea, those farming comparisons have become more literal. Soaring out of the water, twenty-five miles off the Suffolk coast, skeletal giants were spinning in the wind, rotor blades turning as hard as Viking oars. If you could ask an ancient Greek what they reckoned were the most far-fetched details of the *Odyssey*, the sack of winds would probably come ahead of the Cyclops. But here epic fantasy has been engineered to a form of reality. Full circle, turning like a wheel: the ancient Greeks and the Vikings depended on wind power; a millennium later, as we stagger through the twilight of the fossil fuel age, we are learning to farm the wind again.

The Viking raids left a legacy of 'barbarian' savagery as notorious as the Hun, although they were no more violent than the army of Charlemagne or the knights of the First Crusade. In the Icelandic sagas, 'going raiding' is simply what young men do to win a fortune. Instead of looking on Jobs.net or applying for *The Apprentice*, you rig up a boat and sharpen your axe.

A relay of buses carried me across Holland and northern Germany. Early morning in Denmark: dew gleaming on stacks of silage. Turbines harnessed wind over fields of luminous rape. Oily peat bogs flashed back at the morning sun, like smugglers' lamps; and behind forests of beech the rolling tides telegraphed their own signals with sparkling waves. The grey breadths of the Baltic were never far away, straddled by the tunnels and suspension bridges that knit the islands of the Danish archipelago.

It's hard to imagine this calm nation as the land of Grendel and his grisly mother. But over the coming days, I had plans to visit the burial ground where the story's legendary matter took root; and first, in Copenhagen, to learn how the Anglo-Saxon epic has influenced the nation that spawned it. For we may see *Beowulf* today as an English epic, but that wasn't how it was perceived by the men who peeled it out of obscurity.

The painting shows a night sky, half red with fire. Tails of white light dangle in the dark and flame spews from a steeple, while men struggle to control their horses and a bare-armed woman cradles her baby, peering anxiously up at the sky. It could be the stronghold of the Geats in *Beowulf*, when the dragon 'surrounded the people of that region with fire, / flames and cinders'. In fact, the picture, by Christoffer Wilhelm Eckersberg, shows Copenhagen in 1807. Napoleon had his eye on the Danish-Norwegian navy, so the British saw it as a threat. More than four hundred British battleships sailed into Copenhagen harbour, shelling the city with cannon-shot, mortar rounds and the latest weapon of mass destruction – iron-clad Congreve rockets. For four days gunpowder and shot poured down on Copenhagen, killing 195 civilians and burning down a thousand buildings.

One of these was the home of Grímur Jónsson Thorkelín, an Icelandic scholar who had been appointed Denmark's Keeper of the Royal Privy Archives. On a series of trips between 1786 and 1791, in the service of the King of Denmark, Thorkelín travelled to England 'to study the treasures of the British libraries', as he put it. Amongst the transcripts he brought back were two copies of *Beowulf*. Strange to think the siege, which strengthened Britain's naval supremacy, set back the public emergence of Britain's oldest literary masterpiece. Thorkelín's translation of *Beowulf* was destroyed in the bombardment, but the transcripts were unharmed, and eight years later, in 1815, he finally published the epic's first edition.

When we call *Beowulf* an 'English poem', we are following two centuries of absorption into the literary canon. Thorkelín, working at the beginning of *Beowulf* studies, saw it differently. 'Of events concerning the Danish in the third and fourth centuries,' he titled his edition, 'a Danish poem in the Anglo-Saxon dialect.' In the preface, he underlined this Danish heritage: 'I came home with great success and rich reward,' he recalled of his journey to England, 'and with me a poem that had been absent for more than a thousand years returned to its country of origin.'

Whilst Thorkelín was escaping the siege, a young Danish student was taking part in Copenhagen's defence. Nikolay Grundtvig would prove as significant as Thorkelín for *Beowulf*'s early transmission, as well as 'the greatest single influence on the development of Danish society and culture in the last hundred years', according to his biographer, A. M. Allchin. He developed a philosophy of Nordic spiritualism and disciplined creativity, especially in educational life, and is credited as the ideological founder of the Danish Folk High Schools. He is also, according to the scholar Sven H. Rossel, the man who 'laid the foundation for international *Beowulf* research'. Here, once again, we find epic transcending national borders, reminding us of the tangled roots underneath our maps.

Beowulf fascinated Grundtvig all his life. He considered it 'the earliest known attempt, in any vernacular dialect of modern Europe, to produce an epic poem'. At the age of twenty-five (when he wrote a groundbreaking work on Norse mythology), he argued the need for an edition of the poem. A few years later, he reviewed Thorkelín's 1815 transcript, engaging in a feud with Thorkelín over the errors he found in the latter's work. He kept plugging away at *Beowulf*, delivering the first (partial) translation of the epic in 1820, writing an article on *Beowulf* in 1841, publishing his own edition in 1861, and four years later he completed his translation, at the age of eighty-two. Forget Seamus Heaney, William Morris or any of the poem's many celebrated translators – politically speaking, nobody's engagement with *Beowulf* is as significant as Grundtvig's.

His passion for Anglo-Saxon literature is particularly surprising when you consider Grundtvig's influence on Danish identity. This is a man who has transcended his own time, affecting the development of the Danish welfare system, the campaign against joining the EEC in the 1970s, debates about the Maastricht Treaty of 1992 and the referendum against the euro in 2001. And none of this is separate from Grundtvig's interest in *Beowulf*, because it was through his search for the 'Nordic spirit' in Anglo-Saxon literature that he developed the philosophy of Nordic spiritualism for which he is remembered.

A bus ride north of the Lakes and the Zoological Museum, to the Bispebjerg district. The facade of the Grundtvig Memorial Church soars, ribbed like a giant harp, rising up stepped gables that gnaw the sky like castle parapets. Its structure was conceived in homage to Grundtvig. Dizzy verticals and simple brickwork evoke his spiritual depths and humility – although what to make of the spiky parapets; echoing Grundtvig's appetite for the odd feud? Inside, high neo-Gothic arches vault over the nave and light pours through the long, narrow windows over the altar. There are no paintings or sculptures, no statues or burial slabs. The minimalism is breath-taking, amplified by the scale, the orderly arrangement of 6 million gold-yellow bricks.

I sat on a chair of woven wicker, poring through the Danish Psalm Book. Many of the songs were Grundtvig's compositions. Repeated in Sunday services across the country, these are the words that keep him alive in Danish hearts. What few of the country's dwindling congregation realise, however, is that many of these compositions are translations from Anglo-Saxon, including a popular Easter psalm and a song commonly recited on Ascension Day. They represent the enduring legacy of Grundtvig's immersion in Anglo-Saxon literature.

Losing his job was the key for Grundtvig. Forced to resign as a church minister after a libel case, he found himself with plenty of time on his hands. So he appealed to the Danish king for a grant to study the Anglo-Saxon manuscripts of England. At the time, according to Grundtvig himself, 'Even the most meticulous historians of the Island rarely went further back than the Norman conquest of 1066; at any rate they dispensed with the Anglo-Saxon and Danish epochs as horrible barbarisms.' So Grundtvig aspired 'to get in contact with the Englishman and win him for the Anglo-Saxon and so for Scandinavia'. Eschewing recent military entanglements, Grundtvig identified a deeper cultural fellowship. At its heart was *Beowulf*, a tale 'pure Norse in spirit', he wrote. It belonged to the Danes, just as much as to the English, for its eponymous hero was 'humankind's northern hero'.

But Grundtvig's interest wasn't purely cultural: he was engaging with a heated political debate that coloured the early decades after *Beowulf*'s rediscovery. For many high-profile German scholars, Grundtvig's claims for *Beowulf* were wide of the mark. Jacob Grimm took him to task and the German poet Karl Simrock (who won fame as the definitive modern translator of the *Nibelungenlied*) insisted 'the myth is a German one', just as 'the Angles and Saxons were German peoples, and the setting of the poem lies on this side of the North Sea'. British scholars joined in the debate: on one side, J. M. Kemble dedicated the first British edition of *Beowulf* to Jacob Grimm; on the other, George Stephens protested against the 'grasping and stealing Germans, who . . . publish our finest things as pieces in a "dialect of High-German"!'

This was more than just a matter of a few eggheads getting cranky in their studies. The debate synchronised with a period of deep tension between Danes and their southern neighbours, as Prussia pressed its claims on the region of Schleswig-Holstein. Like the *Kosovo Cycle* and many other epics, poetry wasn't just words; it was also territory.

The 'Schleswig-Holstein Question' led to armed conflict, first in Denmark's favour in 1848–51 and later to Prussian gain in 1863, followed by a policy of strategic Germanisation and the industrialisation of the region's valuable ports. It was an important stage in the growth of German nationalism, a stage which would lead to more devastating events in the twentieth century. Showing the continued resonance of *Beowulf* in this debate, a ship built for the German Imperial Navy in the 1890s was named the SMS *Beowulf* (under a ship class named Siegfried) and it took part in an assault on the Baltic port of Libau during the First World War. Although the SMS *Beowulf* was decommissioned after 1915, the name continued to strike a chord: during the Second World War a German mission to occupy islands off the Baltic coast was named Operation Beowulf.

For Grundtvig, then, championing *Beowulf* was part of his Danish nationalism, reflecting a patriotic seam that runs through his work and helps to explain his continuing popularity today. 'Of a people all are members / who regard themselves as such,' he wrote in one of his most popular verses, 'those whose mother tongue sounds sweetest / and their fatherland love much.'

Like many Britons, a large proportion of Danes are wary of EU influence, proud of their independent geography and history. But they are also proud of their nation's liberal, philanthropic reputation, which many Danes continue to trace to Grundtvig's philosophy, and which helps to maintain Denmark's high perch on global 'happiness' surveys. So the influx of refugees in recent years, fleeing countries at the other end of the 'happiness' ladder, has provoked plenty of soul-searching about the sort of country Denmark wants to be.

In Copenhagen, as in so many of Europe's capitals, the refugee population is conspicuous: easy to pick out amongst all the blue eyes, square glasses and topknots. For the sake of my budget, and with Iceland's piratical price tags to come, I saved myself a few hundred kroner by night-spotting at the Central Station. Come the witching hour, many of my fellow nocturnals were chatting in Arabic, or there were African guys listening to their tunes, hunching on the benches, trying the deal on fried dough balls at McDonald's.

I had heard about a refugee welcome centre, and after contacting its administrators, set off to pay a visit. Stepping through the glass doors of the municipality building, I sat under a bright wall mural of a hammer-wielding Thor and photographs of old Copenhagen. To one side of me was a Palestinian man, who had come to Denmark to seek medical help for his autistic son. To my other side was a young Afghan-Iranian who had left home after converting to Christianity. As so often during my journey, I was struck by the range of motivations for flight, stories so much more complicated than the media clichés. Perhaps the most surprising was a Syrian chemist, who had escaped not one but two different war zones.

'I had my own pharmacy,' he explained.

It was a good life. I had a family, a business, a car, a house, but Assad bombed my town, the country became a living hell. My wife was Ukrainian, so we talked about going to the Ukraine – and then what happens? A war broke out in Ukraine as well! It made so many problems for us, so many arguments. My wife took my son to the Crimea, but he hated it there and it stunted his growth. Now he's here with me, and my wife is over there.

I had met dozens of refugees during the course of my journey, and the differences between their stories floored me. They were fleeing broken societies still hot with the ashes of war. 'Syria is finished.' 'If they send me back I will kill myself.' 'There is nothing in my country but pain.' When they talked about their homelands, it was like listening to Wiglaf's prophecy of doom in the closing stages of *Beowulf*.

Epics aren't only foundational texts, they are also climactic, apocalyptic; stories from the end of days. Troy, medieval Serbia, Beowulf's Geats: these are societies on the verge of collapse, endings that will lead to new beginnings. So it goes, and so it always has. Trauma for millions, but also the potential for something new. To start again, like Aeneas building Rome or the Norse and Celtic refugees who founded Iceland and made their own stories there.

Many refugees were busting their guts to reinvent their lives. But for others, it was harder to turn away from their troubled past. They were still caught inside it, unable to step across, sinking into the underworld that spits them into early graves and worse. I had met a few of these troubled souls on my way through Europe.

'Nobody helps me!' complained a young Syrian in Bremen, where I'd stopped on my way to Copenhagen. 'I only want people to see I am a human being!' We shared a sandwich and talked for a while about Syria – I remembered my visit to Aleppo sixteen years earlier. But the conversation unravelled at the bus stop. I was waiting to ride to Copenhagen, and he told me I should pay for his fare – he wanted to go to Berlin, to collect some identity papers. 'I want you to show you recognise a human being,' he said. The cost of this revelation would be thirty-six euros, which was more than my daily spending.

'I'm on a pretty tight budget,' I said, offering five euros and a packet of biscuits. But he threw the biscuits at my chest.

'This is it? Fuck you!'

I remember sitting, tucked against the window of the bus, looking down on the red-lit puddles. Seething a little, twisting inside a curious interlacing of shame and indignation. I'd had a few other difficult encounters during my journey through Europe. They were rare, but they tended to knock me for six, left me wondering if I'd done something wrong. Thinking about the angry Syrian in Bremen, I sat in the bus, wondering over my failure to reach out to him. And for a few moments, I imagined myself through those troubled eyes: glowing with privilege, light with the ease with which I was able to move around. As much a monster as the bright lights of Heorot to Grendel.

25

It came to pass
with speed amongst the men that it was ready,
the greatest of hall-dwellings, named Heorot
by he who widely ruled with words.

Beowulf, First Fit

Leaving Copenhagen, I took an evening train towards Lejre, the old pagan capital of the Scyldings. Against the lights of the station, rain was shooting down arrows, which melted against my coat as I stepped outside. I was tramping towards my final Beowulfian stop: the place where the story begins.

The moon was tombed in cloud, which parted occasionally to show the stars, strewn like precious stones in a high king's barrow. I had to turn away from the sky to focus on the path, otherwise I was dealing out death on the ubiquitous slugs. A fatal squish underfoot and I stopped, pulled off my glasses to give them a wipe-down. I felt a shiver down my back and did up the top buttons of my coat. Rain had been harassing me for much of the summer, but now it wasn't just wet, it was bone-chilling, a couple of degrees below zero. And with wintrier climes to come, it was only going to get worse.

Fortunately, there was a thatched barn near the museum: my refuge for the night. I sat scribbling in my diary, on a table splattered in bird droppings, and lay my sleeping bag under schoolchildren's paintings – warriors in horned helmets and dragon-prowed longships on zigzagging waves. I'd been planning to sleep on one of the Dark Age barrows, but the rain wasn't having it. So I ended up cooped in the barn, listening to my headphones, blocking out the drumming on the roof with the rolling tones of Benjamin Bagby:

Þa wæs Hroðgare heresped gyfen,
Then was Hrothgar granted good fortune,
wiges weorðmynd . . . Him on mod bearn
glory in battle . . . To his mind it came
Þæt healreced hatan wolde,
That a hall-dwelling he would have,
medoærn micel men gewyrcean
A mighty mead hall for men to build,
þone yldo bearn æfre gefrunon . . .
Greater than ever men's children had heard . . .

Although the setting isn't named in the poem, scholarly consensus has long settled on Lejre, for this was the seat of the Scyldings, the ancient kings of Denmark whose dynastic lines are traced in the poem's opening: 'the glory in bygone days of the folk-kings of the spear-Danes'.

I was deep in farming land. Morning light oozed inside the barn and I unsealed myself from my sleeping bag, stepping out amongst slumbering cows and beautiful, sleek brown horses. The sweet, clammy smell of manure, heightened by the rain, mixed with the blasts of methane. It smelt too lively for a burial ground, but there they were: the pagan barrows of Lejre, rising over the fields like a chain of atolls.

Although the rain had softened, the morning was streaked with spittings. Puddles stained the path that trailed, under the unexcavated 'Raven's Mound', past the flat-topped 'Shelf Mound', running between nettles and fans of sorrel. Here, in these barrows, Scylding kings were buried – although many of the barrows were still waiting to unleash their secrets. I climbed the steep camber of the 'Cooking-Pot Mound', where teazles rustled out of darkened earth that still bore traces of ritual ceremonies, soil wounds stretching back more than a dozen centuries. Standing on the grassy lid, I was looking over the 'ship graves' – a line of granite stones, guiding the dead on their last sea journey to Valhalla. I felt like a watchman on a headland, looking out for dragon-prowed ships. Lichen-streaked and tapering, these granite fins scraped the sky, cleaving the tiniest rift through which to spy on *Beowulf*'s pagan, seafaring world.

Long after Lejre was abandoned as a major settlement, travellers continued to be drawn to its legend. The German traveller Ole Worm wandered here in the seventeenth century, learning local names for the barrows and the traditions of the Scyldings; another German, the literary scholar Gregor Sarrazin, followed him in 1865. A few years earlier (in 1850), a hoard was discovered in hills to the west of the village, including a Hiberno-Saxon silver bowl. Later, in the 1940s, a tenth-century burial ground revealed tortoise brooches and a stone spindle whorl, along with the trunk of a beheaded slave. But it was the excavations between 1977 and 2002 that reasserted Lejre's pre-eminence in Danish culture.

Local politics has a habit of shadowing archaeology. In the case of Lejre, many of the mounds were inaccessible because they were on farmland, and archaeologists were kept busy with their involvement in new developments. It was only because a farm had burned down that they were able to excavate the mound of Fredshøjgård, which has since been associated with Hrothgar's mead hall in *Beowulf*. Most of the mounds still haven't been opened, but to judge from what has been discovered so far, there is plenty of motivation for further digs. Among the exhibits in the museum are rune-covered bones, trefoil brooches, spindle whorls, gilded weights, sword pommels, an amulet of Thor's hammer, an iron sword with a Damascus steel pattern on the blade and – the pride of the collection – a tiny hollow silver Odin seated on his throne, one of less than a dozen extant figures of the one-eyed Nordic god.

The museum proudly asserts Lejre's role as the birthplace of Danish identity: 'the story of the kingdom of Denmark begins in Lejre' declares a board depicting Nikolay Grundtvig (mounted, surreally, on Odin's eight-legged horse, Sleipnir, working on his translation of *Beowulf*). But 'with its roots in the Viking social order and belief in Norse gods,' the screed explains, 'Lejre now had to surrender its power.' Round about AD 1000, Lejre was abandoned. The conversion of Harald Bluetooth (famous these days for the wireless technology named after him) transformed Denmark into a Christian country, leading to the establishment of a cathedral and new capital at Roskilde.

'When I was at school,' said Ditta, who worked at the museum, 'they told us nothing about Lejre – everything began with the conversion to Christianity. But my grandparents knew that Lejre was a powerful place, and now with the recent archaeology, that's being discovered again.'

After an amateur digger turned up at Roskilde Museum in 2000, with a handful of jewellery and mounts, archaeologists gathered around the field of Fredshøjgård. Their attention focused on the edge of a prominent bluff, which overlooks the surrounding fields. Deducing from the holes left by long-rotten posts what once existed here, the archaeologists traced the ghostly outline of a 150-foot-long hall. Its walls curved, like the hull of a ship, widening the hall from twenty-six feet at the gable ends to thirty-six feet at the midpoint (twice the width of an ordinary Viking house from this period). The association with Heorot was irresistible. 'What the *Beowulf* poet presents,' as archaeologist John D. Niles put it, 'leaving his superlatives aside, is an image of an Iron Age hall not unlike the one that archaeology has now revealed.'

This has been a rewarding century for the relationship between epic and archaeology. Around the same time as a palace has been revealed in Ithaca, and new discoveries at King Nestor's palace in Pylos; just as treasures have been unearthed in old Mercia, enriching our understanding of Anglo-Saxon craft, so a 'mighty hall-dwelling' has been discovered here in the land of the Scyldings. Not that anyone assumes the *Beowulf* scop would have visited, but it's tempting to imagine the rumours of a great hall reaching across the North Sea, along with tales of an eerie landscape and heroic feats.

Now, wandering the spongy sward, I followed low banks of sod and turf, which mark the extent of the walls. Slugs were sucking at the vegetation, like half-cut warriors whoozy with mead; beetles climbed around the toadstools, as if they were visitors looking for the front door. The drizzle was pattering down, wet grass and nettles drooling on my trousers. A school group stretched out tape measures while their teachers skulked under umbrellas, and a man with a majestic handlebar moustache rode by on a black mare.

South of the mound were the woods of Hearthadal, milky under the spittering sky. Retreating icecaps had moulded this moraine landscape, drilling it with kettle holes and erosion gullies, raising hillocks spiny with oak and beech: a rugged counterpoint to Lejre's soft pastures and hallowed barrows. *Beowulf*, like many monster stories, is often misread as a contest between civilisation and the wild, and Lejre's bipolar landscape teases this division. But *Beowulf* does something more complicated, and if we can dig down far enough, we can glimpse the treasure embedded in this enigmatic poem.

Civilisation has been defeated. As Hrothgar tells Beowulf, 'men have boasted, drunk with beer, officers over their cups of ale, that they could abide in the beer-hall Grendel's attack with a rush of sword terror'. But all have failed, leaving 'benches gory, the hall spattered and befouled'. Tackling Grendel requires more than civilisation: a hero who boasts of slaughtering 'a tribe of giants' and fighting 'sea monsters at night'. Not for Beowulf the tools of civilisation: he grapples the monster with his bare arms, as ferocious as any of nature's devisings. This isn't civilisation's champion against nature – this is a lone phenomenon caught between them. In other words: a hero. The same word, *æglæca*, meaning 'awesome one' or 'terror', is applied not only to Grendel and the dragon, but also to Beowulf. 'Bee-wolf' – the 'bear': it takes more than a man to tackle nature's worst.

This is a paradigm shift splitting north and south. The weapon devising of Odysseus, the technological know-how and verbal guile are stamped down, the disguises and tricks of the Balkan heroes are trampled under a beefy boast of courage and strength. 'I shall perform a deed of manly courage,' declares Beowulf, 'or in this mead hall I will await the end of my days!' Long after Mediterranean heroes had monopolised cunning, the heroes of the north defined themselves by brawn.

But, between the differences, layers of connection can be glimpsed. Beowulf, like Roland, refuses to accept assistance from others and defeats his enemy by mortally wounding his arm. Like Odysseus, sailing with a retinue of followers, battling monsters in faraway places (including a man-eating giant who snacks on his crew), he comes back at last, fighting his final battle around the wreck of his hall. Odysseus had a younger kinsman to stand alongside him – and so does Beowulf. But it isn't enough: the dragon is a more dangerous proposition than a cluster of gluttonous suitors. What Beowulf needs is more support, but his thanes desert him. The poet is unambiguous: they are 'weak traitors'.

What does this mean? Good kings are defined by the loyalty they inspire in the men around them (Arthur and Camelot, Charlemagne and his paladins; even the weak King Gunther in the *Nibelungenlied* is able to count on his followers). By this measurement, Beowulf must be considered a poor king indeed. He leaves his people unprotected, at the mercy of 'the feud and the fierce enmity', as Wiglaf prophesises. Here is a lesson about heroes: great for slaying monsters, sure, but when it comes to the more complicated matters of running a court of loyal retainers and carving a sustainable dynasty, mere mortals are a safer bet.

We may never resolve the question of where *Beowulf* was composed (for my money, East Anglia shades the Midlands — for the synthesis of language, folklore and landscape), but here at the core of the story, we can unravel the poet's motivation: *Beowulf* is European epic's most piercing investigation into the nature of the hero. A Christian poet looking back into a romanticised, tribal past, asking what it takes to slay the monsters; and in the process, revealing his flaws along with his strengths.

For those left behind, there is 'a time of trouble' to come, as Wiglaf foresees. For Saxons in the aftermath of the Norman Conquest, this tale of civilisational collapse must have spoken with tremendous force. Reading it now, Wiglaf's fear of hostility from the European mainland after decades of cordial relations has a telling resonance.

I had a room booked in the village of Kirke Såby that night, seven miles north. Hiking out of Lejre, I forded a shallow stream thanks to a well-placed pallet. Rosehips glistened bloodily, autumn's ripening, and the moss was thick against the trees, luridly green. Open your mouth and you could taste it in the air.

I dived into the Hearthadal (or 'Deer Wood'), feet pressing down on coppery leaves, until a golf course improbably bellied across my path. A couple of shaggy-coated cattle squatted on the fairway like reluctant watchguards. The forest regrouped and a pair of cuckoos called out their two-note query, like border guards ushering in the forest dwellers.

Dusk would be falling soon, and I wanted to get plenty of rest. Tomorrow, I would be camping on a Swedish hillside; the three-day ferry to Iceland was only a few days away. But I was sad to be leaving *Beowulf* behind. Was this my tribalism? I liked the idea that *Beowulf* connected my English identity with Danes and Swedes, and with the wider Germanic sphere suggested by the epic's digressions (the tale of Sigurd/Siegfried the dragon slayer, for example). It didn't feel so much the closely guarded treasure of an isolated nation as a magnificent bounty shared between neighbours. But I wanted more, I wanted to stretch that feeling further, spanning the continent, from the Arctic Circle to the Black Sea and beyond.

In front of me, a stag stood his ground, stiller than anything else in the Deer Wood; stiller than the oak trees, thrashing cable roots over dark troll holes; stiller than the carrs, the forest lakes where thirsty alders probed the water like cartridge pens dipped in ink. His antlers rhymed with the branches of the oaks and his coat with the wrinkling leaves. His eye was a nugget of gold, polished by the lowering sun. Here was the organic intertwining of Anglo-Saxon art; the cross-hatching between Grendel and the sinister moors where he lurks. I yielded the path to the king of the forest and minced between the trees, footfall soft on the falling leaves of the deep, dark wood.

PART SIX

A Wasteland of Equals

Njal's Saga

Gunnar is the mightiest warrior in Iceland, but he has a lot of enemies. Luckily, his best friend is Njal, the finest lawyer in the land, so he's usually able to keep them at bay. But when Gunnar falls in love with the beautiful but prickly Hallgerda, whose last two marriages ended in violent death, Njal warns this could bring down a storm of trouble on his head.

Acts of theft and murder – there's nothing Hallgerda won't stoop to. But it's Gunnar who takes the rap and, after a spell of bloody incidents stirred by a trouble-maker called Mord, he is sentenced to three years' exile. Even Njal's legal finesse can't spare him this time. But leaving his beloved home is more than Gunnar can bear. Forty of his enemies converge on his farmhouse, and when Hallgerda refuses to help him mend his bowstring, he realises his luck has run out. He goes down fighting, a hero to the end.

But Gunnar's death doesn't end the feuding. Some years later, Njal's combative sons satisfy a grudge by killing their rival Thrainn, and Njal adopts the dead man's son, Hoskuld, in the hope of avoiding further bloodletting. But his sons, goaded by the troublemaker Mord, kill Hoskuld as well. Vengeance is demanded by the dead man's wife, Hildigunna. Her uncle, Flosi, enraged by slanderous insults at the Althing (the Icelandic parliament), sets out for Njal's farmhouse with a lynch mob. When they are unable to break inside, they set the house on fire.

Njal is killed, along with his wife, sons and grandson, but his son-in-law, Kari, manages to escape through a window. After a trial over the burning descends into a brawl, Kari sets off overseas, hunting down the arsonists until only Flosi is left. Both men perform pilgrimages of atonement and eventually they meet at Flosi's farmhouse in reconciliation. As a symbol of the truce, Kari marries Hildigunna, widow of the murdered Hoskuld. After decades of feuds, the cycle of violence has finally been broken.

26

Ever will I gods blaspheme,
Freyja methinks a dog does seem,
Freyja a dog? Aye! Let them be
Both dogs together, Odin and she.
Hjalti Skeggjason, *Njal's Saga,*
Chapter 98

T HE SAGAS WERE calling – the tale of a lawyer burnt in his
farmhouse, a curmudgeon who died of magical wounds on a
remote islet, a farmer's daughter who falls in love in a hotpot. But
first, I had a date with a dragon slayer.

It was early morning on a Swedish hillside. I was a few miles out
of Eskilstuna, and a few feet out of my tent, and there he was
standing next to me. The dragon slayer looked quite pushy: chunky
arms, no neck, small bendy legs. A cross between a prizefighter and
a caveman. But since he was carved from the rock I was standing
on, I was safe at least from his blade.

It was deep in the coiling tail of a dragon, which was engraved
with runes, circling the scene like the wrap-around margin on an
illuminated manuscript. Birds, a horse, a decapitated blacksmith: the
storytelling was dramatic, and diagrammatic. I'd seen these details
before, on a church facade in Spain (not far from Roncesvalles, in
the village of Sanguesa); and I'd read about them in the thirteenth-
century *Volsung Saga*, written down two centuries after this carving
was made.

This isn't just *another* dragon slaying – it's the very dragon slaying
I'd followed in Germany. The story tells of Sigurd (the Scandinavian
name for Siegfried), who eats the dragon's heart and consequently

learns the language of birds. They warn him of imminent treachery by Regin the blacksmith, so he kills his former tutor, and loads his horse with treasure. Descended from the same source that morphed into the *Nibelungenlied*, the *Volsung Saga* was plundered by Richard Wagner for his operas and is briefly retold in *Beowulf*, recited to the tune of a harp in Hrothgar's mead hall. The setting remains the same – Burgundian Worms and a climax at the court of Attila the Hun. But the Norse version ratchets up the gore and swaps the Mitteleuropa obsession with rank for the fire of sexual jealousy. Of all the stories I tracked around Europe, this was the most ubiquitous, the most flexible, the most viral.

It was one of the stories carried by ninth-century seafarers fleeing the tyranny of the Scandinavian kings, which is how it ended up being written down in thirteenth-century Iceland. Those medieval emigrants left their peninsula in crowded longships, stowing infant livestock to reduce their cargo, guided by the flight patterns of seabirds north of the Faroes. What they found was a forested island, carpeted with rich pasture, its rivers teeming with fish. Thorolf, one of these early settlers, claimed butter dripped from the grass. His leader, Flóki Vilgerðarson, was less sunny-minded. After glowering into a fjord full of drift ice, he declared this was *Is-land*, a 'land of ice'.

Now I was following them, boarding a pine-panelled train and an air-conditioned bus towards the tip of Jutland to catch the bi-weekly Smyril Lines Ferry. While the flocks were migrating towards their winter nests in Africa, I was northward-bound, keeping up with the cold and the blush of reddening leaves. I was on the track of my final tale, *Njal's Saga* (or, to give its longer title, *The Saga of Burnt Njal*), whose most dynamic hero, Gunnar, is likened to Siegfried and marries a woman descended, so she claims, from the dragon slayer himself. A story that drags epic by the roots and pulls it towards the modern world. With its irascible menfolk, brawling females and climactic massacre, it has plenty in common with the epics I'd been following. But the hero who gives his name to the story is no muscle-bound warrior. Njal is physically unthreatening, passing from middle to old age, a lawyer with the gift of prophecy. He points back towards ancient seers like Tiresias, and forward to the legislators who were beginning to prise power away from the strongmen. As I travelled into Iceland, I wanted to learn how this complex 'valkyrie's web' of a story interacts with the epic tradition, explores and adapts and, eventually, transcends it.

Strictly speaking, *Njal's Saga* isn't an epic but a saga (although the etymology is the same: *saga*, from *seyja* – 'to say'), one of the forty 'family sagas' written down in medieval Iceland. A prose tale, although it also contains verse, based on events that happened around the turn of the first millennium, it was written down by an anonymous author around 1280. So popular did it prove that twenty-one medieval manuscripts have been discovered so far; and as I would discover, there are versions of the tale still being told.

Inside the ferry, I was billeted in a dormitory in the hull, with a Sikh motorbiker's turban as a foot-warmer. The atmosphere was stiff, conversation sporadic. It was the ship that did the talking: cables creaking, engines growling, the 'shook' of pressure when you slid open the metal doors on deck. I thrilled at the curdling waves, the sea darkening as we approached the Faroes, the ship's wake moulded by phosphorescence into braids of liquid metal, like jewellery in a giant's smithy.

Pressing my palms against the shuddering railings, I only had to close my eyes and I was on a steel howdah strapped to a sea dragon. The water was silver-grey, the colour of chainmail. Winched by a stiff north-easterly, the breakers formed tent-like peaks, snapping at the chines like an enemy camp ready for a siege. Gobbets of swell bashed against the bows in flash-powder streaks. *This* is the North Sea, I thought: the 'whale's riding' (to use the kenning from *Beowulf*). Or, as the medieval Arab scholar al-Idrissi put it: 'the sea of perpetual gloom'.

In the glow of dawn after the third night, birds were scudding over the waves. Great skuas wheeled over the radar spinney, rasping their ambiguous welcome: '*Kjo! Kjo! Kjo!*' Fulmars raced alongside us, like conscientious pilots, measuring out the wind along the bows. Blue cloud seethed on the horizon, slowly darkening into something more substantial, fractured with crevasses, silvered by waterfalls. The slopes ran at sheer angles down to the sea: a wrinkly giant, shaggy with lichen. Tour leaders scanned their clipboards, truck drivers flicked cigarette butts and a fleet of traffic slid past the clapboard houses of Seyðisfjörður. The stragglers were herded into a bus to the nearest town, Egilsstaðir. Spongy downs crumbled around us, dissolving into watery cascades that fed the gurgling rills in the meadows. There was no bus north for another three days, but I couldn't bear the prospect of kicking my heels – I'd only just arrived, I was itching to explore! I had plans to hike to a pagan memorial at the north-eastern edge of the island, to tramp among saga sites before sliding south to Reykjavik and the settings of *Njal's Saga* – battle rocks, rivers and fountains, the heroes' farmsteads. But now I could feel the thought like a slap to the head: how the hell am I going to get around?

Meet Lyor. He's got a camper van, with a plug-in for his phone, a TomTom so he can key in his destination, a compartment in the back to store his food and a washing line slung above to dry his clothes. Long-haired and squirrel-eyed, he radiates the positive energy of a traveller at home on the road. A barista from Tel Aviv, he's the first driver to stop for me, a couple of miles out of Egilsstaðir.

'Look at the map – I've put down my route, so if you need to go anywhere along here, I can take you.'

I'm hoping to reach the outpost of Raufarhöfn, a fishing haven with a monument to Norse mythology, 164 miles north-east. This will set me on the way: after twisting my thumb at the traffic for nearly two hours, catching a ride is a relief.

The ring road is a tarred conveyor belt around the country. Traffic is so calm you can see truck drivers working on their laptops or eating bowls of yoghurt-like *skyr*. But the B-roads are less polished. As far as Lyor is concerned, there's only one way to beat them: flat-mash the throttle and drive flat out.

'You gotta show the road who's boss!' He refuses my offer of petrol money – 'I'd feel like a taxi driver!' Instead, he comes up with a curious method of payment. 'You said you're here for the sagas. So, I wanna know what they're all about!'

If only I could use this currency elsewhere! During the long hours on the ferry, I've been reading the sagas. In the absence of ferry conversation, I found myself amongst medieval farmers, outlaws, lovers, poets, sea raiders and sorceresses with atmospheric names like Unn the Deep-Minded, Gunnlaug Serpent-Tongue, Ulf the Unwashed. Now, for a couple of hours, I become a hitch-hiking troubadour.

The one I spend most of our journey narrating is *Njal's Saga*. I rattle through the ill-fated early marriages of the capricious Hallgerda, her feud with Njal's wife Bergthora, Gunnar's bold stand when his enemies descend on his farmhouse, the trail of slander and slayings that leads to the incineration of Njal's farm, and before we've reached the final killing, the landscape has passed through several million years of geological transformation.

'Oh man!' says Lyor, rapping the steering wheel. 'I wish we had stories like this in my culture.'

'But you do!' I peer across the orange pastel sands and cones of black rock like charred dunes. Take away the clouds, soften the tones a little, and this could almost be the Negev.

'Yeah,' says Lyor, 'but the Bible stories are always tied up with religion. You can't just enjoy them as stories.'

I'm not sure the contrast is so stark. The *Song of Roland*, the *Kosovo Cycle*, the Homeric epics . . . Even *Njal's Saga*, which influenced the nineteenth-century movement for Icelandic independence and the re-establishment of the Althing (the Icelandic parliament), has had a considerable impact on its society's codification. That's the trouble with stories: entertaining us isn't enough. The bossier ones can't resist telling us how to behave.

Sulphurous yellow wash trickles down from the sides of mountains. Lava clinkers scatter across plains of palagonite, rising in cairn-like turrets and twisted battlements with pinnacles like gargoyles, casting spears of shadow over crater rings of Martian red. A wasteland, perhaps: there's little vegetation all the way to the settlement of Asbyrgi. But this is an evolving landscape of expanding rifts, congealing cinder hills and surging rivers nibbling at banks of moraine: 25 million years young, a country so juvenile it threw up the world's newest island (Surtsey) in 1963.

This frenzy is given roaring voice by the waterfalls. Ripping through the soft clasps of soil, bursting the tufa, they batter the bedrock with the ferocity of spear-throwing warriors. At Dettifoss, we clamber over basalt boulders to feel the spray, thrilling to the mighty sheets of water that throw themselves over the edge. Dettifoss is the largest waterfall in Europe, but it's the speed that amazes: dust and sand haven't slowed down the brown-grey chutes to much less than 400 cubic metres per second. Sitting beside the falls, Lyor brews some tea on his stove and we sit, hypnotised by the rushing wall of water and the icy sparkles of rebound.

Green-blue cliffs of rhyolite and silky red craters span the track to Asbyrgi, where woods of birch and spruce float between the cliffs of a horseshoe-shaped canyon formed by the Jökulsa, the same river that feeds Dettifoss. Lyor is heading west, so I climb out and wave goodbye, watching his camper van plunge towards the pale hills on the far side of a bridge.

I've broken the back of the journey, but Raufarhöfn and its monument to Norse mythology is still a long way north. Bowled a few miles up the road by a salmon farm manager called Thomas, I pace beside a T-junction, jumping backwards into bog grass to avoid getting splashed when the rare car passes by; and jumping forwards when a rackety pick-up pulls over.

'Get in, you're soaked!'

Kristin and Anna, both from Norway, are volunteering on a couple of nearby farmsteads. I'm grateful for the lift, although I can't help wondering where all the Icelanders are. In the country with Europe's smallest population (just 300,000), foreigners are all the more conspicuous. And unlike the refugees on the mainland, these ex-pats and short-term labourers are mostly affluent enough to drive themselves around – luckily for me.

Tuffets rise out of the peat heaths, in prickly formations that rationalise local stories about trolls. Mountains of scree slide to scrub bushes and birch, and grey trachyte snakes down the hillsides to nourish the vegetable patches. Kristin and Anna drop me beside the track to Raufarhöfn and I set off on a twenty-mile hike, under slate-coloured clouds, towards the edge of Iceland.

For the next five hours, I meet nobody – not a car, a motorbike or a hiker. I slide towards cliffs streaked white with guano. My boots crunch on stony lava chips, and sometimes I think I can hear a motor.

I look behind, a little hopeful, a little wary. But there's nobody behind me: the sound is an illusion conjured by the gravelly tempo of my own footfall. I'm far from any sign of habitation, accompanied only by the shrieking of invisible seafowl and the lugubrious mountain line that follows my steps – a scaly, hibernating beast. With the darkness comes mounting paranoia. What if the path crumbles into a river or an unpassable cliff? I'm winging it, guided only by a squiggly line on my phone, which is rapidly running out of battery. There are no lights on the horizon and for a couple of hours I don't pass a single homestead. I've stepped into a void, like the primordial chasm from which the world is conjured in the *Edda*.

At last, a distant flickering resolves into a bracelet of electric lights strung across the other side of a bay. Pulling my coat tighter, I follow an inky shoreline and trudge into Raufarhöfn. With the eerie timing of a horror movie, the lights snap out, one by one. I've arrived bang on bedtime.

At the edge of town, protected from the sea by a mound of turf, is an uninhabited campsite. I drop my backpack on the duckboard and plunge inside a corrugated-iron toilet cabin. Like something from a dream – a radiator! Even the stench from the toilet bowl can't push me away. My legs are shaking and my hands swollen, shiny pink like rubber gloves. Now they're thawing, recovering enough feeling to uncap a miniature bottle of Chivas Regal that I bought on the ferry. *Mmmmm . . .*

To cross so much of this dramatic landscape on my first day has been thrilling. It's strange to think I'm still on the same continent as those sun-baked hills in Greece, where the blossom burst from the trees and grapes bubbled in the vineyards. Glimpses of the sea have shown a different texture from the beguiling turquoise of the Mediterranean. But, as the *Odyssey* and refugee stories have taught me, the Mediterranean isn't as calm as it looks; and the North Sea, for all its grey thrashing savagery, isn't untraversable: that's one of the lessons of the sagas.

Iceland looks, and feels, like the island at the edge. But one of the many virtues of *Njal's Saga* is its contradiction of the cliché. The hero Gunnar visits Norway, other characters travel as far as Rome and Constantinople. As I cross the island, I hope to learn about the pull and push between its independent identity and the threads of connections with the rest of Europe. Because if a country as far apart as Iceland can plug into pan-European story patterns, surely that's the proof they really do straddle the continent.

Raufarhöfn was the northernmost town in Iceland, and it felt like it. Corrugated-iron blocks locked together in a prefab grid, a chilly atmosphere unheated by all the puffy hearts and balloon faces leering through the windows. Most of the stores and cafes were closed, only opening when somebody phoned up the owner. You wouldn't expect to find grand memorials or pompous statues here. But on a hill behind a horse paddock, there's an evolving monument known as the Heimskautsgerd – the 'Arctic Henge'.

This is the *Edda* in stone – the names of seventy-two dwarves arranged as calendar markers, distributed around a giant sundial to catch the midnight rays of midsummer. On the summit of the hill, a ring of six metre-high stone gates surrounds a central, 11-metre-high column of four leaning pillars topped by a capstone.

Many of the poems that form the *Edda* are composed in what Eddic specialist Terry Gunnell calls 'metre magic'. This draws on the Eddic belief in poetry as the 'mead of Odin', drunk by the god from a giant's cauldron. The *Edda* juggles literature and liturgy: conversion through verse, words as drops of magic potion. I wanted to reach this northern prong of Iceland – to gauge the scale of the landscape before heading towards the saga settings; and to think about the pagan beliefs – the *Ásatrú* – which play such a key role in tales like *Njal's Saga*, as they do in other crossover stories of the Nordic world, like *Beowulf.*

Most of the monuments I had visited were the reassembled ruins of long ago, but here was a monument yet to be completed. Standing on the hilltop, I was looking at the future as much as the past, a monument in double time. There are plans to build a 1.5-metre-high encircling wall and plant a crystal capstone on the central column, reflecting sunlight all over the henge. This is a bridge, not only into Iceland's heritage but all of Northern Europe's. The *Edda* harvests a wide range of matter, including the tale of Sigurd/Siegfried the dragon slayer, Thor's battles with giants, the dwarfish lore that inspired Tolkien (and gave him iconic names like 'Gandalf'). Away from the extinctions and evolutions that purged so much continental storytelling, Iceland became cold storage for mythology, keeping these tales safe from oblivion.

This is what made them dangerous. With their broadly Norse genetic background, the Icelanders represented, for the Nazis, old Germanic bloodlines uncontaminated by miscegenation (although the early Icelanders hailed from many backgrounds, including a large Celtic population, as the title *Njal's Saga* suggests). So powerful was the link that Hitler, in his youth, conceived a pseudo-Wagnerian opera set in Iceland, based on the legend of Wieland, the mythical blacksmith who forged, amongst others, Beowulf's mail-shirt, Siegfried's sword Gram and Roland's sword Durandal. According to the Führer's friend August Kubizek, 'From the *Edda*, a book that was sacred for him, he knew Iceland, the rugged island of the North . . . There he laid the setting of his opera, for there Nature herself was still in those passionate convulsions which inspired the actions of gods and human beings.' The opera was never completed: 'new, pressing problems requiring immediate solution confronted my friend' and the opera was put aside: '"Wieland the Smith", Adolf's opera, remained a fragment.'

It's an intriguing image: the megalomaniac-in-the-making, cherry-picking the myths of northern Europe, hammering out bombastic melodies from his Viennese bedsit. In its own dark way, this reflects the interconnectedness between Iceland and the rest of Europe. But it proved a major stumbling block for the revival of the Ásatrú faith in the second half of the twentieth century. When the poet Sveinbjorn Beteinsson sought official recognition of Iceland's growing pagan community in the 1960s, the Lutheran bishop cited the Nazis as a reason to withhold it, claiming they had used elements of the old religion as a basis for their 'supreme Aryan race'. But recognition came, and in 1973 the first *blót* (pagan gathering) was held since the eleventh century, in front of a statue of Thor on Beteinsson's farm.

A couple of weeks after my trip to the Arctic Henge, I walked through the drizzle of Reykjavik to the first pagan temple built on Icelandic soil since the age of the early settlers. My guide amongst those stacks of rebars and rain-spattered piping was Hilmar Örn Hilmarsson, Beteinsson's successor as chief *godi*, or 'high priest'.

'It's going to take a long time to complete it,' Hilmar admitted. 'But we're very keen to build it out of the landscape, using local stone and the warm springs under the ground for water. For us, nature is alive – you see these ideas in the *Havamal* [one of the most popular poems in the *Edda*].'

Listening to Hilmar, I thought of Gunnar in *Njal's Saga*, whose emotional connection to the landscape is so powerful he is unable to bear the prospect of leaving it. This is the hinge on which his fate swings, and it results in his death. Later, in one of the saga's most iconically 'pagan' scenes, he is depicted, a ghostly presence in his barrow, singing songs with an 'exultant' face. The poetry-reciting pagan warrior who, even in death, cannot be pulled away from his beloved home.

The henge had entranced me. There was something magnificent in building this monument so far from the population heartlands, and the difficulty of the enterprise was reflected in its unfinished state. Now I was looking for the place that symbolised the end of Icelandic paganism – a moment described in *Njal's Saga*.

Delivered out of Raufarhöfn by a kindly local plumber called Indrinn, I walked a couple of miles, past the settlement of Asbyrgi, and struck luck again when a couple of kindergarten teachers, Greta and Tara, offered me a lift. They were on their way to the 'northern capital' of Akureyri to watch a movie. They chatted breezily – everything from horror movies to nicknames for dodgy bankers ('We call them Vikings!' chirruped Greta) – as heaths stretched desolate around us and lonely cinder hills softened to scratchy pasture.

About thirty miles east of Akureyri, I waved back to the shrinking car and made my way past a petrol station. Running from deep in the highlands, the river Skjalfondafljot carves a corridor through the dales of Barda and plunges over the rocks. Chutes of water fling themselves over the edge, forming curtains over a rocky horseshoe. Here, around the year 1000, the law-speaker and godi Thorgeir Ljosvetninga passed by and tossed his pagan idols into the falls, which were named after him – 'the godi's fall'.

In *Njal's Saga*, many battles break out over the new faith. Missionaries are at loggerheads with old-school sorcerers, who use spells to tear open the ground under the missionaries' horses. 'Did you ever hear,' asks one staunch pagan, 'how Thor challenged Christ to a duel, and Christ did not dare to accept the challenge.' Eventually, the high priest Thorgeir is charged with deciding whether the Icelanders should adopt the new faith or stick with the 'old gods'. He spends a day in meditation, covering his head with a cloak, before pronouncing his decision at the Hill of Laws:

> our matters were come to a deadlock, if we are not all to have one and the same law . . . This is the beginning of our laws, that all men shall be Christian here in the land, and believe in one God, the Father, the Son, and the Holy Ghost, but leave off all idol-worship, not expose children to perish, and not eat horseflesh.

Amongst the early followers of the new creed is Njal. 'In my opinion the new faith is much better,' he declares. Dramatising the transition to a Christian nation, from the perspective of a Christian author, *Njal's Saga* gives the moral high ground to the Christians. But underneath the narrative brush strokes are deeper subtleties. For paganism had already buried itself deep in the subsoil of Iceland. It would take more than a high priest's decree to root it out.

27

It does me little good to be married to the bravest man
in Iceland if you don't avenge this, Gunnar!

Hallgerda, *Njal's Saga*, Chapter 35

I WAS SOAKING in sagas (and given how much it was raining, I mean that literally). The landscape was so richly storied, you could travel around Iceland hopping from one saga to another. After a pit stop in Akureyri, I hitch-hiked along the northern ridge to Saudðárkrókur and trekked around the Skagafjord, under the mineral-rich wall of Tindastoll Mountain. Brooks bubbled and burns sliced the infields, between whinnying ponies and sheep so fat I wondered if old Thorolf the settler was right and the grass really was smeared with butter.

In one of the most popular sagas, a curmudgeon called Grettir battles with farmers, ghouls and a troll-woman, until he is forced to seek refuge on a narrow isle. I was now in 'Grettir country', drawn by the connections between his story and Beowulf's (both fight a ghoulish creature in a hall, a female monster in a watery cavern, and both are deserted by their companions – many scholarly papers have traced the correspondences, illustrating how stories from elsewhere were adapted to Iceland's idiosyncratic landscape).

The stocky, sheer-cliffed isle of Drangey soars out of the water, flanked by two rocky needles, hazed in great skuas and nesting guillemots. Here, according to the saga, Grettir holds off his attackers until magic spells bring him low. Near the headland are two hotpots, built on the site where Grettir legendarily bathed. Mr Eriksson, the shock-haired *jarl* (or landowner) who had them built (one of them, in his honour, is known as the 'Jarl's Bath', the other as 'Grettir's

Bath'), was sipping tea in a hut behind the baths, wrapped warm in lambswool.

'It's a true story,' said his friend Ingi, when I asked about the tale. 'And we still read it, even now!'

It was a day for girding your loins and accepting your punishment – so I warmed my feet on black clinker stones and sank into the hotpot. I might not be able to replicate Grettir's battle with a troll-woman, or his duel with a shining moor-beast, but I was right beside him when it came to having a bath.

Splashing around the largest of the hotpots was a party of naked Russians. Under an ice moon, they climbed in and out, skin glowing in the moonshine. One of them had shown me his photos of the Northern Lights over a mug of noodles in the campsite kitchen, and later he invited me to join them for another dipping. So I slipped back into the warmth of the pot, watching the celestial pazazz of shooting stars. I remembered another watery plunge at the end of the world – all the way back in Greece at Cape Tanairon. Not that I was planning to revisit hell: Iceland had enough spectres to keep its authors busy, so the sagas are resolutely clamped to terra firma.

Meandering around the sagas showed their deep interactions with Iceland's landscape. Not since Sicily had I travelled anywhere so richly storied. Every dale or crag links itself to one of the forty family sagas, and I couldn't resist dabbling in a few of them as I travelled towards Reykjavik. But I was also struck by the connections between these stories and broader European epic traditions. Many of them juggled the native landscape with the older narratives that inspired them. Reading *Grettir's Saga* is like coming across a shaggy burlesque of *Beowulf*, stripped of the latter's epic grandeur but retaining the allure of the eerie. Even more plugged into the mainland is the *Laxardal Saga*, a tale of thwarted passions that adapts elements of the *Nibelungenlied* to the milieu of feuding Icelandic farmers. Its setting spans the western side of Iceland, so I decided to dip into this moody tale on my way south.

Wide stretches of peat bog and glaciated rock stiffened into pasture-land – fodder and fertiliser forming plastic pyramids, pick-up trucks carrying flocks down from the highlands. The Laxa River dissects this region in a gentle descent, falling with the soft contours of the valley, a soothing river swelling to a salt lake edged with peat bog. I'd been trekking this melancholy landscape for a couple of hours when a high-browed sports teacher called Arnar picked me up, rushing me forty miles up the valley. He was on his way to shoot barnacle geese near an upland lake. A shotgun rested on the back seat, next to his ten-year-old son.

'He's the dog!' joked Arnar. 'I need someone to fetch the geese.'

I was hoping to reach Laugar, where the heroine of the *Laxardal Saga*, Gudrun, was raised. On the way, Arnar pointed out the new tarred road we were crossing:

'This farm we're passing – it's the biggest in Laxardal, one of the biggest in the country. The farmer's son is in congress, and this new road passes by his house. I'm not saying they laid it because the son is in congress, but . . . you can make up your own mind!'

This snippet of local gossip was connected to a broader debate, currently thrashing around Iceland, about the corruption exposed by the financial crisis of 2008, when Icelandic bankers' reckless spending battered the country's economy. For a brief period the island at the edge was as much an economic basket case as Greece, although decisive management and a refusal to bail out the bankers precipitated a speedy recovery.

'Ever since the Crash,' said Arnar, 'we realised a lot of people are getting away with corruption and living very wealthy lifestyles. We haven't got the trust we had before.'

A couple of days earlier, the prime minister had been forced to resign, after it was revealed he'd been keeping secrets from his cabinet. His father had vouched for the 'restored honour' of a convicted rapist; having withheld this information from his coalition partners, the prime minister had lost their confidence.

After the political news, the landscape was comparatively undramatic – unusually for Iceland. I spent that evening in a stone-lined hotpot, steaming under the stars, and later listening to the paradiddle of rain on my tent. In the morning I wandered around Laugar, climbing up the rain-sodden hills where ferns and the slick ears of fescue grass swabbed my ankles and scree tumbled underfoot.

Gravity pulled me down into corries where mini-cyclones of spin-
drift whirled like fairy dance. The mists were so thick I couldn't
see any of the sheep, although I could hear their agitated bleating.
I didn't envy the shepherds who had to do the round-up. If this is
where the heroine Gudrun lived, I thought, no wonder she married
the first guy who came along.

The man she loves is a silky-haired buck called Kjartan, 'superior
to other men in all skills'. He visits the spring at Laugar, 'and it
usually happened that Gudrun was there as well . . . Everyone said
that, of all the young people of the time, Kjartan and Gudrun
were best suited for one another.' But Kjartan sets off overseas to
win a fortune, hoping Gudrun will wait for him. By the time he
returns, she's hitched with his foster-brother, Bolli. Although Kjartan
also marries, bitterness ensues and a conflicted Gudrun goads her
menfolk: 'After all the abuse and shame Kjartan has heaped upon
you, you don't let it disturb your sleep while he goes riding by
under your very noses.' It is Bolli who delivers the death blow,
when Kjartan throws down his weapons and gives himself into his
foster-brother's hands. Like the queens of the *Nibelungenlied*, Gudrun
is depicted as a hard woman, pleased that Kjartan's widow 'won't
go to bed with a smile on her face'. Intriguingly, she has the same
name as Kriemhild in the Icelandic version of the *Nibelungen* tale.
Like that story, Gudrun's involves the mishandling of a love token,
open enmity between two women, the subsequent incitement by
one of these women for the hero's killing, and later revenge.

Stumbling out of the white-out that morning, drenched and
freezing, I plunged into the hotpot. When I'd basted myself back
to a sufficiently high temperature, I strolled across the heaths to
the main road, hoping to catch a lift to the Snæfellsnes Peninsula,
where Gudrun ended her eventful life. Luckily, a Polish hotel
worker called Jagoda was passing by; she flung her passenger door
open and I jumped out of the latest squall. Marsh grass sprawled
around us and skerries scattered the sound like giant crumbs. Rain
stabbed the car roof and smeared the windows, and a rainbow
hooped over the hills when the sun broke out from the cantan-
kerous clouds.

★

Built around a busy, square-shaped harbour, Stykkishólmur is a pleasant fishing town of painted wooden houses and corrugated-iron huts. Wind strums the spars of the fishing boats, the whip antennas and deck hoists, rattles the sails and tugs the slickers of fishermen clambering on to trollers and trawlers, fixing engines on the after-decks. Gulls ride over a grass-topped cliff, as if to bring news from the ocean, and Arctic terns sweep over a flank of boulders tasselled with kelp.

I'd come here to visit a sacred mountain, and I set off after a restful night in a hostel. Past the gas station and the airport, bog thickened around the fjord and cattle chocks rattled under a pick-up returning with sheep from the highlands. Helgafell – the 'holy mountain' – swelled between the pasture-lands and peat bogs. Its shape suggested a giant's burial mound, as if it had been sculpted to evoke the many pagan heroes it entombed, before being rebranded as Christian Iceland's most hallowed place. It is here that Gudrun settles in the *Laxardal Saga*, atoning for her quarrelsome life by turning herself into 'the first woman in Iceland to become a nun and anchoress'.

At the foot of the seamy mountain cliff, a rock is engraved with Gudrun's most famous saying: 'Theim var eg verst er eg unni mest' – 'To him I was worst who I loved best'. Traditionally, this is inter-preted as a reference to the handsome merchant Kjartan, whose death she engineers. It drills to the heart of what makes Gudrun such a fascinating character: resourceful and bold, selfish but stoically enduring. A Scarlett O'Hara of the north, with a parallel knack for thwarting her own happiness.

She's not alone. The Icelandic sagas are full of tough-hearted, unbreakable women. Bartered by their fathers to brawling husbands, kept out of the Althing and other institutions, they turn to deadly squabbles, needling their husbands until heads have fallen. The most notorious is Hallgerda, who marries Gunnar in *Njal's Saga* and wages a bitter war with Njal's wife, Bergthora, inciting her house-slaves to various acts of murder and theft. After she steals some food from their neighbour and has his storehouse burned down, Gunnar slaps her face and she vows revenge – which she delivers when she refuses to give him the hair he needs to mend his bow.

Reading about these steely women today, there's a deep feeling of unease. We peer through the cracks in their stories, glimpsing the defiance so admired in the male heroes, and wonder how these women might have told their stories in their own voices.

Above the memorial, a path of shards wound between bushels of crowberry, ling and spongy moss. Wind was roaring across the flat hilltop, like some Nordic god that's just freed himself from his chains and is revelling in his liberated powers. It shoved me from one side of the crest to the other, until I was able to crouch beside a trig point, sheltering in the lee of a dry-stone ruin. The panoramic scale was breathtaking – lakes and marshland, drumlins powdered with glacial flour, farmsteads and pastures clotted with sheep. Isles and skerries brooded in the lava firth, and the sea gleamed like frosted glass, melting into a sky that shared its grainy whiteness.

Downhill from the mountain, a church spiked over a graveyard, next to a farmstead, where Gudrun's tombstone juts inside a painted wicket. The saga tells us that Gudrun came to Helgafell in her twilight years, secluding herself on the mountain as 'the first Icelandic woman to learn the Psalter, and spent long periods in the church praying at night' (possibly in the dry-stone ruin where I had crouched). The *Laxardal Saga*, like *Njal's Saga*, articulates Iceland's development into a Christian culture, and Gudrun's biography is entwined with this transformation.

If you want a definition of *taciturn*, go talk to an Icelandic farmer. He was unlatching the gate of his pick-up. Standing there in his wellies and jumpsuit, he tipped his head wordlessly. I made a few vague gestures of help, uttering the word for sheep – *kind* – and shovelling the air with my hands like a terrible mime artist. Still no reply. At last, he lifted a single eyebrow, as if to say, 'you know what, I think I can manage'.

He nodded towards Gudrun's tombstone and I stood there, reading her name under welts of lichen, relishing the timing that had brought me to this spot on the very day the sheep were coming home. The *Laxardal Saga* is an eventful tale, full of feuds and ambushes, adventures at sea, quarrels in the wind-battered homesteads. But it's also a tale about farming life, scraping away the social stratifications of medieval literature, exposing the passions that burn in the hearts of farmers, crofters and shepherds, male and female. They're all fighting against nature, all straining to eke out a life on this wasteland of equals.

28

Let him who now listens
Learn well with his ears,
And gladden brave swordsmen
With bursts of war's song.
The Weavers of Caithness,
Njal's Saga, Chapter 156

TWO HUNDRED THOUSAND people doesn't sound like a lot for a capital city. But coming out of the hinterlands, Reykjavik feels like the Big Smoke. It does, after all, host two-thirds of Iceland's population, along with a seasonal surge of tourists.

Construction cranes slice up the mountain vistas like metallic waterfalls. Pebbledash apartment blocks soar over rain-soaked work sites, where piping straddles puddled cement. Domino's Pizza and Kebab Express squat beside the pink piggy banks of the Bonus supermarkets. Nature's pushed back and the sky loses its fringe. Even the wind can't bowl as hard, ricocheting between stone nineteenth-century state buildings and old clapboard fishermen's huts.

Reykjavik is where Iceland defines itself, whether lifting statues to the 'Settlement Age' or splashing a horse-riding Valkyrie over a knit-wear store. Painted on the side of a restaurant on the main drag of Laugarvegur, a purple-haired woman is embraced by a horned demon, over that famous line from the *Laxardal Saga* – 'to him I was worst whom I loved best'. Nearby, the axe-bearing explorer Leif Erikson perches on his longship, in front of the volcano-shaped Church of Hallgrim. Further down hill, above the sparkling glass hexagons of the Harpa Concert Hall, Ingolfur Arnarson, Reykjavik's ninth-century founder, gazes between Odin's eight-legged horse and the

Middle Earth Serpent, a historical figure embedded in northern mythology.

The statuary recalls the heroes of the sagas. It was the Settlement Age that inspired nineteenth-century nationalists campaigning for Icelandic independence. Rather than drawing inspiration from the numerous independence movements sprouting up across Europe in the 1830s and 1840s, they focused on medieval treaties with Norwegian and Danish kings, and insisted on recreating the Althing – the parliament of the early Icelanders. The sagas were testimonials for a lost paradise. Their pages might be scarred with violence, but they represent a land that is free of monarchical and foreign rule. As the historian Jesse Byock has written, 'collectively the family sagas are the Icelandic foundation myth'.

So central to Icelandic identity was this epoch that, in the wake of independence (which was fully granted in 1944), there was a vigorous campaign for the manuscripts' repatriation. After several years' wrangling, a bill was passed by the Danish parliament in 1961, but passions were still heated, either side of the North Sea, and the first manuscripts didn't return until 1971, with the rest coming back in dribs and drabs over the next twenty-six years. Thousands crowded the harbour-side, waving Icelandic and Danish flags, greeting the Danish naval frigate that bore the first homecoming vellum. In the words of actor Oddur Juliusson, 'we are constantly reminded of these stories. They are our national identity.'

I met Oddur, and his colleague Esther Talia, after their popular show at the Harpa Theatre – *Icelandic Sagas: The Greatest Hits in Seventy-five Minutes*. Ambitiously, and hilariously, they managed to spin through all forty family sagas. They presented the curmudgeonly hero Grettir as a version of the US TV character Dexter ('a serial killer who only killed the bad guys'), travestied Egil, a poet-warrior in the popular *Egil's Saga*, to the opening lines of *Bohemian Rhapsody*, and narrated Leif Erikson's 'discovery' of the Americas by playing out a medieval version of the Superbowl. Talking afterwards, the actors were keen to emphasise the sagas' topicality, especially *Njal's Saga*, which Oddur described as 'the big epic one, the most known'.

'We call our bankers "Vikings", and we talk about strong women as being like Hallgerda,' said Esther, 'so these references are all around us.'

Songs, sport, television shows: the universality of the stories was communicated by their adaptation to so many different forms. Dipping into the sagas for the first time, they can feel alien, welded to Iceland's idiosyncratic frontier culture. But the saga writers were in contact with the rest of Europe, a trend that is dramatised in the many landfalls of *Njal's Saga*. Reading this tale of revenge and counter-revenge, the pursuit of justice, failed efforts at peace-making, violent sea battles, disastrous feasts and tentative reconciliation, is to hear echoes of the storytelling that flourished all over medieval Europe. But its tone, its deadpan humour and surreal imagery are distinctively Icelandic. It's hard to imagine any hero from the continental epics taunting a rival as earthily as Njal's reckless son Skarphedinn: 'You would be better employed,' he declares, 'picking out of your teeth the bits of mare's arse you ate before you came here.'

Now, checking into a budget hostel on the main drag and browsing my emails to set up a few meetings, I was hoping to learn about the tug-of-war between European influences and Icelandic exceptionalism. For Iceland, much like Britain, feeds off the rest of the continent while telling its tales after its own fashion.

A famous painting, by the Danish artist A. H. G. Schiött, hangs in Iceland's National Gallery. It shows a *kvöldvaka*, an 'evening wake'. In the sleeping quarters (*baðstofa*) of an Icelandic farmhouse, a family has gathered. Women are carding wool and working spinning wheels; a small boy leans on the knee of the *kvæðamann*, the 'reciter', who reads from a manuscript by the light of an oil lamp. This is a culture both literate and oral; and it is in the epic poetry of Iceland, the *rímur*, that we glean its power.

Deep in the bowels of Reykjavik University, under a copy of this painting, the rímur curator Rosa Thorsteinsdóttir works among thickly stacked bookcases and shelves cluttered with recording equipment. There's a Mackie Mixer and a Magnetaphone for slow recordings; reel-to-reel machines and compact disc players, a box of cotton buds for cleaning tapes and dozens of files where information about the recordings has been logged. Many date back to the 1930s, when urbanised country folk recorded themselves on silver lacquer discs. These are mostly rímur ('rhymes'), verse tales derived from the sagas and continental stories. There are so many that, when I visited, Rosa had logged 2,368 rímur files (and she was working so fast that when I got in touch a few months later, she was up to 3,700).

The relationship between Iceland and the rest of Europe can be glimpsed through the rímur. They come in different forms, between two and four lines a stanza, with varying rhyme schemes and metres, influenced by continental troubadours and minnesingers, and by fourteenth-century English romances. There are certain constants, such as the *mannsongur* ('maiden-song'), a verse preface derived from continental love-songs, and the alternating metres differentiating each *ríma* from its neighbours in a cycle of rímur.

Among the titles that Rosa showed me were tales based on the legends of Sigurd/Siegfried the dragon slayer, the Trojan War, the *Song of Roland* and the deeds of the Danish Scyldings, illustrating how rímur embraced the full spectrum of European epic. Many of these stories had been brought to Iceland by the early settlers. Many others were carried by merchants trading with the mainland. If you wanted to make a fortune, as the merchant Kjartan illustrates in the *Laxardal Saga*, you needed to leave the island for larger, more prosperous landmasses – the same principle that's fuelled migration for millennia.

Now let's listen to the kvæðamann. His voice is gristly and brittle, raised on weak lungs and a narrow throat damaged by decades of arduous outdoor labour. The atmosphere of Icelandic farming bristles in his voice as he recites the verses of the *Numarímur*, the epic of a legendary Roman king. I sit in front of Rosa's PC, mesmerised, listening to the swell and build of the alliterative lines, leaning back each time the kvæðamann pulls out the *draga seiminn*, a plaintive endnote that resonates like the call of a muezzin. This is storytelling as defence against the wind and cold, imagination and poetry fusing with the warmth of the hearth.

The diverse sources of the rímur illustrate that stories from one end of the continent could find a ready audience at the other. But they also flag up something particular to Iceland: the high literacy that has coloured its culture from the Settlement Age, and unlike in other parts of Europe wasn't confined to a cloistered group of clerics. Rímur stories were read, not recalled; fixed, not flexible. The kvæðamenn shuffled from one farmhouse to another, carrying their manuscripts with them. They were like travelling salesmen or Seventh-Day Adventists – offering rhyme and story instead of Gospels or bleach.

'Rímur is telling a story,' explained Rosa. 'It's epic poetry, yes, heroic stories, good and evil. If you think of the stories in films, Harry Potter, James Bond, that's the same instinct.' But there are certain Icelandic characteristics: 'sailing, travelling between countries, battles and feasts. Every rímur needed these to be popular.' The rímur poets may have taken their material from all over Europe, but they poured the ingredients into a native mould.

Of all the rímur, none was more popular than the *Numarímur* – the one we'd been listening to. But it didn't make its composer's fortune. Sigurður Breiðfjord's was the typical biography of a nineteenth-century Nordic scribbler. Although he found work as a cooper and spent time in the Danish mercantile service, he was prey to drink and struggled for most of his life, dying of starvation at the age of forty-eight. Neglected and maligned by a younger generation who saw the rímur as a relic of the past, Breiðfjord has been reappraised, and now he stands at the peak of the genre.

His works were many and diverse. Amongst them was a deep interest in the sagas, especially *Njal's Saga*. But rather than focusing on the eponymous Christian hero, Breiðfjord built his rímur around the pagan hero Gunnar, and so it was known as *Gunnarsrímur*. The story so captivated him that he also wrote a poem about Gunnar's notorious wife, 'Long-legged Hallgerda'. As something of a social outcast himself, Breiðfjord may well have empathised with Hallgerda, the most vilified of the saga's many intriguing women.

In *Gunnarsrímur*, we find the European epic, hoary and crabby, but still marching on. I heard it twice that week. First was in the office of the Ásatrúarfélagið, the 'Pagan Fellowship', where the polymathic high priest Hilmar Örn Hilmarsson was working on his second job as a musical composer and editor (among his many credits, Hilmar had scored a movie version of *Beowulf*). Sitting in front of a wooden prayer pole decorated with runes, Hilmar hunched over his laptop, where green wave forms patterned a palisade across the screen. He was cleaning up some rímur files he'd been sent by Rosa Thorsteinsdóttir, moving his cursor along the y-axis to improve the amplitude, picking out ambient sounds between the peaks, shearing off unnecessary sounds through digital filtering.

'Some of the rímur are basically shit,' said Hilmar, eyes flashing under his broad, professorial brow, 'but some are quite masterful. You have these really complex locutions to describe things, and really weird ways to connect the dots between them. It's a combination of madness and mathematics.'

Together with Steindór Andersen, the greatest modern reciter, Hilmar had compiled two albums of rímur, which represent the most significant recordings of the material by modern performers. They used a flexible Calrec Soundfield microphone, which enables you to zoom in and out of the recording, 'to feel the acoustic space more precisely', as Hilmar put it, in spaces associated with the old traditions of rímur recital.

'We did one in an old timber church,' Hilmar recalled. 'There was a storm outside and the walls were shaking, you could hear the creaking of the wood. We'd picked out some really vivid rímur about the sea and the wind, and the space around us was changing because of the storm.'

I listened to all of them, and to my mind the most haunting was the passage from Breiðfjord's *Gunnarsrímur*.

'We chose the space for that one very carefully,' said Hilmar.

We went to an old *baðstofa* [farmhouse sleeping quarters]. We tried to imagine the people who would have been there – working with wool, carding and spinning. We went at night, because the light affects you psychologically, and your voice changes during the course of the day. The way the poets constructed these poems was affected by the space – it's very intimate. With the *mannsongur* [maiden-song], which is self-deprecating, it relies on an intimate relation with the people around you, which makes it funnier, or sadder. And also the sound effects of the poetry – the alliteration, the harsh consonants, the endnotes – this all works in a confined space.

Hver einn dregur harðmynntan
Boldly carried each a blade,
hjör og fer að beita.
Biting edges teeth-like.
Gunnar vegur margan mann
Fighting Gunnar unafraid,
mikillega barðist hann.
Fiercely swung till all were slayed.

The patterns of alliteration bound the lines, whilst the rhyme joined them at the tips. This pattern welding had the effect of threaded gold wire in Anglo-Saxon jewellery. I was hoping to talk to Andersen as well – I loved the brooding gentleness of his voice, its care and control. But he was away in the hills somewhere, and a planned meeting never worked out. 'He's not really one for talking about his work,' said Hilmar, puffing sadly on his cigar.

Another morning, in a cosy flat near Hallgrim's Church, score sheets and record sleeves floated among coffee mugs and plates of biscuits, and the folk-singer Bára Grímsdóttir recited some more verses from *Gunnarsrímur.* In her woollen cardigan and thick specs, Bára was a homelier figure than Andersen; but her voice caught the drama and rolled it through the verses, bringing the characters to life at the same time as it lamented their passing.

It was a thrill to hear this nineteenth-century epic through these different voices. Sitting in Bara's flat, sipping my coffee, just as I had with Hilmar, I felt I was tasting something of the mead of Icelandic poetry. Like the reciters I had met in other parts of Europe, these were chains in the stories' oral heritage, keeping the tales alive beyond dots on a printed page.

Out in the Gerðuberg district, opposite a public swimming pool, squats a pebble-dash public library. Stepping inside a spacious wood-panelled assembly room, I joined around fifty members of the Iðunn Society for their monthly gathering.

'Ever since our ancestors came to Iceland, we have written poetry this way, with alliteration,' said Ragnar Ingi Adalsteinsson, a literary scholar and Iðunn veteran. It's the same with Anglo-Saxon: Germanic languages, stressing word roots, lend themselves to alliteration. This is why, reading *Gunnarsrímur* or other rímur, is to be reminded of the sound effects that give *Beowulf* its musical patina. Like the narratives of many rímur, language too reminds us how Icelandic epic connects with the continent.

Most of Iðunn's members are on the venerable side of fifty, and many had vivid memories of their early encounters with Icelandic verse. I was sitting beside Magnea, an expressive lady with a high perm, who grew up on a farm in the Western Fjords in the 1950s.

'The farmers would recite poetry all through the day,' she recalled.

> In the evenings we sat in the *baðstofa* and listened to the sagas on the radio. For the older generations, they had no radio so they listened to the *kvæðamenn*. People still knew hundreds of verses by heart – sometimes people would say, 'Don't get him started or he'll never end!'

For Magnea and many other members, rímur was a cultural heirloom, a fondly cherished connection with the past. But there were a few younger members who saw it differently. Amongst them was Vesteinn: long-haired, wearing an Iron Maiden jacket, bearing a pad full of hastily scribbled verses. Fretting about the failings of the 'bourgeois' government, the 'bubble' of the property market and rising Islamophobia, he aspired for radical change in Icelandic politics. He had written numerous verses communicating his frustrations, which he read during the course of the evening.

Song sheets were distributed and forty voices joined together to recite a rímur by Sigurður Breiðfjord, the long-drawn-out hum filling the room like a tolling bell. Ragnar read from the *Bosarímur* (a medieval tale about a Viking warrior sent on a quest to bring back a vulture's egg inscribed with golden letters) and Vesteinn delivered a burlesque about Trotsky – not the Russian revolutionary but his cat:

Trotski gamla vondan veit,
Trotsky, my old troubled cat,
Vellyst spillir griðar.
Truly he's a bother.
Um daginn aftur skömmin skeit
Recently, that shitbag shat
I skona mina og viðar
In shoes of mine and others.

There's a magic spell to hearing verses in a language you don't know. Barred from meaning, you're sucked into the music – internal rhymes and alliteration, the trochaic beat, the elongated hum of the *draga seiminn* (the final syllable in each stanza). I had followed verse and stories all over Europe, so there was a real pleasure in finding myself surrounded by fellow verse lovers. I felt at home amongst the members of Iðunn, even though I didn't know them, nor their language, because I loved stories and verses too.

The continuing inventiveness of rímur is a riposte to anyone who thinks verse storytelling has no place in the modern world. Most famous of modern rímur is the *Disneyrímur*, by the best-selling author Thorarinn Eldjarn, which manages somehow to weave the life story of Walt Disney through the old Icelandic poetic form. When I met the poet in a Reykjavik cafe, he defended this surreal combination of subject and form on the grounds that 'I was a revolutionary traditionalist!'

> That was my way to do things, the old forms in a new way. The rímur were always based on something else: the sagas or European tales. I thought, well, I've been studying all this foreign literature – why not try and make something out of a paradox? People considered the rímur obsolete. So I thought, why not try it?

Now, the rímur is experiencing a rude burst of health, which was illustrated by the numerous compositions at the Iðunn meeting. Several hours after the meeting began, Vesteinn was up on the stage, reciting verses by his friend Haukur Hilmarsson, a prominent activist who had worked with refugees in Greece and enlisted with a Kurdish militia in Syria, where he was killed a couple of weeks earlier in a Turkish air strike. The poem Vesteinn read was a satirical dig at the constitution that emerged from the 'Pots and Pans Revolution' of 2008. Listening to these lively verses by a young activist so recently stripped of life was the most poignant moment of the evening.

I thought of Sigurður Breiðfjord, whose *Numarímur* swings between ancient Rome and polemical verses against the warmongering of the Napoleonic wars. The skaldic techniques of rímur have remained, but so has their relevance to the lived reality of their composers. You're unlikely to find Greek poets working in Homeric hexameters, or German wordsmiths exploring their themes through the style of medieval ballad. But here in Iceland, the old epic form provides a framework that poets continue to deploy. Of all the European epic forms, it was here that I found the old ways of versemaking to be the most alive.

The poets of the rímur culled their stories from the rest of Europe, but now it is Europe that comes to Iceland. No need for any more Viking raids – just stick an advert on TV, with glaciers and geysers and lingering shots of the Blue Lagoon. The international set rolls up and down the thoroughfare of Laugarvegur, picking up knitted jumpers, jars of birch-leaf syrup and packets of lava cheese. But it's not just the affluent who are making it to Iceland these days. At my hostel, one of my room-mates was a Jordanian called Abdullah. He worked for the UNHCR and was here to set up a group of Syrian asylum seekers. 'It's going quiet,' he said, sipping coffee in the kitchen, 'maybe there's hope. But it's gonna take many years to end this war, and even longer to recover from it.' Even here, at the northern tip of Europe, refugees were finding their way.

Inside a grey pebble-dash building, workers from the Red Cross were helping refugees and migrants with residency permits, job applications and the many logistical challenges of repatriation. The numbers – both the local population and the refugee intake – were manageable, said one of the workers, Anna Lára Steindal, but she had noticed a growing disquiet: 'In Iceland, we have the haves and the have-nots, and it's always the case that the have-nots are worried somebody will come and take away what little they have.'

The high cost of living, along with the weather, was one of the biggest challenges. But for many, Iceland offered a fresh opportunity and, most importantly, freedom. Clutching a form for his job applications was Hony, a Syrian father of three. 'We lived near Dara'a,' he explained, 'where a lot of fighting happened. You could see the explosions all the time.' He shook his head, eyes gleaming over a rueful laugh. 'When they started the war in Syria, we thought it's gonna change the system, we'll have democracy. Now it's been seven years and we still have the war! So now we are in Iceland, my children are in school.' His eyelids drooped over a tentative smile. 'We are safe.'

The opening chapters of the *Laxardal Saga* tell of an exile called Bjorn Ketilson, who decides to flee from the oppression of the Norwegian King: 'I see little honour to be gained in sitting at home waiting for King Harald's henchmen to chase us off our lands, or even in meeting death at their hands.' So he sails for Iceland. Similar stories bristle through much of Europe's ancient and medieval literature. As Thorvald, a member of Iðunn, told me when he and Vesteinn were driving me back from the meeting: 'Our ancestors came here as refugees.'

But it was migration founded on equality and opportunity. 'If you receive people as cheap migrant labour or beggars,' said Thorvald, 'then you marginalise them from the beginning and you create social problems which you could have avoided.' Medieval Iceland got a lot of things wrong, but here's a strange thought: if policy makers could read a saga or two, they might learn some salient lessons about agency and independence.

At times during my journey, I had sensed overlaps between the refugees' journeys and the narratives of epic heroes. But the more stories I heard, the less comfortable I felt with these analogies. It wasn't that the refugees were heroes. The point was they shouldn't have to be. Thinking of Hony and his humble ambitions for his family, I was reminded not of the heroes of the epics but of the less famous characters – the likes of Wiglaf in *Beowulf* or Penelope in the *Odyssey*: characters who aren't aspiring for fame and treasure but security and stability. Characters who simply want to pull themselves out from the shadow of war.

Meet refugees and stereotypes of swarming hordes disintegrate. Read the epics and you can see their stories entwined with Europe's. When Europeans were suffering conflict and persecution, they migrated – from Norse refugees establishing Iceland to the Icelanders who fled famine in the nineteenth century and followed the path of Leif Erikson. In Canada, they arrived in such numbers there is still an Icelandic newspaper in Winnipeg. And let's not forget all those British Puritans, impoverished Sicilians, persecuted Huguenots, Irish famine victims, eastern Europeans crossing the Iron Curtain, Balkan families escaping the latest wave of 'ethnic cleansing'. Can we resent people from other continents when they choose to do the same? Only recently have administrative limitations been set against this primal urge: the journey towards safety, or a better life, on which many of our most enduring stories are founded.

29

None that scattered sea's bright sunbeams
Won more glorious fame than Gunnar,
So runs fame of old in Iceland,
Fitting fame of heathen men.
　　　　　　Gunnar, *Njal's Saga*, Chapter 76

STEAM PLAYED BETWEEN lava rocks, as if it was performing a
mating dance for the rain-clouds. I was in a bus rolling towards
Gunnar's country, but there was no public transport after Hvolsvöllur,
so I would be dependent on my feet – and hopefully a few local
rides. All being well, I hoped to reach Bergthorsvoll, where Njal
and his family lived, in four days' time.

My starting point was the Saga Centre at Hvolsvöllur. Inside this
unprepossessing box-shaped building is a treasure, an experiment in
interactive storytelling. I found it behind wire-faced mannequins,
a model of the Althing and a wood-panelled dining hall: a ninety-
metre-long tapestry that tells the narrative of *Njal's Saga*.

Scrolling over a tongue of cloth was a tightly rolled bale of linen.
Bright characters, flashy with pure vegetable dyes, were framed
between the margins like scenes in the Bayeux Tapestry. They bore
the articulated poses and expressive hairdos of modern animation,
offset by medieval costumes and marginal symbols – longships and
shields, severed heads, sacks of silver. Here is beardless, high-browed
Njal, in his navy-blue mantle, weighing out coins on a set of golden
scales. There is Hallgerda, golden locks frothing around her scowl
like the streams of a waterfall. And here is Gunnar, whose appearance
matches the saga's description: 'blue-eyed and . . . ruddy-cheeked.
His hair thick, and of good hue, and hanging down in comely curls.'

The tapestry was designed by Kristín Ragna Gunnarsdóttir, an artist and author I'd met for coffee one morning in a wood-panelled cafe in Reykjavik.

'I used illustrations from old manuscripts,' she explained, 'and I visited the Bayeux Tapestry and spent a couple of days drinking it up. But it's also based on my own personal style.'

The tapestry had struck a chord. Visitors had flocked to the centre, keen to engage with this long-ago story. Kristín was thrilled about this: the estimated ten years to complete the project had been revised down to six.

'Every time I go to the Saga Centre,' she said, 'I end up talking to people, so I hardly get any stitching done. Last time, I only managed to sew the blood on an axe! We have people who come to Hvöllsvollur especially to sew, and some of them even get hold of the key, so they can spend a lot of time there.'

Of all the characters in *Njal's Saga*, the one who interested Kristín the most was Hallgerda. 'Actually, I am descended from her,' she pointed out (which means, if we believe the saga, she's also descended from Sigurd the dragon slayer, who Hallgerda claims as an ancestor). With her long, icy blonde hair, it was easy to believe. As far as Kristín was concerned, Hallgerda's role was not only central to the saga, it was also woefully under-represented.

'I start the tapestry with a woman, and I end it with a woman,' she pointed out.

> There are quite a few distinctive, strong women characters and often when male specialists talk about *Njal's Saga*, I feel they discard these female characters. But things happen because of them. Like the niece of Flosi, when she throws her dead husband's bloody cape – that is the turning point and there's no going back from it. Both her and Hallgerda, this story couldn't be without them. And I tried to portray their part in the story and give it space.

Recalling Gunnar's slap against Hallgerda, she pointed out that Hallgerda's previous husbands also hit her. 'So this is a pattern and finally she says no. That has a modern relevance and I kept it in mind while making the tapestry.'

We sat in the cafe for over an hour, discussing some of the elements that make up this complicated tale. Now, looking at the tapestry, I was reminded – as by many of Europe's epic tales – of its agile interweaving between the past and the present. As Kristín told me, 'We still have authors who are making new stories out of *Njal's Saga*, because it's alive. Every time I delve into it, I like it even more. I really think it is one of the greatest stories ever written.'

That night, howling winds bullied my tent, yanking the poles and mushing my face with the damp. It was a vindictive gale, thumping like we were stuck in a feud. By four o'clock, I'd given up on sleep. By six, I'd given up on the tent. I bundled it in my arms and tramped over to the gas station, waiting in a birch grove for opening time. As soon as I'd poured some hot fluid down my throat, I was ready to set off.

Clinker plains swelled with lava; farmsteads poked through wraiths of mist, from which I could see the odd cow or sheep. Fertiliser and fodder sacks appeared like smudged thumbprints on a landscape painting. I was setting out on a journey of more than thirty miles, via the old turf house at Keldur and a rock that marks one of Gunnar's most famous victories, all the way to Hliðarendi, where the warrior lived and died. The weather didn't look very promising; and as the rain drilled through the clouds, a passing SUV took pity.

'Thanks! You've saved me from the storm!'

The driver was a mechanic called Baldur.

'It's my day off,' he said, puffing on a cigarette, 'so I decided to go for a drive. It's not such a bad day, after all.' As a rule, the wetter the weather, the drier the humour. And judging by the sagas, this humour's been passed down the generations. In *Njal's Saga*, when men are attacking Gunnar's home, one of them staggers back from climbing up his roof. 'Is Gunnar at home?' someone asks. 'That's for you to find out,' he replies. 'But I know that his halberd certainly is.' As the saga puts it: 'And with that he fell dead'.

Rolling between rain-sodden meadows and mounds of lava, Baldur and I exchanged remarks nearly as dry. After commenting on the sheep – 'they'll be glad they haven't been sheared for a while' – he dropped me at Keldur, and I scrambled towards a turf-roofed, arch-gabled house on a knoll. Cows moaned down the hill, under the pounding of rain, which followed the river running over the clinker rocks, down a gushing stream. A millennium ago, this stave-built house was owned by Ingjald, 'a very brave man and open-handed to his friends', whose wobbling loyalty to Njal steers him into trouble with the burners. Now, the house represents a major survival from medieval Iceland, which has mostly been wiped out by fire and rot.

Behind the stone walls and wooden beams was an underground tunnel leading down to the brook. Here was the dark hall where men of Njal's age sheltered from storms and each other. With the rain thrashing around me, soaking the turf roofs and dripping off the gables, it didn't feel like the hard-graft world of the sagas was very far away.

Keldur is, and was, a working farm; like Gunnar's home, and Njal's. This is one of the hallmarks of the sagas: unlike most of the epics, there's practical agricultural work to be done. We learn about hay threshing, corn reaping, livestock rearing. But there are also the narrative staples of epic – violent feuds and armed battles, men and women set on revenge or spilling blood in defence of honour. Reading the sagas is like discovering a halfway house between *Beowulf* and the novels of Thomas Hardy. It's this combination, evoking medieval values while pointing towards more modern sensibilities, that makes the sagas one of the most significant bodies of literature in Europe.

I didn't linger long. As soon as the rain calmed, the road was beating my feet, but the wind refused to let me read my map, so I put myself in the hands of my orienteering instincts – big mistake. After forty-five minutes bumbling in the wrong direction, I turned myself round. I was cross with myself, but also thrilled by the atmosphere of brewing ordeal. I'd dreamed of stepping inside the pages of the sagas; and here they were, jostling me with gusts like swinging axes.

Lava plains stretched towards the cinder cones of Mount Hekla, under the hoop of a rainbow, an arch so bright I wanted to throw a stone and see if it bounced. Rain bubbled in the peat holes, calming to oily browns, tinged with the same colours as the rainbow.

The Ranga river – 'the Crooked' – gurgled under the hoop, and I followed its northern bank to a gnarly, moss-patched clump: 'Gunnar's Rock', where one of the saga's most ferocious battles takes place.

Climbing over muddy runnels and rocky spikes, I felt like I was mounting some dormant beast, a cross between a sarsen and an armadillo. I wiped the spray off my glasses and peered from the top, imagining Gunnar's perspective – the ambushers sweeping out from the Hill of Knaves, their spears flashing against the tips of Gunnar's arrows; arms and legs sliced into the mud, bodies hurled into the raging current. Rain was splashing my shoulders, dribbling down my trousers; the wind kept bashing against my ribs, chopping me down. True, I didn't have any warriors to fight off, but I was still getting my share of 'battle sleet', to borrow a phrase of Gunnar's. If ambushers are analogous with terrible weather, surely the image works the other way round?

But the racketing elements couldn't obscure the richness of the countryside. Shuffling southwards, bogland sparkled alongside downs so lushly green they looked as if they had been hosed down with malachite paint. Approaching the cliffs of Thrihyrning (the 'Three Peak Mountain'), I waded between bushes of deep yellows and burning red. There were huts dug into the hillsides – storage containers roofed in turf – poking out of the grass like hobbit houses. Verandahs spun around wooden chalets on stilts, raised over the lava fields like observation posts.

Ahead, wrinkled slopes of tuff stone slid from the distinctive pinnacles of Three Peak Mountain – like giant troll ears billowing either side of a knobbly crown. The rain-swept perspective was distorting, stretching ever further, until at last the dirt track turned alongside the foothills. Only now, I could feel my heart sinking. Close to the mountain base was the gleam of a river: dashing over the bed, pleating across the boulders in the middle, as clear and bright as whisky. The wind was bawling too hard to hear the river's hiss, but as I drew closer, I realised it wasn't running out. The river had ambushed me. In order to trek further south, I would have to ford it.

I climbed up lava knolls, mud softening underfoot, taking the high way in search of a dry way. But there was no other option.

No way was I turning back now: it had taken hours to get this far. Besides, how much wetter could I get?

Off came my shoes, socks and trousers, stuffed inside my backpack, and in went me. Those first steps in the stream, it felt like I was wrapping my ankles in ice cubes. Treading over a pebbly islet, I dropped into a deeper stream, about five metres across, which lapped my thighs with its icy touch. The current tugged at my balance and it took a few mincing steps to adjust to its rhythm. On the last stretch, I went too fast up the bank and had to drop back into the river before I could mount it.

Wading through Icelandic rivers in my underwear – this wasn't an activity I'd been planning before the trip, and not one I had any wish to repeat. My feet had turned ivory-white, the soles wrinkled, blisters bubbling around my toes. I rubbed them down with my towel, coddling them in my thickest socks, stifling the pain where my blisters had leaked. A road trickled over the hillside ahead. If I was reading the map correctly, this should carry me around the shoulder of the mountain, towards Gunnar's home-place of Hliðarendi. I crossed my fingers there wouldn't be any more rivers to ford.

I'd walked nearly twenty miles today – but there were still several more to go. The track turned to gravel and carried me over a couple of streams (now channelled, thankfully, through pipes) towards the waterfall of Knittafoss. Beryl-green hills flooded the cascade, which plunged down crevasses of steamy froth and icy seracs like mammoth tusks. This valley is known as Flosidalur, or 'Flosi's dale', after the arsonist who leads the burning of Njal's farmhouse. According to the saga, this is where they gather after murdering the lawyer and his family.

Over the last hour, my body was beginning to give way, my right knee twinging, my legs starting to buckle, my fingers throbbing from the cold. The road curled through pine and fir, down to the main road, where farmsteads gleamed with metal and glass and other artificial materials – exotic sights after so many miles of raw nature. I hadn't eaten anything since morning, and now I was so hungry, I drooled at the sight of a crowberry bush. Standing on the stoop of a roadside guest-house, a kindly lady held back a curious toddler and pointed me towards a pine cabin across the road, which functioned as a kitchen for her guests.

As I stepped inside, my breath poured out like steam from a hotpot. The cabin was occupied by three couples. They were watching movies on their iPads, faces lit by the screens' clamshell glow, and none of them looked up. Thank God – I was too weary to talk. Slowly, relishing the calm ambience of the place, I boiled up a mug of soup, savouring the heat on my lips even more than the taste of the broth.

The last dabs of light had been sucked out of the sky, so I followed the path towards Gunnar's old home with the torch application on my phone. Climbing uphill through the spittering rain, I saw asylum – a tiny shed, a hoop of corrugated iron, cluttered with planks of rotten wood and blocks of stone. Crawling inside, I tucked myself into a ball, hugging my damp knees. I was really spent, and it was only later that I mustered the energy to unroll my sleeping bag. This was the place Gunnar loved so much that he gambled his life on the chance to stay there. In the morning, it would show me its beauty.

Like some old-school footman, the snipe announced dawn with a piccolo fanfare. Above me, a pointed steeple poked out of corrugated walls. How ironic, here at the home of a great pagan hero, the landmark is a church! But it reinforced a truth embedded in Gunnar's tale: his appreciation for the landscape of Hliðarendi is rationalised by continuous habitation. Sitting in the open shed, I could see cattle on the plains of Landeyjar. Geese were riffling their wings over the hay fields, tightening formations towards the stool-shaped Stora Dimon and the broad delta of the Markarfljot, which wriggles along the edge of the ice-capped volcano of Eyjafjallajökull. Above me hung the dark crest of the Three Peak Mountain, and waterfalls cascaded down the cliffs of Thvera. The perspective was astonishingly broad: a good defensive position from which to view your enemies; the quality of pasture proven by the bunching of three neighbouring farmsteads. No wonder Gunnar couldn't bear to leave it.

It's a crucial moment in the story. Condemned at the Althing to three years' exile, the hero rides out of Hliðarendi to board his ship.

Slipping off his horse, he steals a glance at the beautiful landscape he has always called home. 'Fair is the Lithe,' he declares, in the saga's most iconic speech, 'so fair that it has never seemed to me so fair; the corn fields are white to harvest, and the home mead is mown; and now I will ride back home, and not fare abroad at all.' His brother, Kolskegg, also outlawed, sets sail and ends up as a captain of the Varangian Guard in Constantinople; but Gunnar stays at home, awaiting his attackers. Like Odysseus, he is defined by a homeward yearning. But Odysseus is travelling back, whereas Gunnar determines never to leave. A hero he may be, but that doesn't make him an adventurer. And, crucially, Gunnar lacks Odysseus' knack for strategy.

Here is yet another northern hero with his back to the wall, let down by those nearest to him. Forty of Gunnar's enemies ride over the Pass of the Three Peak Mountain. He shoots down several with his bow, and even manages to hold them off when they peel the roof off his house. But when his bow is damaged, he asks Hallgerda to 'Let me have two locks of your hair' to twist a new bowstring. She refuses: 'I shall now remind you of the slap you once gave me.' Gunnar continues to fight, but his fate is sealed. In an intriguing artistic choice, the author skates over the bloody details of his death, focusing instead on the awe with which his enemies appraise him: 'His last defence,' declares the attackers' leader, 'will be remembered for as long as this land is lived in.'

It was a day for waterfalls. That morning, I walked down to a rowan-wood guarded by the bust of a local poet, Thorstein Erlingson. Sparrows were holding avian Althings among the berry bushes, and the autumn colours flared to coppery and yellow crispness. Behind them, the velvety slopes creased and folded, laced with watery crevasses, which gleamed like plunging zip-lines. Sunlight pulsed against a membrane of cloud, like treasure hidden in a bundle of shorn wool; but the clouds tightened, and darkened, burying the glow.

Samshun, a chain-smoking huntsman, bailed me out of the latest gale, driving me across the plain and putting me to use – 'Keep your eyes on the field, the ptarmigan are out there!' A flicker of black-and-white feathers, swallowed by the moor, was enough to designate the kill-zone. He hurriedly dropped me by the main road, and spun his car back round. I was grateful for the lift: the sky had cleared, but a new obstacle presented itself. I had come too far west and needed to sideways scuttle to reach the foothills of the volcano.

All along the main road, the wind was throwing fierce jabs and right hooks. I hunkered down, bending low, but the effort was draining. Exhausted, I rested in the lee of a cargo container. I still had to cross the Markarfljot River, which was straddled by a bridge. Boulders nosed against the broad grey water, which swirled around shoals of gravel, bearing off the debris it had looted from the banks. I thought of Njal's son, Skarphedinn, skating across this river on an ice floe, swinging his axe against his enemy, Thrainn, and knocking his teeth out. In its meandering way, this feud leads to the saga's fiery climax.

Still braced against the headwind, I moonwalked into the foothills of Eyjafjallajökull. A torrent crashed down the hillside – the massive waterfall of Seljaland – dousing the tourists who clambered up the rocky path around it. Dwarfed by the cascade, they looked like Lilliputians marching up Gulliver's arms.

Another waterfall, smaller and more mysterious, the Gljufrabui ('dweller in the gorge') lurked behind a splintered cave nearby. Ferns fanned the stony bank, and sprigs of willowherb sprang out of cracks in the rock. Through a mossy fissure, you could glimpse the shimmering curtain of water, but you had to breach the cave to feel its rush. I pulled off my shoes and socks, rolled up my trousers, and joined a Japanese couple in waterproofs.

Gljufrabui has long been associated with the 'hidden folk', the elvish creatures that still hold surprising sway in Iceland. The previous year, after highway workers accidentally buried an 'elf rock', a series of mishaps occurred and they were compelled to clean the rock. There had been several cases of road construction altered or even cancelled because of elf-related accidents, which were reported in the media with relish.

Now, in that water-walled cavern, it was easy to imagine yourself in the company of the supernatural. I thought of the hero Grettir, wrestling a troll-woman who disappears in a waterfall; and of the supernatural visions – witch rides, blood rain, prophetic dreams – sprinkled throughout *Njal's Saga*. Although it was written long after the conversion to Christianity, the saga still captures much of the pagan spirit. And in a land so dominated by nature, there remains a healthy respect for the spirits that dwell in the earth.

It was another blustery, rain-soaked night. The wind jabbed at my tent poles until it brought them down, hurling rain through the crack where I hadn't pulled the zipper tight enough. The top of my sleeping bag was soaked, water was spraying my head. After a couple of hours of watery torture, I pulled my damp gear out of the tent and broke into the campsite kitchen. Once again, I found myself drying out by a radiator, eyes half closed with dreams of the bed I had booked at Njal's farmstead, just a single day's walk away. There were no more mountains to cross, no more rivers. Still, I doubted the irascible Icelandic weather was going to leave me in peace for the final run.

30

Since the men their brands abusing
Burned last autumn guileless Njal,
Burned him house and home together,
Mindful am I of my hurt.

Kari, *Njal's Saga*, Chapter 131

'WITH LAWS SHALL our land be built up,' says Njal, 'but with lawlessness laid waste.' Throughout medieval northern Europe, the legal profession was beginning to flourish, developing an authority to equal and eventually surpass that of the Church. Njal, the clever beardless peace-broker, represents this growing art: a hero who never wields a weapon in anger, who uses mental agility rather than physical prowess. Echoing the word guile of Odysseus, but without his warrior strength, he signifies the institutionalisation of the pen, on its pathway to supremacy over the sword.

But Njal dies, burned in his home by the wrath of Flosi. *Njal's Saga* is a strangely ambiguous tale, celebrating the power of the law – which invests parts of the narrative with the procedural compulsion of a courtroom thriller – while recognising its limitations. When Njal tries to broker the atonement for his sons' slaying of the high priest Hoskuld, he is unable to lock down the peace. Flosi is on the verge of accepting blood payment when Njal's impetuous son, Skarphedinn, launches a vicious taunt: 'if you are, as I have heard, the mistress of the Svinafell Troll, who uses you as a woman every ninth night' (in short: 'up yours, you dickless phantom-fucker!'). All hopes of a settlement are dashed. In the multiple failed legal cases of *Njal's Saga*, we are reminded of a reality that shadows our world today: peel away the veneer of due process and you'll find something pretty savage underneath. Flosi may not be the transgender sex toy of a fairy-tale creature, but he is enough of a monster to burn a family to death.

South and seaward I wandered, meandering between fringes of mat grass and velveteen pincushions of sphagnum moss. This was practical farming country – a couple grooming horses, a JCB slicing into a bank of peat. Rain lashed me at the end of this stretch, in its usual alliance with the wind, so I barrelled over to the Gunnarsholmi farmhouse and waited under the narrow gables for the rag clouds to clear.

Another turn-off was signed for Bergthorsvoll – named after Njal's wife. The clouds turned fluffy, and blue sky unfurled a few serene-looking banners. Geese honked overhead, flying in a tight V, like a military squadron surveying the field after a battle. The track was puddled, but a rainbow looped, linking lava mounds on one side with farmsteads on the other. I walked on, perfumed by the rich smell of peat, teetering towards my destination.

A new blister was swelling on my right foot, and aches were twitching at my back. It felt like a toll was being collected – the price for all the hikes and climbs of the last few months, the nights outdoors, the raggedy disrepair of my shoes. The track curled out indefinitely, creeping past one farmstead after another, until at last it rolled beside a postbox and a set of cattle chocks. I drooped against the steel bars, falling over them like a runner at the end of a race.

My host was Runolfur – lean and gaunt, eyes hooded in deep sockets, cautiously wrinkled. He strode out of his house on a knoll, two dogs yapping by his side. The female's belly was hanging low, scraping the ground.

'No sleep,' said Runolfur, in a voice of hoarse fatigue. 'Hopefully she'll deliver tonight.'

He'd lived on the farm for ten years, with his wife and their son, Sigurhurdur, who had Down's syndrome. They had their house, the sheepfold (with over three hundred sheep, including the lambs), a horse paddock, a chicken shed and a hut for their goats, as well as a pebble-dash cottage, which used to be a rectory. This was where I was billeted.

'You see over there,' said Runolfur, pointing to a gravelly patch on the hill beside his house, 'they believe that is where Njal lived. Some archaeologists found the remains of a farmhouse and some bodies – there was a burning in the medieval period. It doesn't quite fit the dates in the saga, but it's true that something happened there.'

He gestured to the knoll, where sheep were squatting. The Icelandic annals record the 'burning of Njal' in 1010, but it was a couple more centuries before the saga was written down. By then, the story had transcended into the realm of myth. The Icelandic scholar Einar Palsson posited Bergthorsvoll as the 'primeval hill' in the keyline of an 'Image of Creation', one spoke in a cosmic wheel identified in the Icelandic landscape. For now, it was a sheep dorm and a stomping ground for chickens, skulking out of a turf-roofed hut originally built to grow potatoes.

'They think Flosi and the burners came behind this hill,' said Runolfur, 'and that's why nobody saw them. But I'm not sure about that. The hill isn't very high, around here nothing is, so they would have been easy to detect.'

'Do you think the author knew this area?' I asked.

'Not if you read the saga. Or maybe he just used what he needed to make his story work. And he succeeded, it's a great story!'

In the afternoon I visited the goat shed. Hose pipes and saws hung from the slats, among hammers and harnesses, iron scuffles and tines. Feeding troughs were scattered across the straw and weighing scales rested against a wooden fence. The goats were tupping each other's horns, scrambling around the loose metal fencing, eyes mischievously intelligent under thick old-man brows. Before they could make a break for the open air, there was a shout behind me. Runolfur's son, Sigurhurdur, stood in the doorway, silhouetted against the sunlight. Storming inside, he hollered at the goats until they were back in their stable. He pulled the most recalcitrant from the door, holding their horns and riding them back behind the gate.

In his cap and jumpsuit, Sigurhurdur was in his element. He looked back at me with a satisfied grin – the goats were all in the pen, buckling under his authority. He was on a roll, and he gestured to the three-wheeler, parked on the other side of the chocks. I had no idea where he was going to take me, but I was curious to find out. In the end, we just looped around the farm and slid back to the chicken coop. As we rattled along, words came thick and fast, but I couldn't understand them. Comprehension only sparked around the names for animals, and I chided myself for not working harder at Icelandic (apart from a bout of vocab learning on the ferry, I hadn't made a lot of progress). *Hestur* – 'Horse!' *Hundur* – 'Dog!' *Kjúklingur* – 'Chicken!' At least we had a few nouns in common.

I climbed down from the grassy crest and we waved each other off, Sigurhurdur to ride back to the goats, me to walk over to the horse paddock. I'd imagined Bergthorsvoll as a place of the dead, a shrine to a long-ago tale. But it turned out to be alive, connected to the long-ago because of the same natural advantages, the flat land and fertile pasture, that had brought Njal and his family here a millennium ago.

But across the field, a couple was riding on horseback, bobbing on the path behind a frisky-looking dog. I would meet Ara and her partner the next day, when they gave me a lift back to Hvollsvöllur. They were renting a stable at the neighbouring farm, a place called Karagerdi.

'It's named after Kari, the guy in the saga,' said Ara, 'because they say it's where he went after he escaped from the fire. And some people say there's been a curse around this place ever since.'

When I mentioned I'd been staying in the guest-house, they both laughed. 'Well, that used to be the priest's house,' said Ara, 'but he hated the people on the hill. The people at Karagerdi and the people at Bergthorsvoll, they always have problems, they're always suing each other. Who gets to use the road, who owns the fences, who's got rights over which piece of land. We call it a war zone!'

Feuds handed down over the generations: as if the ghosts of the saga writers were presiding over these fields, stirring up their old storylines, mixing the past into the present. Thinking of Kari, the final hero of the saga, I remembered his grief after the burning. He has lost his son and the arson is ever-present in his mind. 'My heart was raging,' he declares, composing verses on the spot:

When Njal's rooftree crackling roared;
Out I leapt when bands of spearmen
Lighted there a blaze of flame!
Listen men unto my moaning,
Mark the telling of my grief.

This is poetry as memory and pledge, articulating Kari's deepest feelings. After a trial over the burning descends into a violent brawl, he sets off to pursue revenge in his own way. One of the most memorable episodes takes place in Orkney, where he overhears a gloating arsonist in the earl's hall. Reciting verses against 'their burning zeal', Kari leaps across the hall and decapitates the arsonist. Blood is shed, and so is poetry, fused together in the reckoning of Kari's grief.

Grief . . . that saturating emotion again, which had been a theme throughout my journey. I could never be sure if I was projecting my own experiences and memories on to the epics, or if I was drawn to them, in part, because of the way they handled grief. Sure, the epic poets may relish their battles, but they are conscious of what comes after: the bills run up by every war. I had found many of these stories cathartic, and although the characters handled grief in very different ways, they had helped me to reflect on some of the issues I'd struggled to resolve in my own mind.

Literature makes us less alone, it can salve the hurt, especially for those of us who don't find it easy to discuss the feelings we harbour. We can share the burden with the characters we meet in stories. I thought of Njal, grieving over the death of Hoskuld 'so much that he could never speak of it unmoved'. I thought of Odysseus meeting his mother in the underworld, distraught that he can't hold her in his arms. I thought of the Mother of the Jugovichi, breaking to pieces in her grief for her fallen sons; and Wiglaf lamenting Beowulf, 'the man he loved best'.

I had always struggled to talk about my grief. For years, I kept my feelings locked inside, little knowing they were leaking through me like battery acid. Guilt, as much as grief, because I had been in the wrong place when my father died and I had found that difficult to live with. I remembered, years ago, banging on the door of a locked church in Jerusalem, the day I knew my father was going to die, because I wanted to pray, or so I thought, although I knew it was too late. But I didn't want to pray, not really. I wanted the priest to shout at me, which he did. I wanted combat, and he gave it to me. It made me feel better, for a moment, and then it made me feel worse.

Time can't heal, not the big wounds, but there are other cures. This journey had started for me, the previous year, on my road trip with my family across Europe. My children, more than anybody, had taught me about letting go of the past, thrilling at what's in front of you. In some ways, this journey had been a retreat from those lessons, but in more ways it was a renewal of life, a recognition of the present. Odysseus refuses to submit to the Sirens' call to linger in their songs about Troy. He sails away from them, as he sails away from the stagnant paradise of Calypso's island, towards the real life of Ithaca. The story of the *Odyssey* is the story of a war survivor breaking away from the past. In *Njal's Saga*, there is a similar trajectory for Kari. He cannot stay mired in the past. He finds a way to free himself from it, after so much death, and reconcile himself to the present with Flosi's niece.

The epics may be stories *from* the past, but they are *about* the present. And in them are valuable lessons about not letting the past control you. For the past is as powerful as the sun, and if we look into it too long it blinds us. I couldn't wait to get home. I wanted to put my arms around the people I loved, I wanted to hug them and hold them tight, and tell them how much I had missed them.

In the fading light, I took my nearly empty whisky bottle and climbed up the knoll to sit on the turf roof. My journey was coming to an end, and I could feel a strange equilibrium, as if something in my body was balancing out. Every few years, it happens to me: I'm shaken by this ridiculous need, to fling myself on some long trajectory towards a half-mythical destination. To run away from my life and float along stories and pathways. 'Far from home is far from joy,' says the warrior Hrut near the beginning of *Njal's Saga*. I needed to travel far away to feel the truth of the saying; and I suppose I always will.

The sound of a shotgun split the air – hunters in search of geese, or grouse. I thought of the hunters I had met, but also of the refugees escaping gunshot and incineration. Reading the dramatic attack on Njal's farmhouse – the ruthlessness of the arsonists, the defiance of Njal's sons, his little grandson's finger poking out of a hide – I couldn't help thinking of other burnings in other, troubled places.

I lay back, whisky hot on my tongue. Above me, the moon was as bright as a pot of fresh skyr. I thought about the saga, the final segments falling in soft declensions, like pale hills across a broad dale. When Kari returns from his pilgrimage of atonement, he visits the home of the chief burner, Flosi, declaring that he wishes 'to put Flosi's nobility to the test'. Flosi opens his arms and welcomes him into his house. Kari even marries Flosi's niece, Hildigunna, the widow of Hoskuld, whose killing led to the burning that Kari has been avenging. There has been too much bloodshed for this to feel like a triumph. Still, there is at least a break from the cycle of violence. At the end of the *Odyssey*, only the gods can stop the fighting. At the end of the *Nibelungenlied*, there is barely anyone left to kill. But *Njal's Saga* offers something more hopeful – that people can rise above the violence, at the very end, putting away their axes and extinguishing their brands.

Sitting on the hillock, whisky swilling in my head, I thought about the pulses of anger and violence that had throbbed at my journey: the fights in the refugee camps, the anarchists of Athens, the political tensions over Kosovo, the Mafia's lingering stranglehold in Sicily, the frustrated aspirations of the Basques, the right-wing demagogues of Germany, the bitter fallout of Brexit. The most civilised continent on earth? So Europe might like to think . . . But is it any happier than the others? From what I had seen over the last few months, I doubted it.

The strange, sad tale of Njal and Gunnar echoes the European epics: the burning of Troy, the brands that Kriemhild rains down against her brothers, the dragon burning Beowulf's throne hall. And it echoes, too, the hell-fires still burning in the saddest corners of the world. As I write these words, somebody, somewhere, is burning in their home, like Njal and his family, and somebody is fleeing across Europe, like Kari, trying to make sense of the destruction they've so narrowly escaped.

'The hand's joy in the blow is brief': *Njal's Saga* snuffs the flames of heroic epic, the burning smelter in which Europe was forged. Epic would continue to be composed all over the continent (the *Kosovo Cycle* still lay in the future, and Dante Alighieri's *Divine Comedy*, contemporary with this saga, would reinvent the epic tradition for a literate audience), but the possibilities of prose were becoming increasingly apparent to gifted storytellers.

Swinging from dream prophecies and heroic last stands to intricate legal processes and cautious reconciliation, this complicated masterpiece explores the landscape of epic only to turn away. The epic, encapsulated in the figure of Gunnar, can no longer support the layered rigging on which our world is built, so the saga argues. In this respect, *Njal's Saga* looks ahead to the psychological complexities and formal subtleties of the novel, just as its multifaceted picture of a society torn between legal processes and violence, the old faith and the new, offers a vivid window on medieval Christendom. Which makes this tale from the outer reaches of the continent as European as any of its epic forebears.

Grass fell down my back as I pulled myself up. I stepped between slumbering sheep, treading slowly so I wouldn't stumble over them. Luminous violet shapes were stalking the sky, like the bruised faces of long-dead heroes pressing against the skin of the living world. I gazed up for a while, hypnotised by the mysterious pulses of the aurora, before retracing my steps towards the old rectory. I had seen the turn of the continent, and of the year, from the sap of springtime Greece to the wind-blasted verge of Icelandic winter. Gunnar never wanted to leave his home, and Odysseus focused all his ingenuity in getting back to his. The two great tales that framed my journey were homeward-bound. And now, at last, so was I.

Epilogue

Eight months after I reached Njal's farm, I was back on the road, travelling between Munich and Vienna. I had timed my trip to coincide with a theatre festival, for the Theatre an Wien was hosting a show I'd been hunting for the best part of a year. It had eluded me during my journey across Europe, but now I had a chance to make up for the omission. For now, leaning over the upper balcony, I was about to experience *The Song of Roland: the Arabic Version*.

On the stage, cross-legged and turbaned, were eighteen *fidjeri* singers from a pearl-diving community in Bahrain. They sang in classical Arabic, directly translated from the medieval French, while German subtitles rolled over the proscenium arch. Deep bass rolls, punctuated by the percussion of tabla drums, boomed over the painted cherubs and stucco eagles, sonorous as a muezzin's call to prayer.

Throughout my journey, I had sought out the epics in public spaces: the participatory *Odyssey* in Athens, guslars reciting from the *Kosovo Cycle*, theatrical revisions of the *Nibelungenlied*. These were public stories, after all, devised for large audiences. And now I was watching the biggest surprise of all: a French epic about an eighth-century clash between Christians and Muslims, thrown back at this twenty-first century audience by Arabic-singing Muslims. It was the most radical interpretation of European epic I had seen. Which made it a fitting final stop on the road.

The production had already played in Hamburg, Frankfurt and Athens, but from my perspective, Vienna was the most suitable place to hear the story. When the 'Bavarians and Germans' are listed in Charlemagne's army, when the 'King of the Franks' returns to his capital at Aachen, we are reminded this is a story of Germanic imperialism, as well as French. Or, to quote the show's deviser, the Egyptian artist Wael Shawky: 'European imperialism'. And few places signify the heart of European imperialism like the former capital of the Holy Roman Empire.

'It's a story from before the time of the Crusades,' said Wael, sitting beside me in the auditorium before curtain-up – an impish, curly haired figure. 'But it became very important during the Crusades for propaganda. I'm not saying history repeats itself, but we can see the result, we can see what happened a thousand years ago and how to connect that with what's happening today.'

For Wael, the *Song of Roland* and the attitude that inspired the Crusades is a form of 'Christian jihadism' that is feeding into more recent geopolitical struggles. By retelling this medieval French poem in the voices of Arabic speakers from Bahrain, he was consciously drawing a link with the 'oil imperialism' of the twentieth century: 'The discovery of oil changed everything for the pearl-diving community,' he said. 'Western oil companies came and they were looking for money and power, which is the same thing behind the Crusades.'

Listening to the deep choral chanting of the singers, there was an ironic dissonance between their classical Arabic and the content transmitted by the subtitles: 'pagans are wrong,' the Bahrainis sang, 'and Christians are right.' In their voices, the words sounded not only contradictory but accusatory, twisting back against the audience. But they also sang about the Alexandrian silk in which Roland's body is wrapped, the ivory stools, the oriental jewels that mesmerise the traitor Ganelon. Listening to this inside-out telling, I was reminded of the strange ambiguities embedded in this most European of epics. As Wael pointed out, 'the whole story is people cheating each other, and this is happening in the world today'. For all the polarisation it broadcasts, the *Song of Roland* also offers insights into human weaknesses on either side of the geopolitical faultlines.

In its ambiguous dialogue with Europe's neighbours, the *Song of Roland* isn't alone. It's there in the *Nibelungenlied*, in the Nineveh silk from which Brunhild's girdle is made, in the Arabic silks

Kriemhild uses for Siegfried's robes, in Menelaus' Egyptian treasures in the *Odyssey*. In every European epic there are reminders, however deeply buried, that Europe is not an island but hinged to other landmasses – geographically, of course, but in other ways as well. The story of Europe can only be appreciated if we recognise its impact on other continents, as well as theirs on it.

Setting out on my journey across Europe, I wanted to find out what the epics tell us about the continent today. The *Song of Roland*, like the *Kosovo Cycle*, has much to say about the historical conflict between Christians and Muslims, their mutual ignorance, the devastation that follows from war. We are still negotiating the categorical divisions these stories dramatise, and we are still a long way from resolving them. The *Nibelungenlied* sheds light on the cost of rigid principles, the relish for violence and the corrosive power of grief. *Beowulf* is eloquent on the value of alliances and the toughness required to deal with a significant threat. The *Odyssey* reminds us how dangerous the Mediterranean can be, and is revealing about the challenges of dealing with the aftermath of war. *Njal's Saga* is a study in law and feuds, dramatising the tension between public systems and more primal instincts, showing how conflicts can fester down the generations if they aren't properly resolved. Collectively, these stories illustrate the violence that is every European's inheritance, reminding us that our 'civilised' continent was built on the ash-heaps of a very bloody past; but they also show us the development of the systems that have formed this 'civilisation', from the emerging city-states of Greece to the feudal courts and legal innovations of the north.

Each of these epics has left its fingerprints on history. Some helped to radically change their societies within a few generations of composition (the *Song of Roland* as a clarion-call for Crusaders and Norman armies, the Homeric epics driving the formation of Greek identity and the Athenian Empire). All have influenced the development of the modern nation-state. The Greek War of Independence and the Serbian Uprising were touched by the Homeric epics and the *Kosovo Cycle*. The *Song of Roland* played a key role in French identity around the Franco-Prussian Wars. The

Nibelungenlied cast a shadow from the Napoleonic conflicts to the Second World War. *Beowulf* influenced modern Denmark's spiritual father (not to mention its impact on twentieth-century fantasy fiction). *Njal's Saga*, as the most beloved of the sagas, was an important text for the establishment of Icelandic independence.

These stories have powerful legacies, clearly not all of them positive. The *Nibelungenlied*'s abuse by German politicians, and the *Kosovo Cycle*'s by Balkan warlords, are particularly egregious examples, showing how dangerous these stories can be. The seeds of the horrors are there, within the stories themselves, for these are dark tales dealing out death by the score. Like so many of our most stimulating pursuits, they can be very exciting, and very dangerous. Which is why their handlers need to beware.

Does that discredit the epics? Certainly not. It is because they are so powerful that they can be so grossly manipulated. Because they burn with such vitality, because they push deep roots into our cultural soil. 'Njal's Saga is alive,' Kristín Ragna Gunnarsdóttir told me, and the same can be said of all these stories. They continue to turn under new lights, to show new ways of examining the world. These are the stories on which Europe was founded, and they will be there until the end, still warning and tempting, goading and bemusing, like prickly gods whose motivations remain hidden to mere mortals. Getting rid of these stories, burning the books, would be like stoking a bonfire for the panther or the snow leopard.

And are they still worth reading? Absolutely! These stories have moulded Europe and without them we miss a crucial part of the continental narrative. Without them, we are blinder, our path into the past mistier. There is no better way to understand how people felt in the past, what they believed, how they projected images of themselves, responded to those images and shaped them; and to understand the structural accumulations that have manufactured the world we live in today.

But these stories are also worth reading because they remain so readable. Forget *relevance* – that overused term. Relevance comes, first and foremost, from the brilliance of the storytelling. The *Nibelungenlied* and *Beowulf* are as compelling and dramatic as any fantasy blockbuster, but with the added plausibility of their authorial voices, reminding us these stories are embedded in the dangers they write about, not tapped out from the comfortable distance of a modern author's laptop. They were written by authors who faced raiding, plague, sorcery, spiritual terrors and dishonour as daily threats in their lives, and these dangers fizzle in their verses. *Njal's Saga* is as engrossing as any courtroom thriller. The *Song of Roland* and the *Kosovo Cycle* are both troubling, overlaid with tribal allegiances, but they contain multiple pleasures, exciting battle scenes and intriguing ambiguities. And let's not forget the *Odyssey*. Will we ever? Some have called it the first novel, the first romance, the first fantasy tale, the first travel book. Whatever genre you pick, you'd be hard pressed to find its equal. In Odysseus, we have Europe's greatest hero, and its most enduring, in every sense.

During the course of my journey, I had followed a tangle of threads joining the European epics across north and south, east and west. When Gunnar strings his bow to fight off his attackers, or when he wins an athletics contest abroad, or disguises himself as a pedlar to trick his rival, he recalls the behaviour of Odysseus and throws out an invisible line from north to south. When Prince Lazar gathers his knights for the feast before the Battle of Kosovo, he recalls the feudal codes that joined kings and their retinues in Charlemagne's court, as well as the court of the *Nibelungen*. When Beowulf slays the dragon, he throws out a line of connection to Siegfried, his fellow dragon-slayer, whose use of disguise casts another line to Odysseus in the south and Gunnar further north.

But it wasn't the individual motifs that made me feel any more European, so much as the pleasures of reading the stories and meeting people who enjoyed them too. When I talked to Albert Ostermaier about his *Nibelungen* plays, or when I met reciters of the *Odyssey* in Athens, I felt a bond with these people, united by our love for these stories. My favourite experiences of the journey were these moments of connection – sitting with the readers of Iðunn in Reykjavik, listening to Eberhard Kummer playing his lap-harp, reciting *Roland* with other readers in Roncesvalles, drinking rakija with the guslars of Višegrad. Epic was never as alive for me as when I saw it alive in the eyes of others.

There was another surprise: it wasn't only the heroes who made the stories. There are so many other characters, and it was some of the less celebrated ones who stayed with me long after I had put the books down. Characters like Telemachus, who grows from a diffident youth to a man who can stand beside his father in battle (and, troublingly, who can hang the house-maidens without flinching); or Rudiger of Bechelarn, who sacrifices his life for a point of honour; or Wiglaf, Beowulf's kinsman and fellow dragon fighter, the very definition of loyalty. Characters like Nausicaa, the confident Phaeacian princess who takes pity on a naked Odysseus; or Gunnar's combative wife, Hallgerda; or the crafty, much enduring Penelope.

Heroes are dangerous, and they rarely offer us a feasible route map. This is why they have to die, or head off into exile. Does the return of Odysseus portend a rosy future for Ithaca? It is steadier Telemachus who represents the island's future; just as Iceland after Gunnar rests its hopes on the peace deal between Kari and Flosi. European epic is the story of the collective death of the hero and their replacement by a system, a state, a rapprochement; from the legal system of medieval Iceland to the super-state engineered by Charlemagne. In this respect, it *is* the story of Europe: how it was created, how its institutions developed and took over from the stranglehold of powerful individuals.

But heroes never disappear entirely. Individuals can be killed, but ideas endure. Crowd-pleasing mavericks will always draw a following, especially when they present themselves as alternatives to the status quo, appealing to popular frustration. But they are rarely reliable guides into a sustainable future.

What makes the epics really sing, still, isn't the heroes so much as the broader pictures of medieval and ancient societies. We can step inside the frames of these pictures, reach across the centuries, and recognise ourselves in the people who inhabited Europe before us. We can meet our predecessors, and glimpse the world through their eyes. Epic gives us this possibility, it time-travels us, with a vividness that nothing else – not archaeology, not genetic evidence, not philosophical tracts or scientific treatises – can match. It places us there, and gives us scale. At its best, it helps us to understand each other. It turns us into Franks and Geats and Serbs, into Icelanders and Saracens, Burgundians and Greeks. It rides us around a treasure mound, singing songs of mourning. And it carries us to a wooded isle, sunlight drying the sea spume on our arms, as we peer into the deep, dark woods and wonder what lies in wait.

Acknowledgements

I am grateful to the many people who gave me their time during the journey described in this book, and the many people who helped me with my research and writing. Some of them can't be named, and in a few cases names have been changed. I am very grateful to all of them for their time and for sharing their experiences with me. I hope that by writing about the refugees entering Europe I have drawn some attention to the continuing problems faced by the many thousands of people who are trying to escape conflict in other parts of the world. I would recommend any readers concerned about this situation to consider donating to the NGOs Be Aware and Share (www.facebook.com/beawareandshare.baas/) or Action for Education (www.actionforeducation.co.uk).

I would particularly like to thank the following people: Nikos Xanthoulis, the staff of the Archaeological Museum in Athens, James and Lewsha in Athens, the staff of the Andrić Institute in Višegrad, the staff of the Museum of Crimes Against Humanity in Sarajevo, Eset Muracević, Marcella Croce, Michael Buonnano, Fabrizio Corselli and his mother Nadia, Gaetano Lo Monaco, Aitor Pescador, Albert Ostermaier and his assistant Sabine, Anna Rosmus, Thomas Eichfelder and the Nibelungen Gesellschaft, the organisers of the Nibelungenfest in Worms, Florian Mahlberg, the staff and owner of the Damaskus Restaurant in Worms, Irene Diwiak, Eberhard Kummer, the volunteers at the Priory Church of Breedon-on-the-Hill, the staff of the Potteries Museum and Art Gallery in Stoke-on-Trent and Birmingham Museums Trust, Jenni Butterworth, Fred Hughes, Vicky Hyden, Jeff Kent, Martin Newell, Dr Sam Newton, the staff of the Vålby Centre in Copenhagen, Dr Terry Gunnell, Hilmar Örn Hilmarsson, Rosa Thorsteinsdóttir, Bara

Grimsdóttir and Chris Foster, Thorarinn Eldjarn, the members of the Iðunn Society, Vesteinn Valgardsson, Kristín Ragna Gunnarsdóttir, Anna Lára Steindal and the Icelandic Red Cross. For their feedback on the book, I am especially grateful to Ben Bagby, Fabrizio Corselli, Marcella Croce, Irene Diwiak, Aitor Pescador, Anna Rosmus, James Simbouras, Rosa Thorsteinsdóttir and Nikos Xanthoulis. I apologise if I have forgotten anybody.

On the publishing side, I am grateful to my agent Carrie Plitt, my editor Joe Zigmond, Nick Davies who commissioned the book, and all the team at John Murray, including Abigail Scruby, Caroline Westmore and Hilary Hammond.

Finally, thank you to my family for their support and forbearance. This book is dedicated to my children Milo and Rafe, who inspire me in so many ways. The biggest thanks of all, as ever, go to Poppy, for all her support and encouragement – editorial, logistical and moral – and for kicking off this journey with our European road trip.

Sources and Further Reading

The European epics have attracted some surprising, multi-talented translators. Amongst the editions I consulted, there were translations by the explorer/adventurer T. E. Lawrence (*The Odyssey*), the crime writer Dorothy Sayers (*The Song of Roland*), the poet Seamus Heaney (*Beowulf*) and the host of the TV quiz show *Mastermind*, Magnus Magnusson (*Njal's Saga*). For readers interested in delving into the epics described in this book, I would recommend the following editions:

The Odyssey: either Lawrence's translation (Ware, Hertfordshire: Wordsworth Classics, 1992) for the breakneck spirit of adventure, or Robert Fagles's (Harmondsworth: Penguin, 1997) for the poetry.

The Kosovo Cycle: in *Marko the Prince: Serbo-Croat Heroic Songs*, translated by Anne Pennington and Peter Levi (London: Duckworth, 1984).

The Song of Roland: Dorothy L. Sayers's translation (New York: Penguin, 1957), which is particularly enjoyable for capturing the rhythms of the original text.

The Nibelungenlied, translated by A. T. Hatto (Harmondsworth: Penguin, 1965).

Beowulf: either Seamus Heaney's translation (London: Faber & Faber, 2000) for the poetry, or R. M. Liuzza's *Beowulf: Facing Page Translation*, 2nd edn (Ontario, Canada: Broadview Press, 2013) for its accuracy and accessibility.

Njal's Saga: either George W. Dasent's first English translation (Edinburgh: Edmonston and Douglas, 1861) or Magnus Magnusson and Hermann Palsson's version (London: Penguin, 1960).

Prologue

The quotation from Derek Walcott is taken from *The Poetics of Derek Walcott: Intertextual Perspectives*, p. 235. Walcott (whose masterpiece *Omeros* relocates Homeric epic in the Caribbean) was talking especially of the relationship between his work and the *Odyssey*. I have quoted Aristotle from *Aristotle's Poetics*, p. 15. The quotation from the swineherd Eumaeus is from Fagles's translation of the *Odyssey*, p. 299.

Part One: *The Odyssey*

My Homeric quotes are from the two above editions. Quotes from the Fagles translation are as follows: 'a brazen, shameless beggar', p. 296; 'Nobody – that's my name', p. 151; 'riptooth reefs', p. 93. From Lawrence, I have quoted 'so that blood gushed', p. 182; 'Have we not vagabonds', p. 177; 'You frame and bedeck this tale', p. 120; 'a skilled musician', p. 213; 'Ever jealous the gods', p. 43; 'How will you find some madder adventure', p. 122; 'the earth's verge', p. 113; 'I am your father', p. 166; 'a cup of wine', p. 33; 'as if I were a naked, needy man', p. 32; 'our islands which rise', p. 49; 'unaccustomed face', p. 139; 'abandoned . . . for spiders', p. 164; 'under the overhang', p. 154; 'See how it rises', p. 175; 'their bodies all crusted', p. 227; 'The vast mischief', pp. 236–7. In an effort to capture the spirit of the Homeric metre, I have adapted the verses that open the chapters ('O would to God' from Book 18; 'But still the night' from Book 11; 'My dearest son' from Book 11; 'Telemachus, the time' from Book 3; 'I cannot credit' from Book 13; also 'Now spoke up many-sided' from Book 9).

On the refugee crisis, I recommend *Refuge: Transforming a Broken Refugee System* by Alexander Betts and Paul Collier. The Alexis Tsipras quote is from p. 108.

The quotation from the *Hymn to Delian Apollo* is from *Hesiod: The Homeric Hymns and Homerica*, p. 337. The Albert Lord quotation is from *The Singer of Tales*, p. 158.

The comparison of Gorgythion to a poppy in *The Iliad* is taken from Fagles's translation of *The Iliad*, p. 135. Rupert Brooke's verses are taken from John Victor Luce's *Celebrating Homer's Landscapes*, p. 39.

Shelley's declaration, 'We are all Greeks', is from *Hellas: A Lyrical Drama*, pp. viii–ix.

On the Greek War of Independence, I recommend *That Greece Might Still be Free* by William St Clair and *Byron's War: Romantic Rebellion, Greek Revolution* by Roderick Beaton. The quotation from Bollmann is from St Clair, p. 76; Beaton's observation about 'The Greece that Byron fought for' is from p. 272. Byron's Ithacan rhapsody ('If this isle were mine') is from Beaton, p. 164.

Greece is described as the 'cradle of European civilisation' on www.europa.eu, the official website of the European Union.

Carl Jung writes about the *nekyia* in *Psychology and Alchemy*, p. 53.

The quotation from Cavafy is from his poem 'Ithaca' (*Collected Poems*, p. 36).

Papadopoulos's claim for the excavation of Odysseus' palace is from a press briefing by the Hellenic Republic General Secretariat for Media & Communication in August 2010 (see www.greeknews-agenda.gr).

Part Two: *The Kosovo Cycle*

The quotations from the *Kosovo Cycle* come from the Pennington and Levi edition, *Marko the Prince*, and are as follows: 'do not ride off', p. 3; 'the blood of the heroes', p. 24; 'build a great church in Resava', p. 109; 'the nine widows are lamenting', p. 25.

Most of the Serbian verses are written in decameter (ten-syllable lines), but translations usually are not. In an attempt to communicate something of the tempo of the verses I heard in the Balkans, I have made my own adaptations, consulting the Pennington and Levi translation as well as John Matthias and Vladeta Vuckovic's *The Battle of Kosovo*. These include: 'My Lord, I beg' (*Marko the Prince*, p. 3); 'Lazar, Lazar, prince', p. 17; 'As God is witness', p. 11; 'And now the heroes red', p. 21; 'Unhappy! Evil luck', p. 24; 'Were I to touch',

p. 24; 'Then Miloš saw', p. 6; 'He leaves a fame', p. 12; 'I never have been faithless', p. 15; 'This army is not packed', p. 16.

Marko Živžovic's observation ('With the advent of war') is from his essay in *Balkan Epic: Song, History, Modernity*, p. 268.

The Florentine comment on Miloš ('Blessed above the rest') is from Tim Judah's *The Serbs: History, Myth and the Destruction of Yugoslavia*, p. 30; the comparison of guslars to 'jumping like goats' is from p. 5.

Milošević's speech ('The Kosovo heroism has been inspiring') is quoted in *History and Popular Memory* by Paul A. Cohen, p. 25. King Petar's son ('got it into his head') is from Iain King and Whit Mason's *Peace at Any Price: How the World Failed Kosovo*, pp. 31–2.

Ismail Kadaré's *Three Elegies for Kosovo* offers an interesting, polyphonic perspective by a major modern novelist. His quotation ('both a curse and blessing') is on p. 32.

On the curation of the *Kosovo Cycle,* I read Duncan Wilson's *The Life and Times of Vuk Stefanović Karadžić 1787–1864: Literacy, Literature, and National Independence in Serbia.* The quote from Karadžić's childhood ('I was born') is on p. 23.

The observation by Svetozar Koljević ('On this threshold') is from the introduction to *Marko the Prince*, p. xvii.

'Oh Radovan, you steel man' is taken from the 1992 BBC documentary *Serbian Epic*, directed by Pawel Pawlikowski. The quote from Karadžić's poem 'Sarajevo' is from Julian Borger's *The Butcher's Trail*, p. 257.

Alexsander Hemon's observation on Karadžić ('he saw himself as the hero') is from 'Genocide's Epic Hero', *New York Times*, 27 July 2008.

Ivo Andrić's *The Bridge Over the Drina* is one of the greatest works of modern Balkan literature. The quote ('his sharp profile was outlined') is from p. 34.

On the oral nature of Balkan epic, nothing has surpassed the groundbreaking investigation by Milman Parry and Albert Lord, which was published (after Parry's death) as *The Singer of Tales* by Albert Lord. The quote 'the laboratory of the living epic tradition' is from p. 3.

On General Mladić's 'memory disorder' see 'Mladic Refuses to

Testify for Karadzic at ICTY Trial', BBC News, 28 January 2014, www.bbc.co.uk/news/world-europe-25923102

The quotes from Evans and Baernreither are both from Vladimir Dedijer's *The Road to Sarajevo*, p. 258. Dedijer's book remains the outstanding contextual account for Gavrilo Princip's assassination of Archduke Franz Ferdinand. The quote from Čabrinović about Vidovdan is from p. 260; Dedijer's observation about 'The historic circumstances' is from p. 236. I have also quoted Čabrinović on Miloš Obilić ('became the first assassin') from Judah's *The Serbs*, p. 64.

Eset Muračević's poem 'Sloboda Je' is published in his collection, *Zapis O Bosni*, p. 87.

Part Three: *The Song of Roland*

I read two versions of the *Song of Roland*: Glyn Burgess's bilingual edition and Sayers's translation cited above. Amongst the quotes are the following: 'the sorcerer who'd once' (Sayers, p. 105); 'Ten mules laden', p. 76; 'inscribed and painted', p. 150; 'Spend all your life', p. 59; 'Ne'er shall base ballad', p. 108; 'His every limb wrenched', p. 202. The bilingual quotation ('Ço sent Rollant') is from the Burgess edition, laisse 174. 'Pagans are wrong' is from laisse 79 (in the original French: 'Paien unt tort e chrestïens unt dreit').

Several quotations are my own adaptations: 'Whoever is the cause' (laisse 45); 'My good sword Durandal' (laisse 172); 'In many lands' (laisse 41); 'hair sweeps down to the ground' (laisse 78); 'Slices off his coif' (laisse 104); 'In Roncesvalles this Roland' (laisse 77); 'The Knights on seats' (laisse 8); 'With Durandal' (laisse 84); 'From Spain does Charles' (laisse 268).

Master Wace reports on the singing of a 'Song of Roland' in the *Roman de Rou*, p. 181; William's attendants compare him to Roland on p. 191. Although some sources contest the singing of a *Roland* at Hastings, it is also mentioned in William of Malmesbury's *Gesta Regum Anglorum*.

On the Sicilian tradition of the *opera dei pupi*, I read two fascinating accounts: Michael Buonanno's *Sicilian Epic and the Marionette Theater* and Marcella Croce's *The Chivalric Folk Tradition in Sicily: A History of Storytelling, Puppetry, Painted Carts and Other Arts.* I recommend all of Croce's books (see www.marcellacroce.com) as she is the leading authority on this subject. The critic on rogues who 'spin for themselves a genealogy of the Paladins' is from Buonnano, *Sicilian Epic*, p. 106; Buonnano outlines Rinaldo's 'Mafia' credentials on p. 12.

The quote from Einhard is from *The Life of Charlemagne*, p. 34.

Marianne J. Ailes on 'The Christian warrior' is from *The Song of Roland: On Absolutes and Relative Values*, p. 20.

On the 1870 siege of Paris, I read Felix Whitehurst's fascinating, often humorous and surreal *My Private Diary of the Siege of Paris.* The details quoted are from vol. 2, pp. 60 and 202.

I read several books about the nineteenth-century impact of the *Song of Roland*, including *Classics and National Cultures* by Susan A. Stephens and Phiroze Vasunia; I also read 'Politicizing National Literature: The Scholarly Debate around *La chanson de Roland* in the Nineteenth Century' by Isabel N. Divanna. The quotes are from Stephens and Vasunia, *Classics*, pp. 205, 206 and 209; and Divanna, 'Politicizing National Literature', pp. 128 and 131–2.

Cécile Alduy on Marine Le Pen is from her article 'La rhétorique diabolique des Le Pen', published in *Le Monde*, 6 July 2013 (my translation).

Rochet on his brother's statue is from *The Statues of Paris: An Open-Air Pantheon* by June Hargrove, p. 363.

Napoleon compared himself to Charlemagne on several occasions. This quotation is taken from his 1806 letter to his uncle, Cardinal Fesch (in *The Mind of Napoleon: A Selection from His Written and Spoken Words* by Christopher J. Herold, p. 109).

Graf Coudenhove-Kalergi's speech for the Charlemagne Prize is published on the website www.karlspreis.de/en/

'*Europae . . . pharus*' is from the poem 'Karolus Magnus et Leo Papa', see Peter Goodman's *Poetry of the Carolingian Renaissance.*

Part Four: *The Nibelungenlied*

The quotations from the *Nibelungenlied* are from the edition of *The Nibelungenlied* cited above, and include: 'came to be a beautiful woman',

p. 17; 'I never broke', p. 261; 'the boldest warrior', p. 288; 'if any had found its secret', p. 147; 'A liegewoman may not', p. 113; 'My dear husband', p. 114; 'Are we to rear cuckoos?', p. 117; 'shall always be as you wish', p. 86; 'Then, as Siegfried bent', p. 130; 'The news that', p. 166; 'Since Attila has', p. 162; 'The strangers were comfortably', p. 166; 'water fairies endowed', p. 193; 'broad palace', p. 169; 'men from Greece and Russia', p. 171; 'Whichever course I leave', p. 267; 'giving ample demonstration', p. 273; 'they all wept', p. 272; 'magnificent golden goblets', p. 169; 'through one man', p. 159; 'every morning I hear', p. 215; 'my heart has none', p. 260; 'a fearless warrior', p. 204; 'Siegfried was in no small fear', p. 71; 'splendid fortress', p. 170; 'the Christian life', p. 170; 'What terrible vengeance', p. 19; 'to the dead', p. 243; 'If any of you are plagued', p. 261; 'There lay the bodies', p. 291.

The quotation ('Uns ist in alten', with my translation) is from *Das Nibelungenlied, Paralleldruck der Handschriften A, B & C*, p. 2.

The *Nibelungenlied* has the most regular rhyme scheme of all the epics in this book, and I have attempted to catch its rhythm in the following cases: 'In Worms they held', adapted from p. 17; 'Now Brunhild, you have brought', adapted from p. 114; 'The conflict could not reach', adapted from p. 263; 'To steep in blood', adapted from p. 269; 'To mercy's kindness', adapted from p. 259; 'His tunes are red', p. 247.

Quotations from Albert Ostermaier's *Glut* are as follows: 'the trick is not minding', p. 20; 'You can prove your Nibelungen loyalty', p. 13 (my translations).

Amongst the critical texts I have consulted are Edward R. Haymes's *The Nibelungenlied: History and Interpretation* ('Siegfried follows the chaotic model' is from p. 102).

Jörg Friedrich's *The Fire: The Bombing of Germany, 1940–1945*, translated by Allison Brown, is a standard account of the Rhineland bombings in the Second World War ('national epic of self-destruction' is from p. 237; 'four weeks earlier', p. 240).

Irene Diwiak kindly sent me a copy of her play *Die Islanderin*, and I have quoted from the play-text with her permission: 'I dreamed I reared a falcon', p. 2; 'Who should take seriously', p. 3; 'She will bring new wind', p. 4; 'a girl isn't worth', p. 5; 'do you know what it means', p. 44; 'Your honour is', p. 44.

Freud on the 'weak spot' is quoted in *Richard Wagner, Fritz Lang and the Nibelungen: The Dramaturgy of Disavowal* by David J. Levin, p. 16.

Von Hindenburg ('Just as Siegfried fell') is quoted from *Shell Shock Cinema: Weimar Culture and the Wounds of War* by Anton Kaes, p. 145.

The poem's early translator, Von der Hagen ('with pride and trust') is quoted from *The Return of King Arthur and the Nibelungen: National Myth in Nineteenth-century English and German Literature* by Maike Oergel, p. 192.

Tom Shippey writes about the New Mythology in *The Shadow Walkers: Jacob Grimm's Mythology of the Monstrous*, p. 3.

Quotations from the Nazi period are from *Hitler's Nibelungen* by Anna Rosmus ('A thousand years long' is from p. 138, 'We know a', p. 16). The most illuminating first-hand account I have read of the Nazi obsession with Germanic mythology is a memoir by Hitler's childhood friend, August Kubizek: *The Young Hitler I Knew* ('had been intoxicated' is from p. 82). Goebbels's rhapsody on Fritz Lang's *Nibelungen* movie is in *Fritz Lang: The Nature of the Beast* by Patrick McGilligan, p. 104.

Helmut Berndt describes the geography of the *Nibelungenlied* in *Die Nibelungen: auf den Spuren eines Sagenhaften Volkes*. The Baedecker comment is on p. 179.

Kierkegaard's discussion of grief can be found in *Either/Or*, vol. 1, pp. 33–4.

Part Five: *Beowulf*

In addition to the two translations cited above, I also consulted Robert Kay Gordon's *Beowulf* and Michael Swanton's *Beowulf*, revised edition. Most of my quotations are from Liuzza, and are as follows: 'I shall grapple', p. 81; 'the riders sleep', p. 203; 'with skill', p. 107; 'Take this cup', p. 125; 'two armlets', p. 127; 'gifts of treasures', p. 227; 'eagerly gaze on', p. 219; 'the great ravager', p. 65; 'greedy, grim-minded', p. 131; 'holy God brought about', p. 147; 'I have never entrusted', pp. 93–5; 'surrounded the people', p. 193; 'men have boasted', p. 83; 'a tribe of giants', p. 79; '*æglæca*' ('awesome one' or 'terror'), pp. 99, 211; 'I shall perform', p. 93; 'the feud and the fierce enmity', p. 235. The Anglo-Saxon quotations ('Ða com of more' and 'Þa wæs Hroðgare') can be found on pp. 96 and 58; and 'wrætlicne wyrm' is on p. 108. From Gordon I have quoted as follows: 'the King of Glory', p. 50; 'the splendour of the saints', p. 51; 'Now I have sold', p. 50; 'a time of strife', p. 52; 'then the monster began', p. 42; 'a secret pursuer', p. 6; 'Bid the men', p. 50; 'They laid on the barrow', p. 57; 'Then the woman of the Helmings', p. 12; 'I sent old treasures', p. 9; 'foamy-necked floater', p. 5; 'plough the deep water', p. 34.

There are a few verses that I have chosen to translate myself, consulting the Anglo-Saxon text along with multiple interpretations. These include the following: 'Then from the moor came' (see Liuzza, p. 97); 'It came to pass' (Liuzza, p. 59 and Gordon, p. 2); 'Then was Hrothgar granted' (Liuzza, p. 59 and Gordon, p. 2).

On the association of *Beowulf* with Breedon-on-the-Hill, I consulted Richard North, *The Origins of Beowulf: From Vergil to Wiglaf* ('a house filled' is from p. 159).

On Tolkien and *Beowulf*, I read *Interpretations of Beowulf: A Critical Anthology* ('It has been said of *Beowulf*' is from p. 10). I also read Tom Shippey's *The Road to Middle Earth* (Shippey's observation 'Tolkien felt more' is from p. 19).

Nigel Farage on 'The Anglo-Saxons' is taken from his book, *The Purple Revolution*, p. 275. His explanation for his Bayeux Tapestry tie ('the last time we were invaded') is from the *Daily Telegraph* ('Nigel Farage's Bayeux Tapestry Tie Sold Out in Online Stores', 24 November 2014). Steve Baker on Sun Tzu is quoted in Tim Shipman's *All Out War*, p. 81. Daniel Hannan's claims about feudalism are from his book *How We Invented Freedom and Why it Matters*, p. 89.

Wat Tyler is quoted from *History of the Conquest of England by the Normans: With its Causes*, vol. 3, by Augustin Thierry, p. 519.

On the 'Norman Yoke' and the history of anti-Normanism in England, the most thorough account I have found is in Christopher Hill's *Puritanism and Revolution: Studies in Interpretation of the English Revolution of the 17th Century* ('In no better condition,' pp. 63–4; 'Norman bondage', 'Norman Yoake', pp. 75 and 84).

For more on the campaign for Independent Mercia, I refer readers to the organisation's website, www.independentmercia.org ('regular folk, leet' can be found in the Constitution, Article 2.3).

James Campbell on 'constitutional liberty' is from *The Anglo-Saxon State*, p. xxix.

Martin Newell's haunting ballad *The Black Shuck* was a fascinating introduction to the subject of the East Anglian monster ('sees the wounded wolfcoats' is from the 31st stanza; 'And Shuck', the 6th stanza).

Sources on King Rædwald include H. M. Chadwick's 'The Sutton Hoo Ship-Burial: Who was He?', *Antiquity*, 14 (1940) ('All probability is in favour', p. 87); and *The Venerable Bede's Ecclesiastical History of England,* edited by J. A. Giles ('in the same temple', p. 98).

Thorkelín's preface to his original edition of *Beowulf* appears in *De Danorum Rebus Gestis Secul. III & IV. Poëma Danicum dialecto Anglo-Saxonica* ('Of events concerning', p. 1; 'to study the treasures', p. viii). His errors and legacy are analysed by Magnus Fjalldal in 'To Fall by Ambition – Grímur Thorkelín and his *Beowulf* Edition', *Neophilologus*, 92 (2008), pp. 321–32 ('I came home', p. 323).

On Grundtvig, I consulted *Heritage and Prophecy: Grundtvig and the English-Speaking World*, edited by A. M. Allchin ('the greatest single influence', p. 3; 'the earliest known attempt', p. 50; 'Even the most meticulous', p. 35; 'to get in contact', p. 48; 'pure Norse in spirit', p. 48; 'humankind's northern hero', p. 55). Sven Rossel ('laid the foundation') is quoted from *A History of Danish Literature*, p. 198. The verse ('of a people') is from Ove Korsgaard, *N. F. S. Grundtvig: As a Political Thinker*, pp. 82–3.

On the disputes over *Beowulf*'s origins, I have quoted from *The Modern Origins of the Early Middle Ages* by Ian Wood ('the myth is a German one', p. 167) and Andrew Wawn, *The Vikings and the Victorians: Inventing the Old North in Nineteenth-century Britain* ('grasping and stealing' is from p. 242).

On the excavations at Lejre, there is a comprehensive account in *Beowulf and Lejre*, edited by John Niles ('What the *Beowulf* poet presents' is from p. 176).

Part Six: *Njal's Saga*

I read *Njal's Saga* in a couple of different translations, including George Dasent's 1861 version (the first in the English language). I have used this as well as Magnusson's and Palsson's translation, cited above. The following quotations are taken from Dasent: 'Ever will I gods blaspheme', vol. 2, p. 71; 'our matters were come', vol. 1, p. 79; 'Let him who now listens', vol. 2, p. 341; 'None that scattered', vol. 1, p. 247; 'blue-eyed and', vol. 1, p. 60; 'Fair is the Lithe', vol. 1, p. 236; 'Since the men', vol. 2, p. 197; 'When Njal's rooftree crackling', vol. 2, p. 207. The following quotations are from the Magnusson and Palsson translation: 'exultant', p. 173; 'Did you ever hear', p. 221; 'In my opinion', p. 217; 'It does me little good', p. 98; 'You would be better employed', p. 249; 'Is Gunnar at home?', p. 169; 'a very brave man', p. 240; 'Let me have two locks', p. 171; 'His last defence', p. 171; 'With laws shall our land', p. 159; 'If you are', p. 256; 'My heart was raging', p. 283; 'their burning zeal', p. 343; 'so much that he', p. 233; 'Far from home', p. 48; 'to put Flosi's nobility', p. 354.

From Liuzza's *Beowulf* is taken 'whale's riding' (p. 53) and 'the man he loved best' is taken from Gordon's *Beowulf*, p. 139.

Al-Idrissi on the 'sea of perpetual gloom' is taken from *The Edge of the World: Light, Life and Brilliance in the Dark Ages* by Michael Pye, p. 14.

Njal's Saga is described as a 'valkyrie's web' by Wawn in *Vikings and the Victorians*, p. 143.

Terry Gunnell on 'metre magic' is from an interview with the author in Reykjavik, September 2017.

The details about Hitler's opera are from Kubizek's *Young Hitler I Knew*, p. 195.

I read several other sagas in *The Sagas of the Icelanders* including the *Laxardal Saga*, which I would recommend to anybody interested in Icelandic literature. Quotations are from this edition and are as follows: 'superior to other men', p. 322; 'and it usually happened', p. 344; 'After all the abuse', p. 369; 'won't go to bed', p. 372; 'the first woman in Iceland', p. 420; 'the first Icelandic woman to learn', p. 418; 'to him I was worst', p. 421 ('Though I treated him worst, I loved him best'); 'I see little honour', p. 277.

One of the best historians of medieval Icelandic society is Jesse L. Byock, whose *Viking Age Iceland* is a standard text ('collectively the family sagas' is from p. 22).

The quotation from *Gunnarsrímur* ('Boldly carried each a blade') is my translation using the text from *Rímur: A Collection from Steindór Andersen*.

On Bergthorsvoll as a 'primeval hill' in the 'Image of Creation', see Petur Halldorsson, *The Measure of the Cosmos: Deciphering the Imagery of Icelandic Myth* (pp. 7 and 12).

Bibliography

Source Texts

Homer, *The Iliad* (trans. Robert Fagles) (Harmondsworth: Penguin, 1996)

Homer, *The Odyssey* (trans. T. E. Shaw (Colonel T. E. Lawrence)) (Ware, Hertfordshire: Wordsworth Classics, 1992)

Homer, *The Odyssey* (trans. Robert Fagles) (Harmondsworth: Penguin, 1997)

Marko the Prince: Serbo-Croat Heroic Songs (trans. Anne Pennington and Peter Levi) (London: Duckworth, 1984)

Battle of Kosovo, The (trans. John Matthias and Vladeta Vuckovic) (Athens, OH: Ohio University Press, 1987)

Song of Roland, The (trans. Dorothy L. Sayers) (New York: Penguin, 1957)

Song of Roland, The, bilingual edn (trans. Glyn Burgess) (Harmondsworth: Penguin, 1990)

Das Nibelungenlied, Paralleldruck der Handschriften A, B & C (Tübingen: Max Niemeyer Verlag, 1971)

Nibelungenlied, The (trans. A. T. Hatto) (Harmondsworth: Penguin, 1965)

Beowulf: Facing Page Translation, 2nd edn (trans. R. M. Liuzza) (Ontario: Broadview Press, 2013)

Beowulf (trans. Robert Kay Gordon) (New York: Dover Publications, 1992)

Beowulf, rev. edn (ed. Michael Swanton) (Manchester: Manchester University Press, 1997)

Njal's Saga (trans. Magnus Magnusson and Hermann Palsson) (Harmondsworth: Penguin, 1960)

Sagas of the Icelanders, The (London: Allen Lane, 2000)

Story of Burnt Njal: Or Life in Iceland at the End of the Tenth Century, The (trans. George Webbe Dasent) (Edinburgh: Edmonston and Douglas, 1861)

Primary Sources

Andrić, Ivo, *The Bridge Over the Drina* (trans. Lovett F. Edwards) (London: Harvill Press, 1994)

Aristotle, *Aristotle's Poetics* (trans. E. S. Bouchier) (Oxford: B. H. Blackwell, 1907)

Bede, *The Venerable Bede's Ecclesiastical History of England* (ed. J. A. Giles) (London: Henry G. Bohn, 1847)

Cavafy, Constantine P., *Collected Poems* (trans. Edmund Keeley and Philip Sherrard) (Princeton, NJ: Princeton University Press, 1992)

Diwiak, Irene, *Die Isländerin* (author's copy, 2016)

Einhard, *The Life of Charlemagne* (trans. Samuel Epes Turner) (Michigan: Michigan University Press, 1960)

Grahame, Kenneth, *The Wind in the Willows* (London: Walker Books, 2000)

Hesiod/Homer, *Hesiod: The Homeric Hymns and Homerica* (trans. Hugh G. Evelyn-White) (London: William Heinemann, 1914)

Kadaré, Ismail, *Three Elegies for Kosovo* (trans. Peter Constantine) (London: Harvill Press, 2000)

Kierkegaard, Søren, *Either/Or,* vol. 1 (trans. David F. Swenson and Lillian M. Swenson) (Princeton, NJ: Princeton University Press, 1944)

Muračević, Eset, *Zapis o Bosni* (Tešanj: Štamparija Planjax, 2015)

Newell, Martin, *The Black Shuck* (Wivenhoe: Jardine Press, 2016)

Ostermaier, Albert, *Glut* (Frankfurt am Main: Korrektur Verlag, 2017)

Plato, *Republic* (ed. Lewis Campbell and Benjamin Jowett) (New York: Garland, 1987)

Shelley, Percy Bysshe, *Hellas: A Lyrical Drama* (London: Reeves & Turner, 1886)

Wace, *Roman de Rou* (trans. Glyn Burgess) (Woodbridge: Boydell Press, 2004)

Secondary Sources

Ailes, Marianne J., *The Song of Roland: On Absolutes and Relative Values* (Lewiston, NY: Edwin Mellen Press, 2002)

Allchin, A. M. (ed.), *Heritage and Prophecy: Grundtvig and the English-Speaking World* (Aarhus: Aarhus University Press, 1993)

Andersen, Steindór, *Rímur: A Collection from Steindór Andersen* (Hong Kong: HNH International Ltd, 2003)

Andersson, Theodore M., *The Growth of the Medieval Icelandic Sagas* (Ithaca, NY: Cornell University Press, 2006)

Beaton, Roderick, *Byron's War: Romantic Rebellion, Greek Revolution* (Cambridge: Cambridge University Press, 2013)

Berndt, Helmut, *Die Nibelungen: auf den Spuren eines Sagenhaften Volkes* (Oldenburg: Gerhard Stalling Verlag, 1978)

Betts, Alexander, and Collier, Paul, *Refuge: Transforming a Broken Refugee System* (London: Allen Lane, 2017)

Bohlman, Philip V., and Petković, Nada (ed.), *Balkan Epic: Song, History, Modernity* (Lanham, MD: Scarecrow Press, 2012)

Borger, Julian, *The Butcher's Trail* (New York: Other Press, 2016)

Buonanno, Michael, *Sicilian Epic and the Marionette Theater* (Jefferson, NC: McFarland, 2014)

Byock, Jesse L., *Feud in the Icelandic Saga* (Berkeley, CA: University of California Press, 1982)

——, *Viking Age Iceland* (Harmondsworth: Penguin, 2001)

Campbell, James, *The Anglo-Saxon State* (London: Hambledon and London, 2000)

Croce, Marcella, *The Chivalric Folk Tradition in Sicily: A History of Storytelling, Puppetry, Painted Carts and Other Arts* (Jefferson, NC: McFarland, 2014)

Dedijer, Vladimir, *The Road to Sarajevo* (London: MacGibbon & Kee, 1967)

Divanna, Isabel N., 'Politicizing National Literature: The Scholarly Debate around *La chanson de Roland* in the Nineteenth Century', *Historical Research*, 84, no. 223 (February 2011), pp. 109–34

Farage, Nigel, *The Purple Revolution* (London: Biteback, 2015)

Fenwick Jones, George, *The Ethos of the Song of Roland* (Baltimore, MD: Johns Hopkins Press, 1963)

Fjalldal, Magnús, *The Long Arm of Coincidence: The Frustrated Connection Between Beowulf and Grettis Saga* (Toronto: University of Toronto Press, 1998)

——, 'To Fall by Ambition – Grímur Thorkelín and his *Beowulf* Edition', *Neophilologus*, 92 (2008), pp. 321–32

Friedrich, Jörg, *The Fire: The Bombing of Germany, 1940–1945* (trans. Allison Brown) (New York: Columbia University Press, 2008)

Fulk, R. D. (ed.), *Interpretations of Beowulf: A Critical Anthology* (Bloomington, IN: Indiana University Press, 1991)

Godman, Peter, *Poetry of the Carolingian Renaissance* (London: Duckworth, 1985)

Halldorsson, Petur, *The Measure of the Cosmos: Deciphering the Imagery of Icelandic Myth* (Reykjavik: Salka, 2007)

Hannan, Daniel, *How We Invented Freedom and Why it Matters* (London: Head of Zeus, 2013)

Hargrove, June, *The Statues of Paris: An Open-Air Pantheon* (New York: Vendome Press, 1989)

Haymes, Edward R., *The Nibelungenlied: History and Interpretation* (Urbana, IL: University of Illinois Press, 1986)

Herold, J. Christopher, *The Mind of Napoleon: A Selection from His Written and Spoken Words* (New York: Columbia University Press, 1955)

Hill, Christopher, *Puritanism and Revolution: Studies in Interpretation of the English Revolution of the 17th Century* (London: Secker & Warburg, 1958)

Hitler, Adolf, *Mein Kampf* (*My Struggle*) (London: Hurst & Blackett, 1933)

Holmes, Urban Tigner, *A History of Old French Literature: From the Origins to 1300* (New York: F. S. Crofts, 1937)

Judah, Tim, *The Serbs: History, Myth and the Destruction of Yugoslavia* (New Haven, CT: Yale University Press, 1997)

Jung, Carl, *Psychology and Alchemy* (trans. R. F. C. Hull) (London: Routledge & Kegan Paul, 1953)

Kaes, Anton, *Shell Shock Cinema: Weimar Culture and the Wounds of War* (Princeton, NJ: Princeton University Press, 2011)

King, Iain and Mason, Whit, *Peace at any Price: How the World Failed Kosovo* (Ithaca, NY: Cornell University Press, 2006)

Korsgaard, Ove, *N. F. S. Grundtvig: As a Political Thinker* (trans. Edward Broadbridge) (Copenhagen: DJØF Publishing, 2014)

Kristjansson, Jonas, *Icelandic Manuscripts: Sagas, History and Art* (Reykjavik: Icelandic Literary Society, 1993)

Kubizek, August, *The Young Hitler I Knew* (London: Greenhill Books, 2006)

Levin, David J., *Richard Wagner, Fritz Lang and the Nibelungen: The Dramaturgy of Disavowal* (Princeton, NJ: Princeton University Press, 1998)

Lord, Albert Bates, *The Singer of Tales* (Cambridge, MA: Harvard University Press, 1960)

Luce, John Victor, *Celebrating Homer's Landscapes: Troy and Ithaca Revisited* (New Haven, CT: Yale University Press, 1998)

McGilligan, Patrick, *Fritz Lang: The Nature of the Beast* (London: Faber, 1997)

Newton, Sam, *The Origins of Beowulf and the Pre-Viking Kingdom of East Anglia* (Cambridge: D. S. Brewer, 1993)

——, *The Reckoning of King Rædwald* (Colchester: Red Bird Press, 2003)

Niles, John (ed.), *Beowulf and Lejre* (Tempe, AZ: Arizona Center for Medieval and Renaissance Studies, 2007)

North, Richard, *The Origins of Beowulf: from Vergil to Wiglaf* (Oxford: Oxford University Press, 2006)

Oergel, Maike, *The Return of King Arthur and the Nibelunen: National Myth in Nineteenth-century English and German Literature* (New York: De Gruyter, 1998)

Pye, Michael, *The Edge of the World: Light, Life and Brilliance in the Dark Ages* (London: Viking, 2014)

Richter, Michael, *The Formation of the Medieval West: Studies in the Oral Culture of the Barbarians* (Black Rock: Four Courts Press, 1994)

Rosmus, Anna, *Hitler's Nibelungen* (Grafenau: Samples Verlag, 2015)

Rossel, Sven H., *A History of Danish Literature* (Lincoln, NE: University of Nebraska Press, 1992)

St Clair, William, *That Greece Might Still be Free* (Oxford: Oxford University Press, 1972)

Shipman, Tim, *All Out War* (London: William Collins, 2016)

Shippey, Tom, *The Road to Middle Earth* (London: Grafton, 1992)

—— (ed.), *The Shadow Walkers: Jacob Grimm's Mythology of the Monstrous* (Tempe, AZ: Arizona Center for Medieval and Renaissance Studies, 2005)

Smith, David James, *One Morning in Sarajevo: 28 June 1914* (London: Weidenfeld & Nicolson, 2008)

Stephens, Susan A., and Vasunia, Phiroze, *Classics and National Cultures* (Oxford: Oxford University Press, 2010)

Thierry, Augustin, *History of the Conquest of England by the Normans: With its Causes*, vol. 3 (London: G. B. Whitaker, 1825)

Thorkelín, Grímur Jónsson, *De Danorum Rebus Gestis Secul. III & IV. Poëma Danicum dialecto Anglo-Saxonica* (Copenhagen: Havniae Typis Th. E. Rangel, 1815)

Walcott, Derek, *The Poetics of Derek Walcott: Intertextual Perspectives* (Durham, NC: Duke University Press, 1997)

Wawn, Andrew, *The Vikings and the Victorians: Inventing the Old North in Nineteenth-century Britain* (Cambridge: D. S. Brewer, 2000)

Whitehurst, Felix M., *My Private Diary of the Siege of Paris* (London, 1875)

Wilson, Duncan, *The Life and Times of Vuk Stefanović Karadžić 1787–1864: Literacy, Literature, and National Independence in Serbia* (Oxford: Clarendon Press, 1970)

Wood, Ian, *The Modern Origins of the Early Middle Ages* (Oxford: Oxford University Press, 2013)